1

*PROPHET OF THE PEOPLE*

# PROPHET OF THE PEOPLE

### A Biography of Padre Pio

By

### Dorothy M. Gaudiose

*Illustrated by*
George Lallas

ALBA · HOUSE    NEW · YORK

SOCIETY OF ST. PAUL, 2187 VICTORY BLVD., STATEN ISLAND, NEW YORK 10314

*Library of Congress Cataloging-in-Publication Data*

Gaudiose, Dorothy, 1920-
    Prophet of the people; a biography of Padre Pio.

    1. Pio da Pietrelcina, Father.   I. Title.
    BX4705.P49G38    271'.36'024[B]    74-7123
    ISBN 0-8189-0351-1

Nihil Obstat:
Msgr. Thomas E. Madden, P.A., V.G.
Censor Librorum

Imprimatur:
† James J. Hogan
Bishop of Altoona-Johnstown
October 1, 1973

Designed, printed and bound in the United States of
America by the Fathers and Brothers of the
Society of St. Paul, 2187 Victory Boulevard,
Staten Island, New York 10314, as part of their
communications apostolate.

**Printing Information:**

| Current  Printing  -  first  digit | | | | | 11 | 12 | 13 | 14 | 15 | 16 | 17 | 18 | 19 | 20 |
|---|---|---|---|---|---|---|---|---|---|---|---|---|---|---|

Year of Current Printing - first year shown

| | | 1992 | 1993 | 1994 | 1995 | 1996 | 1997 | 1998 | 1999 |
|---|---|---|---|---|---|---|---|---|---|

# For

*My Dear Friend*
*Mary Adelia McAlpin Pyle*

# FOREWORD

*From the moment J saw him,* I was drawn, and almost compelled to examine the life of Padre Pio, the stigmatist. I had to know more about the man whose body bore five bleeding wounds, and who possessed so many incredible powers. This book is the result of my search for the truth about him. Although in his quiet Franciscan humility he concealed the greatness of his powers and the saintliness of his life, I discovered almost endless accounts, as well as controversies, revealing his strange, supernatural gifts and the terrible suffering he endured.

A newspaper report about Padre Pio influenced my two sisters, Helena and Carmelita, and me to include San Giovanni Rotondo in our itinerary of Europe during the Holy Year of 1950. (This town was near the scene of the earliest apparition of the Archangel Saint Michael.) At least an hour's drive by car, and about twenty-four miles from Foggia, San Giovanni Rotondo lies in a remote and sparsely-populated area on Gargano Mountain in southern Italy, near Monte Santangelo. The road follows a zig-zag course up the side of the mountain. We took the express train from Rome and arrived five hours later in Foggia. Today, those who prefer faster travel can go by plane from Rome to Foggia in less than an hour. For a fifty-cent fare we took a bus from Foggia which passed directly in front of the Capuchin monastery on the way to San Giovanni Rotondo.

San Giovanni Rotondo is an attractive old city perched on the mountain ridge. The Capuchin monastery of Our Lady of Grace, where Padre Pio had been sent, is one and a quarter miles from the town. In former times the monastery was connected to San Giovanni Rotondo by a muletrack, used only by a few carts that transported gravel from the pits behind the monastery, and by shepherds and peasants who went up the mountain to graze their flocks or gather wood for the fires.

However, to reach the monastery in 1950 we travelled on a pleasant, well-kept mountain road bordered with flowers and a profusion of magnolia trees. As the bus approached the monastery we saw an enormous new white stone building, still under construction. This, we learned, was to be Padre Pio's new hospital, or as he called it, Home for the Relief of Suffering—a vital and necessary institution, becoming world renowned today for its advances in the medical field, and one of the great contributions that he and his followers made to mankind.

The road continued on past the hospital and led to a cobble-stone clearing just below the top of Gargano Mountain where, almost directly in front of the monastery door, stood a single elm tree. We eagerly surveyed the whitewashed monastery and a small church with an old bell. When I looked at it, I thought: *So this is where he lived—what a simple-looking place this is!* Perhaps I was expecting the grandeur of the Vatican, but what was lacking in grandeur was more than compensated for later by my tremendous impression of Padre Pio, an impression that would be renewed many times, but in no way changed.

When we entered the seventeenth-century monastery church I had a *carte blanche* impression of this Franciscan Capuchin priest. I had heard only of his stigmata, the five bodily wounds like those of the crucified Jesus, and of his ability to read the minds of his penitents. But as far as Padre Pio's other gifts were concerned—miracles, perfume, conversion, bilocation, discernment of spirits, and prophecy— I knew nothing. I accepted only what I saw and later experienced.

It is staggering to think that one man could have been given so many gifts. In the history of the Church there have been many saints who were given one or the other of the gifts possessed by Padre Pio; for example: St. Francis of Assisi is known for the stigmata, St. Anthony of Padua for bilocation, St. Frances of Rome for discernment of spirits, St. Dominic for the gift of perfume, and St. Lawrence of Cipriano for the gift of prophecy. But it is hard to find one saint who had as many supernatural gifts as Padre Pio.

We caught our first glimpse of the Padre about ten o'clock that morning of our arrival at the monastery. In those days Padre Pio celebrated an early mass. Because so many people wanted to receive communion from him, the superior of his order had designated the early hour. We remained in the small church watching this scene for more than an hour. Then, thinking our knowledge of Italian might be in our favor, we asked how to arrange a meeting with the stigmatist. It was necessary, we were told, to get tickets and wait for him to cross the corridor on his return to the monastery. So we did this and joined the crowd of women and children.

Just as the crowd was becoming restless, someone suddenly shouted: "Here comes Padre Pio!" The sound of his name triggered an explosion of enthusiasm. Women milled around the approaching dark-robed figure, stretching out all kinds of objects for him to bless, and putting questions to him. To the barrage of requests he responded with patience and humility, and when he spoke, the crowd became more subdued.

My sisters and I maneuvered to a position before the bearded friar. Padre Pio asked us where we were from, and upon saying we were Americans, he smiled, and said, "Americans, yes, but of Italian extraction," which was true. One of us said, "Padre, we are sisters." At that his expression became more serious, and he said, "Yes, but each of you is a different type." Other women were requesting his prayers for favors, and he turned away, nodding, saying yes to some requests and remaining silent at others. "Ah," he remarked then, "some of you women never seem to end a story." Everyone laughed. Finally, he blessed the group and moved on toward the adjoining monastery.

There was nothing spectacular about this first encounter with Padre Pio; yet I was intrigued by him, and I already had a feeling that I had to know more about him. I couldn't get his intense, penetrating gaze out of my mind—it made me feel as if he had known me before. And I had been impressed with the strength he radiated, and with the degree to which the women were obviously carried away by him. Although in dress and in general appearance he seemed to be a simple Capuchin, the air around him was electrified, almost in anticipation of some extraordinary happening, while his searching, restless eyes suggested some intense secret that went far beyond human comprehension. At the time, I was seeking someone like him, someone who could give me advice on pertinent problems, but initially I was puzzled and hesitant. However, when I visited him later, witnessed the spectacle of his mass, and went to confession to him for the first time, the encounters produced in me a pervading sweetness and trust. And my faith in the reality of Padre Pio's powers grew as I was able to add my own firsthand experiences to the endless list of other documented accounts. Now I know that all he has said and done will be etched upon my mind forever.

I want to reveal in this book some of the mysteries that shadowed the life of this profound mystic, and to let the world know more about the supernatural gifts through which he was able to help so many people and direct and guide the lives of those who believed in him. For them, he was an oracle—hence, the title of this book: *Prophet of the People.*

After meeting him, people left refreshed with a new understanding that somehow gave them hope for a better tomorrow. His own faith inspired them to begin their lives anew, and his hope roused them to return to their work. His charity extended to every corner of the world.

You may wonder what kind of man could attract such strong devotion and faith. Those who met him would agree that he had what theologians call "holy simplicity." He was an original figure— what we would call a "natural." His authenticity, originality, and genuineness were indisputable, and the sincerity of his spirit was above suspicion.

He never yielded to the agony and temptation that constantly tormented him. The suffering he endured from his never-healing wounds was only a part of the pain that pursued him; he was forever plagued by the appearance of strange, fearful beings—evil spirits— that even attacked him physically and left him bruised and scarred.

But he never permitted these forces to sway him from his duty to God and man.

He always met his everyday toil serenely, as one who personally neither expects nor requests anything from anyone. However, he believed that both the powerful and the weak should walk in the ways of justice and respect the law, without giving way to disorderly instincts. He revealed such strength of character, such vigorous personality, that everyone was compelled to speak with reverence in his presence. The whole atmosphere of the place seemed permeated with the mood set by the inscription over his door: "The Glory of the World Has Sorrow for Its Companion."

Although he knew how to be firm, he was always patient, painstaking, and quick to detect what was good in others. You might say that he won an empire with his wide and affectionate sympathy. He occupied himself with the *spiritual* condition of the people who came to see him, regardless of race or creed, and not at all with the fortunes of the world.

As if by design, into a world filled with the sorrow of World War I this new victim soul appeared, humble and innocent, dwelling high on the rocks of Gargano Mountain. Many leading doctors, scientists, and theologians went there to examine his wounds—and inevitably were baffled by them. Thus, the *"Padre Pio case"* was opened, never to be closed. According to records, Padre Pio was the first stigmatized priest in the history of the Church. (St. Francis of Assisi was a deacon, not a priest.)

Multitudes went to see the humble friar and flocked around him, drawn by his great virtue. And those who saw him, as well as those who merely read about him, experienced a profound and lasting impression of hope. Similarly, those who were suffering in hospitals, and in prison or in squalid dwellings began to live again with a new spirit. All of them shared the feeling that Padre Pio conveyed: that innocence triumphs over corruption, and a smile over tears and hate.

You would think that the poverty and simplicity of Padre Pio and his monastery would have kept him distant from people, and also that the growing commercialism around him would have alienated them. Yet, they somehow realized that here in this mountain town of San Giovanni Rotondo lived Padre Pio who could point out an imitable and reachable example of a simple way of life.

Crowds besieged him daily, in fact, all seeming to have a secret story, perhaps bearing a heavy cross, or perhaps merely carrying a shred of hope. Important persons of all ranks came to his monastery: royal families, statesmen, men of culture and art, and millions of people of all races. They came from every country and every religion. They were people of every social condition and every class of society —industrial magnates, laborers, film stars, housewives, prelates, humble priests, scientists, the ignorant, the wise, believers, and nonbelievers. They all came invoking the man of God. Some of the poor even slept under a tent for a glimpse of him. Children prayed to him like a saint, and strange figures of hermitage stood before him for a word of salvation. And when they asked to be received, Padre Pio accepted all of them as they came. Never did he in any way discriminate.

Perhaps it was the wide assortment of people who visited Padre Pio that led to the wild and unlikely stories that were published about him. There were many controversies and disputes over him, some which were given great emphasis by both the Italian and foreign press. But to all charges, Padre Pio said nothing to justify himself and he gave no explanation for his actions.

One man became a defamer of Padre Pio and was extremely violent and venomous. A long time later he became genuinely repentant and sent a close friend to Padre Pio to apologize, feeling too ashamed to go personally. When the friend told of the man's retraction and genuine sorrow, Padre Pio replied: "I hope so for his sake. I myself have no need of it." Padre Pio returned good for evil, especially in cases of those who offended him the most.

Though the pious friar did everything to discourage curiosity and excitement, remarkable things did happen around him. Through the years there were dramatic reports of miraculous cures, some of them apparently true, and also reports of bilocation which could not be disproved. There were people who claimed that during periods of crisis they had been given notice of Padre Pio's intercession for them by suddenly detecting the sweet, unearthly odor associated with him, though at the time he was nowhere near. But concerning all these reports, ecclesiastical authorities to date have remained silent.

I heard of one cure while I was a guest at a hotel in San Giovanni Rotondo. Every morning for a week I met Mademoiselle Ginette Estebe from Royan, France, and we were able to converse in French on the way to Padre Pio's 5:00 A.M. mass. When she learned that I was gathering information on Padre Pio, she told me this story:

"I was paralyzed on my left side. My face was drawn, deformed by paralysis, and so were my arms and leg. I was discharged from a hospital after having been examined by eighteen doctors who declared I was incurable. Then I met a man who said to me, 'Why don't you get Padre Pio to help you?' He gave me a book written about him and a medal blessed by him. After reading the book I became determined to write to Padre Pio. It took me three days to write the letter with my right hand. After I sent the letter I found that I could move my arm, hand, and leg. After a short time I was entirely healed. I came here to thank Padre Pio. I was in the hall among a crowd of many other people. He recognized me and beckoned me to him. He blessed me and put his hand on my head."

I was amazed at what she told me. She was an attractive woman, and there was no indication from her appearance or her actions of having been a paralytic.

In another instance I heard that one of the doctors on Padre Pio's hospital staff had been cured of leukemia, and I questioned him about it. He assured me that he had received such a grace, but when pressed for a statement for publication, refused, explaining, "I am a man of science, and do not personally wish to submit myself to all kinds of official probing. Doesn't the cure speak for itself? I am here working at Padre Pio's hospital without personal financial gain."

Perfume is another power associated with Padre Pio, and I personally have experienced such odor. On my first visit to his monastery my two sisters and I joined the throngs who received Holy Communion from his hand. When I received the host I caught the scent of carbolic acid and assumed he used a disinfectant for his wounds, but later I learned he never used one. Afterwards I mentioned this to my sisters and was surprised when one of them said she too detected the same carbolic odor, while the other told of receiving a sweet perfumed scent.

Once, having learned of the stigmatist's desire for a new church, we collected some literature to distribute in America. While passing the small church of Our Lady of Grace on a bright sunny day, a sweetly-scented wind suddenly enveloped us and even blew some of the leaflets from our hands. It lasted only for a few minutes and then vanished. We commented on it and quickly glanced around. But there was no wind blowing and absolutely no flowers were in sight. It dawned on us then that it was the sweet perfumed odor we had noticed in the presence of Padre Pio.

On subsequent visits I became aware of a sweet and pleasant perfume coming from Padre Pio when I was about five or six feet from him. It lasted only for about a minute. Later, when I moved closer to him, I noticed nothing since he never used anything scented. Three or four times on different visits I sensed the same sweet perfumed odor when I arrived home in America after having requested his prayers for a safe trip. However, once I was standing beside him while acting as interpreter for visiting Americans and I sensed the ordinary smell of blood, distinctly unpleasant and quite different from the sweet scent of perfume.

Another of the Padre's gifts, his psychic ability to read minds, brought consolations and conversions to hundreds of thousands of people who contacted him—even to those who were unable to contact him personally but turned to him to feel his protection and his help in some way, or just his nearness and his presence. Once, my sister Helena told me that with travelling on a Sunday she missed mass and upon arrival in Rome confessed this to a priest as a sin. A month later she repeated this same sin to Padre Pio; she was dumb-founded when he replied, "Yes, but you have already confessed it."

Standing before him with two Charity nuns one day, I said,

"Padre Pio, these are American nuns." The Padre said, "And what about you, aren't you American?" I told him I was, and my sister said, "Padre, these nuns say they have a question to ask you." He glanced at them, and said in Italian, "I know what they want; they want to know how they stand before God. Tell them to follow the rules of their order and continue as they have been doing." Out of curiosity, I turned to the nuns, and asked, "Sisters, what question have you for Padre Pio?" They answered, almost in unison, "Tell him we want to know how we stand before God."

Padre Pio prayed, celebrated Mass, heard confessions, and helped those who turned to him, spiritually and sometimes physically. He could make you smile with a witty remark. When he looked at you with his dark, penetrating eyes, he made you feel as though he had known you before. He could speak entire sentences with just a look or a gesture. And he expressed gratitude for all the attention shown to him with a "thank you" said so sweetly that you could hear it over and over in your heart for a long time to come.

Padre Pio often rendered assistance through prayer. He burdened himself with sufferings in hope that the Lord would accept them in the name of those who asked for his prayers. He began each day of prayer by rising at two in the morning, heeding neither fatigue nor the weight of sacrifice. In the church, beginning at eleven in the morning, he prayed for an hour where the public could see him. Then at midday he showed himself at the balustrade of the chapel of the old church and prayed the Angelus with the crowd beneath him; after this he blessed his devotees and made his way to the dining room of the monastery. But he prayed incessantly. Across his heart, hidden beneath his robe, was a tiny rosary which he said constantly, perhaps a hundred times a day. His face suggested that he was always absorbed in prayer. Prayer was his mission, and the promise of it was a message of hope directed to the entire world.

In 1940, in fact, Padre Pio gave the original impetus to a movement called "Prayer Groups." His spirit, even now after his death, seems to permeate these groups no matter where they are conducted. I have attended various prayer groups in different cities of Europe and America, and have often discovered that sincere prayers to Padre Pio give me a feeling of the presence of God, as though Padre Pio were nearby. Other members of different prayer groups have told me that they, too, have had similar experiences.

Padre Pio liked to describe himself as a "humble servant of God." He did or said nothing to attract attention to himself. He had great courtesy for everyone he met, but had little time for the inquisitive who asked nothing but to see him. And he was most clever in hiding himself. He seldom went out of the monastery except to vote or on rare occasions to visit his hospital. Yet, he was the center of an apostolate that has caused a profound transformation of the place where he lived. It was certainly not his initiative that his monastery became a center of pilgrimages to which buses came from all parts of Europe. But now, there is even an Avenue of the Capuchins, two miles long, lined with villas, shops, boarding houses, and hotels.

One can never insist enough on this elementary but oft-forgotten fact: that everything which has arisen on this mountain city is a result of the presence of this extraordinary friar. Everything there revolved around this Capuchin priest who did not make speeches, delivered no sermons, did not denounce communism, and received no training as a businessman. He did not do any of the things usually judged to be indispensable for the success of enterprises such as patronizing committees, presiding over meetings, and sending memorandums to powerful leaders.

People who suffered felt sympathy for the holy man who bore five bleeding wounds on his body; the despondent were thankful for having met him; converts to the Catholic faith were happy to have found him; and the poor, those who wept, those who hungered for justice, and those who tried to find Christ in a materialistic world, were refreshed, encouraged, and inspired by him. His magnetism was indescribable. No one ascended the mountain in vain, and each person who came and saw him experienced a strong desire, an irrepressible longing to return again and again.

There is a wealth of evidence that Padre Pio helped change lives for the better, and volumes of other names and experiences could be added to those that will be recounted in this book. The ones given here, however, will help to acquaint people not only of other faiths but of my own Roman Catholic faith with the incredible story of Padre Pio of Pietrelcina, Italy.

The Padre Pio story—his suffering, the temptations, and his unswerving goodness—is a seed of hope for humanity. Man is in such a hurry these days, he doesn't take time to reflect and meditate. But if we stop to consider carefully the significance of Padre Pio's life, perhaps some of us will feel in an often arid heart the dew of his example which sweetly invites us and exhorts us to do what we can in our everyday lives.

In addition to all that was accomplished while he lived, since his death there have been added: a Prayer Group Center; a mammoth Way of the Cross; a Center for Spastic and Retarded Children, four children's nurseries and day-care centers; a home for aged men and women; a home for aged priests; and a retreat house.

On November 4, 1969 Padre Bernardino of Siena, Postulator General of the Capuchin order, presented Bishop Cunial the papers of the first phase of the cause of Padre Pio's beatification. The Bishop accepted the request and wrote an official letter to this effect, saying, "The long procedure for canonization has now begun. In patience we wait for the final hour."

Not long after Padre Pio's death, Pope Paul VI spoke to the Superior General and several hundred Capuchins who had met there for their general chapter. The Pope said: "I say we had devout affection for Padre Pio of Pietrelcina who left us a short time ago."

For Padre Pio, the Church and the pope always occupied first place. His brethren tell that often he wept at the ills that tormented them. And on the other side, he participated spiritually with filial gladness in the great manifestations of faith both on a national and international level.

An example of his love for the Church is demonstrated by a registered will made by Padre Pio. He left the Home for the Relief of Suffering, and all other possessions in his name, under the jurisdiction of the Vatican in the name of the reigning pope.

The town where he is buried will doubtless become a shrine, similar to Lourdes or Fatima, where people of the world will come to worship God, honor Padre Pio, and be healed.

You may wonder how much of the story that follows is true. Although the dialogue had to be imagined in many instances, the facts surrounding all incidents portrayed were taken from published and unpublished sources which were represented as actual occurrences; to that end the book is entirely true.

*Dorothy M. Gaudiose*

Lock Haven, Pennsylvania
May 15, 1973

# Contents

# Acknowledgments

It would be a never-ending job trying to thank those who have in any way rendered assistance to the publication of this book on the life of Padre Pio. To all I shall say a profound "thank you." However, I would like to acknowledge the assistance rendered to me by the Capuchin friars of the monastery of Our Lady of Grace in San Giovanni Rotondo, especially to Padre Pellegrino who was with Padre Pio to the end of his life.

I also wish to acknowledge the services and encouragement given by my three brothers, V. James, Joseph and Martin, who helped in supplying materials.

I am also aware of the tremendous debt I owe to Father John Schug, O.F.M. Cap., of Broken Arrow, Oklahoma and Mary A. DeVries, of Concord, New Hampshire, whose critical reading of the manuscript and suggestions were greatly appreciated.

# Illustrations

*PROPHET OF THE PEOPLE*

## I.

*"Come on, Francis,* don't you want to play?"

The slight little peasant boy smiled faintly but shook his head no at the three older boys. They were fourteen and known to be boisterous and rowdy in their games.

"Why not?" demanded the tallest, stepping in front of him. Francis avoided the boy's menacing glare and asked to be excused.

"Let the baby pass," mocked one of the boys, taking a poke at Francis' wiry frame.

Francis felt a dull pain inside. With tears filling his eyes, he glanced at the third boy who merely observed him curiously. It was all so pointless, so unnecessary to be unkind. He saw an opening between two of them and bolted through it, leaving their laughter behind.

The two older boys roared at the sight of the unhappy little boy fleeing before them, but the third waved his hand for them to stop. "Leave him alone. You are twice his size."

Francis followed the road, walking now, and turned into a narrow lane leading to the poorest section of the village. He had been born here in Pietrelcina, in the province of Benevento in southern Italy, on May 25 in 1887, eight years ago. His parents owned a poor, one-story, two-room stone house at twenty-seven Vico Storto Valla. The rough, narrow street, which means "street of the crooked valley," runs in an area off the main thoroughfare where the village becomes a maze of cobblestone streets and small, unpretentious, stone houses, greyed with the years, with tiny crude windows that are little more than loopholes.

Shadows were spreading across the medieval face of Vico Storto Valla when Francis reached the small house where he lived. The morning after he was born in the small, desolate-looking room at the back, he was baptized in the parish church of St. Mary of the Angels and christened Francesco in honor of St. Francis of Assisi. But his birth was hardly noticed. He was just another baby coming into the world in a poor house in a poor country town, and for his parents, he was another mouth to feed.

Later, in addition to his brother Michael, there were three more, Felicia, Pellegrina, and Grazia. Two others, Francesco and Amalia, died a few months after birth.

"Francis!" his mother called, startling him as he opened the door. "Where have you been?"

"Walking," said Francis, realizing he had been gone too long. But he didn't want to tell his mother that he had been detained by a few town ruffians.

"Walking? For three hours? Do you think we are rich and can idle away each day walking?"

"No," said Francis meekly, apologizing. It made him unhappy to see his mother worried. Her forehead had wrinkled into a frown above her intense brown eyes, and her thin, colorless lips were unsmiling. Her dark brown hair was pulled back, accentuating the sharp features of her solemn face. Although she was still young, she was always tired; life was not easy for her and he did not want to make it harder.

"I saw the most beautiful bird," he said, hoping to give her something lovely to think about. "It had wide golden wings and glided like a spirit high in the sky, beneath the clouds, very close to God."

She could not help but smile at her son's beaming eyes, and the deep wine lips spreading across his pale, thin face. She shook her head. He was such a good boy, and handsome, but so frail and so different from the other children. What would become of him?

Maria Giuseppa de Nunzio Forgione was Giuseppa's real name. She had married Orazio Forgione, a dark-skinned, ruggedly handsome farmer, with deep brown eyes and dark chestnut hair. Together, with their children, they worked two acres of land they owned not far from Pietrelcina. Her husband was sometimes known as Zi' Orazio. Zi (uncle) and Zia (aunt) were colloquial expressions used as a prefix for elderly persons in central and southern Italy.

Giuseppa left Francis to watch his three little sisters while she went to the field to help her husband and eldest son bring home the baskets of vegetables. "You must mind your sisters," she said sternly to Francis. "No more walks today."

He hid the hurt in his dark brown eyes. "Of course, Mother," he said softly. He wouldn't dream of ignoring his responsibilities.

While his mother was gone Francis stayed by one of the many windows in the small house, sensing the change in the breeze passing through the open windows as the sun dropped low in the summer sky over Pietrelcina. He could hear children playing not far away in the square by the ancient little church dedicated to St. Pius V. But he had no desire to join them. He was content to stand by a window and watch the evening shadow creep out from the stone wall across the street where a fig tree burst from the cracks and mysteriously darkened the crevices in the narrow street.

Darkness had shrouded the narrow, dimly-lit Vico Storto Valla when Francis heard the familiar clatter of the small wooden cart pulled by the Forgione's treasured possession—a small brown donkey. His brother, a tall, thin boy with dark brown hair and laughing brown eyes, walked ahead with his father, prodding the beast along. Their faces were masked with dust and perspiration. Behind them, Giuseppa carefully balanced a basket of vegetables on her head. Beneath the large basket, her long brown hair had slipped loose from a clasp and fell over narrow shoulders which she held straight and firm against the burden of the vegetables.

"Help your mother, Francis," Orazio called wearily. He removed his zappa (hoe) and motioned to Michael to unload the heavily-laden cart.

After washing them, the vegetables would be taken early the next morning to a market. Except during winter, from sunup to

sundown the routine continued, day after day, year after year, without end. They shared their small plot with an older relative who helped pay the taxes, and there was always plenty of food, although in spite of their hard work, there were never five liras (in those days, one dollar) in their house.

With the evening chores nearly completed, the Forgiones gathered in the austere, sparsely-furnished kitchen to recite the evening rosary. Like all the villagers for whom religion was the beginning, the end, and the *raison d'etre,* Orazio and Giuseppa reared their children in the stern, staunch manner of peasants, placing God above all things.

Giuseppa watched her young son kneel reverently on the bare stone floor beside their crude wooden table. She placed a sunburned, calloused hand on his dark chestnut hair and brushed the short fringe away from his pale forehead. Orazio sat on the iron bed a few feet away, making a dark silhouette against the undecorated, white-washed walls. He studied her from the corner of his eye as she stroked the boy's locks. He, too, knew that Francis was not like the other children. In the silence of his thoughts he echoed his wife's sentiments: *what would become of him?*

## II.

Giuseppa found her son sleeping on the floor one August morning. "It's time to wake up, Francis!" she called. His small body was curled almost into a ball, while his head rested on a thin, white arm. His bed had not been slept in.

"Good morning, Mother," said Francis, opening his dark eyes to the early morning light. He sat up quickly.

"Why do I find you sleeping on the floor again?"

"I was praying."

"When were you praying?"

"I don't know. It was very dark and everyone was asleep. Then I fell asleep."

Giuseppa wrung her hands hopelessly. "What must I do with you? Don't you know the floor is cold and hard? You will become sick again." She knew he was susceptible to colds, and once a serious intestinal infection and high fever had even alarmed the family doctor. But when no one was around, Francis had taken some hot peppers from his mother's larder, had eaten them, and to everyone's surprise, had recovered by the next day.

"Do not worry," said Francis assuredly. He smiled at his mother, hoping she would forget about it.

"Do not worry," she mumbled. "How can I not worry when sickness and death have visited so often?" She turned to his older brother who was in the corner, grinning as he dressed to go to the fields. "You are not to speak of this to anyone," she warned him. "The older boys will make fun of Francis again."

Michael nodded obediently. He wondered why in the world Francis would want to get up in the middle of the night to pray and how anyone could possibly fall asleep on the bare floor.

Francis slipped out of his night shirt and into a pair of knee-length, black, home-spun trousers similar to those his father and brother wore. His short-sleeved, white shirt, frayed and yellow with age, was one that Michael had outgrown. He was old enough now to accompany his parents while they worked in the fields, and his job was to carry water in the hot sun to the men and women. As this was the last day before the feast of the Madonna of Liberation, the protectress of the village who, more than a century ago, freed the town from cholera, everyone would be working especially hard to complete his tasks in time.

"Are you going to the festival?" asked one of the dusty, hot laborers.

"Yes," said Francis, smiling politely. No one, including Francis, in the town of 5,000 would think of missing the celebration. It was a good time for the weary peasants—a time when they could forget the long hours of toil in the hot sun, and could dance and sing and pretend they had no cares.

Life for the hard-working, gentle peasant farmers was difficult and often cruel. Dampness and poor living conditions made sickness common, and each year floods threatened the village, often driving people and livestock into the piazza of the church away from the narrow, dangerous streets. But there was nowhere else to go, and each time it ended they returned to start all over again.

Francis was daydreaming when he spotted a thirsty farmer with a hoe trying to wave him over. "I'm coming," he called. Francis did not mind his work in the fields. Although he tired easily, it gave him a chance to stare for hours at the rolling, rocky, green and ochre fields of wheat, corn, and potatoes, and the distant olive groves and fruit trees. To him, it was beautiful country, and he was happy here; it made him feel near to God.

On the day of the festival the boys and young men were forming circles on the cobblestone streets of Pietrelcina, dancing with the girls and young women. Francis felt the wind lift his chestnut hair as he skipped up and down with the others, around and around. A pretty little girl with long black hair and a lemon-yellow dress watched him with large misty eyes, and then slipped into the circle next to him, clasping his small hand tightly.

"Look at Francis!" the young men teased.

Francis blushed momentarily but recovered in time to chide back, "Too bad you are all so ugly that no one wants to dance with you!"

The villagers laughed with Francis. He was very popular among them, with his quiet, polite ways. As far as the women were concerned, he was a good influence on everyone, particularly the wild and troublesome youth of the town. They, too, knew he was not like the others. From their houses and the fields they would sometimes watch him going off alone, across the meadows, to climb to the top of the nearby mountain, where he would sit for hours and meditate. They didn't understand it, but they were certain his solitary hours were not without meaning.

Giuseppa and Orazio observed their son closely. He had worked his way out of the circle and away from his young admirer in the lemon-yellow dress.

Orazio looked at his wife, and without speaking they seemed to be agreeing on something. He remembered what a neighbor had said once, when Francis was tending some sheep and was clearly overwhelmed with his solitude and the natural beauty around him: "Look at your little saint."

"He doesn't belong here," sounded a voice behind Orazio. Don Salvatore Pannullo, the parish priest and also a distant relative of the Forgiones, nodded a greeting at Giuseppa and placed a hand on Orazio's shoulder. He was a tall, heavy man with brown hair, kind brown eyes, and a friendly apple-red glow to his cheeks.

"What do you mean?" Orazio asked.

Don Salvatore laughed. "I mean that Francis has better things to do."

"I don't know what."

"He knows," said Don Salvatore, pointing to Francis who was disappearing on his way out of town. "Do you know he once told me he wanted to become a Franciscan priest?"

Giuseppa was surprised. "When did he tell you that?"

"I think when he was five."

Orazio smiled and nodded. "Once he saw a Capuchin and told me he wanted to be a monk with a beard."

Everyone started to laugh.


### III.


"Father, I want to become a friar," Francis announced one day.

"Very well," said Orazio, thinking about it, "if you do well in your studies in school, I will make a monk out of you, but not a beggar monk. Monks who beg are welcomed by some people when they knock, but often the door is slammed in their faces, and sometimes people turn their dogs loose on them."

Until the war, the Capuchins, who are really friars or brothers and not monks, went begging for food with a sack over their backs. One of three independent branches of the Franciscan order, the

Capuchins were founded by Matteo da Bascio in 1525 to restore a literal observance of the rule of St. Francis of Assisi, and became the fourth largest order of priests and brothers in the world. Sometimes bearded, they wear a brown habit girded with a white cord, sandals, and a long pointed hood (cappuccio) attached to the habit—hence the name Capuchins.

Francis' ardent desire to enter the priesthood among the humble sons of Saint Francis of Assisi presented Orazio and Giuseppa with a serious problem: how could they educate him to become a priest when they were so poor? They realized that to enter a seminary, solid cultural preparation was necessary, and that would cost much money.

Orazio began to talk among his family and friends about leaving Pietrelcina and finding work to earn money for Francis to begin his studies.

"I could go to Naples or Rome," he told Giuseppa, but finally he decided to go to America the following spring.

It was both a happy and a sad day for the Forgiones. Although Francis' dream was going to become reality, everyone would miss Orazio.

On the day Orazio left, Giuseppa stood sadly with her five children, already feeling the loneliness that waited for all of them. A white cloth was folded over her dark hair and a dark shawl covered the top of her plain, white cotton dress. "It is time," she said quietly, motioning for each child to take his turn saying good-bye.

"I'll pray to the Lord for you," Francis whispered, and Orazio's sad, dark eyes filled with tears.

Each week Orazio faithfully sent nine American dollars to Giuseppa. Along with others from Pietrelcina, he had found work as a laborer, laying rails for the railroad, in Jamaica, Queens, in New York City.

Before long Giuseppa told Francis, "You can begin your studies."

Francis was overjoyed; he almost cried with happiness.

Since schools in southern Italy were few and overcrowded, Giuseppa retained a private tutor, Don Domenico Tizzani, an ex-priest in Pietrelcina who had forsaken his vocation and married. Among the villagers he had the reputation of being a good teacher, but after some time it was clear that little progress was being made. Francis seemed to have a mental block in his presence. He ran to church in the morning to attend mass before classes, and he was the first after school to pay a visit to the church before going home.

"Francis is wasting too much time running off to Mass every morning," Don Domenico bluntly complained to Giuseppa one day. "I think he would be better off returning to the fields as a farmer."

Giuseppa stared at him, dumbfounded. "But you cannot be serious!" "We have worked so hard, and my husband has sacrificed so much going to America. I know Francis wants to learn. Please be patient," she pleaded. "I'll speak with him."

Young Francis reacted angrily to Don Domenico's complaint: "Does he say my brain is no good? What about his? Doesn't his own brain tell him he is living in sin in his own house?"

Giuseppa sighed, wondering what to do, but in her simplicity she understood that Francis would have to have another teacher. She approached Maestro Angelo Cavacco, but he hesitated to take Francis as pupil because he owed money to Don Domenico Tizzani. Desperate, Giuseppa appealed to Cavacco's brother-in-law who said that if he didn't take Francis as a pupil he would never permit his wife, Cavacco's sister, to step into his house again. Maestro Cavacco gave in.

It all went well, and Francis received his first real instructions in reading and arithmetic. He showed a keen mind and studied willingly and diligently. Soon he was even studying Italian grammar and Latin.

"Your son will soon be teaching me," Cavacco told Giuseppa.

She was elated and rushed to Don Salvatore to have him write a letter telling the good news to her husband.

When Orazio heard this he happily replied, "Everything will be all right now."

## IV.

Francis was fifteen years old when he left home on January 3, 1903 to join the Capuchin order in Morcone and begin his year of postulancy: He was tense and could feel the muscles tighten in his arm when he knocked at the door of the friary.

Without speaking, a shy young Capuchin led him through the dimly-lit monastery to Padre Thomas of Monte Santangelo, Master of Novices.

"Welcome to Morcone," said Padre Thomas, a medium-tall man with grey hair and a grey beard. He had a long thin face and deep-set dark brown eyes that looked long into the dark eyes of the thin, serious youth. He seemed pleased.

Francis managed a humble greeting, though he was nearly struck motionless by the impact of the large, solemn room and the Padre's plain and simple brown habit. This wasn't a game, he knew. His days of playing in the streets of Pietrelcina or wandering about the nearby fields were gone forever.

"Are you homesick?" asked one of the novices he met later. They were sitting on the narrow bed in Francis' small room.

Francis shook his head no, saying, "I have no regrets. This is where I belong." But he often thought of Giuseppa, Orazio, his brother, and sisters, and sometimes tears would fill his eyes as he remembered the love and goodness he had known.

But each day he watched the other Capuchins eagerly, longing for the moment when he could wear the brown habit and choose a saint's name. On the day of investiture his heart was pounding, and he could hardly control his excitement while he stood between two acolytes as the priest helped him into the brown habit.

"And what name have you chosen?" he was asked.

"Pio," replied Francis. He was moved with joy, but he took a deep breath and hid his overabundance of enthusiasm behind a serious expression. "I have chosen Pio (Pius) in honor of Saint Pius V, the patron saint of Pietrelcina.

The celebrant nodded soberly. "From now on you will be no longer called Francis Forgione; you will be called Frater (Brother) Pio."

At this time the family name of Forgione was replaced by the name of his birthplace, so henceforth Francis would be known as *Fra* (short for frater) Pio of Pietrelcina.

Francis soon learned that the life of Fra Pio was going to be much harsher than the life of Francis Forgione, and he was going to be severely tested.

"Do exactly as you're told," warned a nervous young student.

Fra Pio searched his friend's features. "I had no intention of doing otherwise," he stated, somewhat puzzled.

Fra Pio returned to his room. It was narrow, almost like a prison cell, with whitewashed stone walls, and allowed just enough space for a bed and a small table with washbasin and jug of water. Over his bed was a metal crucifix, and the only thing on the walls, over the bed, was an inscription: "Without solitude and diligence you will never come to acquire virtue."

"I have no need of physical comforts," he had declared when one of the students probed for a reaction to the austere surroundings.

"That's good," said the student, amused, "because you won't find any here."

And he didn't. Fra Pio spent many hours in his room, meditating and praying. Sometimes he would concentrate so hard or become so involved in prayer that he would rise later and find his head throbbing and his legs stiff and aching. He would fall into a restless sleep on the hard straw mattress, only to be roused suddenly after midnight by the harsh wooden gong that summoned students to the chapel for morning prayer three times a week.

"Keep your eyes to the ground!" cracked the voice of the stern Padre Thomas whenever the students walked outdoors.

"I don't even know if there are trees in Morcone," complained a student, and another agreed: "Since I've been here I haven't dared to look around."

"Tell us what it's like, Fra Pio," they said with straight faces. Fra Pio was shocked. "Surely you don't think I—" He caught the twinkle in their eyes then and shook his head. "Such foolishness," he growled, and left them.

"See that you don't pass here without saying a Hail Mary," said the sign over the faded picture of our Lady, at the top of the stairs. Fra Pio kneeled faithfully, as he did whenever he passed a picture of Mary from that day on.

"This boy, Francis Forgione, seems to know and observe the rules better than we do," commented the superior to another Capuchin one day. Everyone, including the students, agreed that Fra Pio was mastering his discipline and training very well.

There was a notice posted later that said two days leave would be granted to those who successfully completed their examinations. The postulants crowded around the notice and began to discuss their plans excitedly.

"It's not enough time," someone insisted. "I will spend a day in travel alone."

Not all agreed. "Be thankful we have even two days."

"But I don't live nearby as you do," the student persisted.

"Nor do I," shouted another.

"Then it's agreed, we need more time. The question is, who will ask for it?"

Fra Pio was unanimously elected. He felt sorry for his friends but went to his superior with some misgiving. "Padre, we humbly request another day of vacation. We fear that two days will not permit us to make the long journey home."

Padre Thomas peered suspiciously at Fra Pio from behind his large desk. "But you live close to here; you do not need the extra day!"

Fra Pio didn't reply. He looked embarrassed and quickly bowed his head, asking to be excused.

"Wait," called Padre Thomas before Fra Pio closed the door. "Please tell your friends something for me."

"Yes?"

Padre Thomas smiled then. "Tell them an extra day of vacation is hereby granted."

## V.

Fra Pio's year of postulancy was nearing an end. But the rigorous year of prayer, severe penances, and fasting had left him emaciated. His two dark eyes looked out hauntingly from a sickly grey face flanked by sunken cheeks. Beneath the brown habit his slight frame showed the results of frequent fasting. Late at night, in his sleep, he could be heard coughing and moaning from fatigue.

He was weak from weariness and hunger and shivering with a fever on the day when his father, back from America, and his mother came to visit him. They found him in his small room.

"Francis!" his mother cried, seeing the way he looked. "What has happened to you?" Orazio simply stared at his son, not believing his eyes.

"I am fine, Mother," he replied with such enthusiasm that they were taken back.

"But you are so thin, and so pale. I know you have a fever."

Fra Pio shook his head and tried to calm his startled parents. "Believe me, I am fine. You must understand that it is necessary to show my devotion and my obedience."

Giuseppa put her head in her hands.

"You must show some sense," said Orazio, "and take care of yourself."

Fra Pio smiled. "God will take care of me."

Giuseppa pleaded with him. "I know he sees your goodness, Francis, but please, let us take you home until you are well again."

Fra Pio tried to console his mother. "I think you suffer more than I," he joked.

But Giuseppa and Orazio were not amused, and the more they looked at their son, the more determined they were to take him out of the monastery.

"It is not that simple," the father provincial told them later. "I understand your concern, but Fra Pio has chosen a way of sacrifice, and you must understand that he will continue along this way with dedication, whether here or in your home. Do not tempt him to abandon his path of duty. He is near to taking his vows, I urge you not to deprive him of that great moment. I assure you, though his body is weak, his spirit is good and strong . . . and he is happy."

Giuseppa and Orazio relented, and Fra Pio stayed to begin his year of novitiate. He took his vows of poverty, chastity, and obedience on January 22, 1904.

Fra Pio and fifteen other novices were then transferred to the Capuchin Monastery of Saint Elia near the secluded Alpine town of Pianisi. Naked winds sometimes swept harshly through the valley and into the town, but the mountains were majestic and the country was inspiring. Fra Pio was completely taken with it and he was excited at the prospect of immersing himself in the solitude and beauty of nature.

The monastery bore reminders of Padre Raffaele who was a native of Saint Elia and died there in 1901 with the reputation of a saint. His room had been made into a small chapel, and a white statue of him stood in the middle of a flower bed in front of the monastery. Young impressionable students were roused to saintly thoughts of emulation and Fra Pio was not at all immune to the lingering influence of Padre Raffaele.

"It's grand here," a novice was saying one brisk winter day as a group of them were enjoying a recreation period in the spacious garden.

"Yes," said Fra Pio, "and another fine place to go would be San Giovanni Rotondo."

"Very true," another novice, Fra Clemente, agreed, "but the Capuchin monastery there has been closed for many years. I wish it would reopen and I would have the good fortune to go there. It is my home"

Fra Pio looked him in the eye and startled everyone by saying, without blinking, "The monastery will be opened, but I will be the one to go there."

Unexpectedly, then, Fra Pio received word that the monastery of Saint Elia had to be repaired. "I am sorry to leave this beautiful place," he said to his friends.

"We all are," a novice agreed. "Where will you go?"

"San Marco la Catala."

This monastery was located in a mountain region of southern Italy—a forbidding land of poverty and solitude.

Padre Benedetto, his teacher, was impressed with Fra Pio— or "Sweet Fra Pio" as he called him. "He is so enthusiastic," he told the others, "and observes the rules so strictly."

Here Fra Pio began to write, zealously filling notebook after notebook with endless pages. He even developed a refined and beautiful penmanship.

In April 1906 Fra Pio returned to San Elia to continue his studies. He was feeling quite well, and it showed. His face was fuller, although now it was partially hidden by a closely-trimmed beard and a thin moustache that dipped down and past the corners of his lips, disappearing in his dark low chestnut sideburns. Above his high forehead he kept his dark chestnut hair sheared close to his head.

Fra Pio made his final, solemn profession of the vows of poverty, chastity, and obedience less than a year later on January 27, 1907 under the direction of Padre Raffaele of San Giovanni Rotondo, in the presence of the religious family and especially the Reverend Fathers Egidio of Fragneto and Giustino of San Giovanni Rotondo.

After completing their studies the students were divided into two groups and assigned to the study of theology. Some were sent to Vico Garganico but Fra Pio went to Serracorpiolo where he began to study fundamental theology under the guidance of Padre Agostino who later became his confidant and confessor.

Once again, Fra Pio adhered to a rigorous life with long hours of study, prayer, and fasting. It was only a short while before his young body began to waste away, and his fever and cough returned.

"I think he is tubercular," one of his superiors announced in a meeting.

"There is no question," said another, "that he is ill and growing worse."

"I see no choice then but to send him to a more favorable climate."

"I think he should return to his home in Pietrelcina."

It was settled, and Fra Pio, who had weakened steadily and was near collapse, did not protest.

# The Devil

## I.

*It was late.* Fra Pio had been praying for many hours and that day he was unusually tired. He sank wearily onto his bed, closed his eyes, and soon fell into a deep sleep. If the door opened, he didn't hear it—only the thundering sound that nearly made the small room tremble.

"See, the saint is going to bed!" a voice taunted.

Fra Pio's eyes were open in an instant and his head snapped upward. A huge, menacing figure hovered over him in the darkness. He caught his breath, trying to see.

Two arms shot out, jerking him from his bed and throwing him against a stone wall. There wasn't even time to struggle. Pain sped through his body as he felt something strike him again and again. His knees suddenly gave way and he fell face down on the floor.

It was some time later that night when he pulled himself back onto the bed. He ran his hands over his body, wincing at each bruise. A few drops of blood slid down his cheek and into his beard. He breathed deeply and took time to regain his strength before going to his washbasin to clean himself up.

He didn't want anyone to see him. What would be the point? He knew that he had no enemies except for the devil and his disciples. Certainly no one in the friary would do such a thing and no outsider would have any cause.

Having recovered sufficiently from his earlier illness, Fra Pio was at the monastery of Montefusco, a place that had been famous since 1625 as a health resort. The monastery, surrounded by fruit trees and rich foliage, was built on a hill on the outskirts of the province.

"He has been ill," said a classmate, Joseph Orlandi, to the other young friars.

They watched Fra Pio walk slowly and stiffly toward the chapel. His face was ashen and his body jerked every few steps as a cough erupted from his chest.

"If you ask me," said a bright-eyed young friar, "he still is ill."

"Do you think it's contagious?" someone asked uneasily.

"I shouldn't be surprised," said the young friar. "I don't want to cause a stir, but ... well ... have you ever thought how many germs we must be picking up having our habits hanging side by side with his?" The young friars looked stricken.

"See here," said Orlandi, "why couldn't we have a separate closet?"

The others approved, and they cornered two of their superiors that evening on the way to mass.

"Why couldn't you have *what*?"

"A separate closet." The students begged, "It's very important or we wouldn't ask, Padre."

Reluctantly the request was granted. That night Fra Pio opened the closet door, finding only his own habit and personal articles. For a moment he was bewildered. Then he realized what had happened.

*I understand,* he told himself, thinking more about it. *They mean well.* But something was tightening in his throat, and his eyes grew watery.

With every passing day he turned more and more toward meditation. He even studied his theology lessons on his knees, his mind lost in the contemplation of the mysteries contained in the texts. For him theology was actually a meditation not only of the mind but also of the heart and emotions.

Fra Pio had been ordained in December of 1908 to the Minor Orders in the Cathedral of Benevento from Bishop Bonazzi. He also

received the first Major Order of Subdiaconate from Bishop Paolo
Schinosi, Archbishop of Marcinaopoli. The year 1909 was the year
of the Diaconate which he received July 18 at Morcone from Bishop
Benedetto of Termopoli. When Fra Pio received his last order before
the priesthood, an old abbot foretold that he would someday be one
of the greatest lights in the Church.


## II.

"Are you awake, Fra Pio?" asked his mother. It was the day
before the ordination ceremony, and they had to leave for the Cathedral of Benevento.

Fra Pio sat up in his bed, eyes wide open. "How can I sleep
with my heart bursting with joy?"

He thought the next morning would never come, but it did, and
it was the happiest day of his life. He was tingling with excitement.
He caught himself talking too fast, his mind constantly skipping to the
coming ceremony.

It was August 10, 1910, and Fra Pio was twenty-three years old.
In spite of the illness that had left its mark, his kind sensitive face
looked more youthful than usual.

The Cathedral of Benevento was crowded as Bishop Paul
Schinose began the long services of ordination for Fra Pio and ten
other young deacons. The ordinands prostrated themselves on the
stone floor of the sanctuary as a sign of their unworthiness and need
of divine assistance. The Litany of All Saints was chanted.

Fra Pio's eyes were shining. He stole a glance to the place where
his family was sitting. Michael was married now; Pellegrina was
a slim, dark, young woman of eighteen; Grazia, tall and thin, was
sixteen; and Felicia, shorter and more robust, was twenty-four. Orazio,
in America again, was absent. But his mother was there, sitting next
to her daughters, all wearing their special dresses—Grazia and Felicia

in blue linen with blue lace mantillas covering their heads and Pellegrina in black silk trimmed in white. Michael grinned at his young brother, and the others watched attentively. Fra Pio thought for a moment how much he loved them.

The ordinands rose, and the bishop began his preparatory instructions, reminding them of a priest's fundamental obligation. Then came the touching ceremony of the imposition of hands. All the priests in the sanctuary joined in the bishop's gesture. At this decisive instant they became priests. Fra Pio was now *Padre* (Father) Pio, and he joined the bishop in offering the Sacrifice of the Mass. His heart was filled with such happiness that he wondered how it could stand the strain.

Giuseppa, Michael, his wife, and the three girls came to the altar rail to receive their first blessing from Padre Pio. Giuseppa couldn't stop the tears from flooding her dark eyes. *If only Orazio could be here,* she thought.

The rest of the day was celebrated like a wedding feast. The newly-ordained priests, their families, and friends were treated to dinner in the church social rooms, and later in the day women from the parish prepared more refreshments.

That night Padre Pio and his family took the train back to Pietrelcina. Everyone was tired but too excited to rest; they laughed and joked every mile of the way.

As is customary, Padre Pio celebrated his first mass, a low mass, at his home church, Saint Mary of the Angels. It was another important day for him, particularly since he had been baptized here twenty-three years ago.

A few days later, on Sunday, he sang his first solemn mass. People from nearby towns had heard of his dedication to prayer and meditation and flocked to fill the church. It seemed as if all the peasant farmers were there, many remembering the quiet, sensitive little boy who used to bring them water in the fields.

It wasn't long before Orazio left America again and returned to Pietrelcina. He was very proud of Padre Pio and felt glad now for all the years of loneliness in America.

But Padre Pio was having another coughing spell when Orazio saw him.

"What can be done for him?" Orazio asked Dr. Cardone. "My neighbors say he must surely have tuberculosis."

Dr. Cardone fingered his glasses and was silent for a moment. Then he took the arm of the troubled Orazio. "Perhaps, but I don't believe it. I have taken test after test and always the results are the same—negative. But if you wish, why don't I take him to Naples for consultation with Dr. Peter Castellino. He is a well known physician and I would be confident with his diagnosis."

Orazio thought that sounded like a good idea, and they went to Naples the next day. But Dr. Castellino also rejected the possibility of tuberculosis. Instead, he confirmed a weakness and susceptibility to bronchial inflammation.

"You will have to live quietly," Giuseppa told him.

The young padre shook his head and smiled at his worried mother. "If I worried half as much as you do I would not have time left for my duties."

"If you worried half as much as I," Giuseppa scolded, "you might be well again."

"Very well," he teased, "I promise to find time to help you worry about me."

Coming back, he stopped to rest at the monastery of Venafro for forty days.

There he began to fast again and for twenty-one days sustained himself only with Holy Communion.

"You must eat," said a superior, and finally he was ordered to take food.

"Please," said Padre Pio, "I cannot eat."

"You must," the superior insisted, and within minutes Padre Pio vomited everything he tried.

It was a mystery to everyone, but this time he did not show any loss of weight. Even his mother and father were unaware of his fast.

Orazio had returned from America for another visit, and he

and Giuseppa smiled with satisfaction as her eyes settled on her son. He was standing tall and straight in a freshly-pressed brown habit, and his dark eyes were shining from his handsome face. He looked thin to her, but not unusually so.

"You look well, Francis," said Orazio.

Giuseppa nodded happily, and Padre Pio quietly listened to them marvel over his good health.

But things were worse than they appeared, and his health soon gave way. Once again he went home to Pietrelcina.

"Each time he comes back, he is worse than the time before," said Dr. Andrea Cardone, the family physician, "but as soon as he can walk he climbs the steps of the church to say his prayers and hear Mass."

Padre Pio was returning from such a trip one Sunday when he spotted two women from the village, sitting in their doorways, patching clothes.

Sunday is the Lord's day," he said to them, frowning, "a day of prayer...of meditation!"

They stared blankly at him as he walked away. He would have stayed to reproach them further but the Easter season had arrived, and today he had to hurry off to teach the children of the district songs to be sung during the Passion on Good Friday.

Later, he was walking in the open country with Don Salvatore Pannullo, the parish priest who had always been his friend and advisor. It was a balmy spring day and the fields had turned green with life beneath a hazy blue sky. His health seemed to improve by the minute as the high yellow sun warmed his young body, bringing color to his pale cheeks and making his dark hair sparkle.

"This life agrees with you," Don Salvatore observed. "Perhaps, Francis, you should have become a secular priest...give up the hard religious life before it does you in."

Padre Pio shook his head. "I cannot." He smiled. "Don't you remember? I pledged my loyalty to Saint Francis when I was five years old."

Don Salvatore nodded. "I remember."

"I could not be unfaithful to him."

"I don't know, Francis. You may be making a mistake to—"

"No," Padre Pio interrupted. "No mistake."

A group of young people from the village had fallen in step behind them just as the church bells began to ring.

Padre Pio stopped. "Those bells remind me of the bells of the friary which once stood here. Someday it will be here again, larger and more beautiful than before!"

The young people behind them snickered. Padre Pio, they thought, tended at times to be a trifle optimistic.

But Don Salvator sighed. "Would that this were true. It would be a help to an already overworked parish priest!"


### III.


Padre Pio slept on a narrow bed in the small kitchen of his parents' home. There wasn't much privacy with the three girls still there, and he was relieved when everyone was asleep.

On a warm Septemper evening he was sleeping restlessly, having prayed into the early morning hours, long after everyone else had fallen asleep. He heard a soft rap at the door, and the familiar voice of Padre Agostino, his confessor, asking to come in.

"Come in, Padre," he called quietly, so as not to awaken the others.

"I had to speak with you tonight," said Padre Agostino, stepping toward Padre Pio's narrow cot in the kitchen. "Forgive me for coming at this hour."

Padre Pio squinted in the darkness. A streetlight shone into the room from an open window, illuminating one half of Padre Agostino's face. He saw the familiar long, fuzzy, grey beard and the round, metal-rimmed glasses.

"But why have you come? My family is asleep."

Padre Agostino nodded. "I'll be brief."

"How did you get here?"

"God sent me. He is displeased with you."

Padre Pio was stunned. "What?" He swung his legs over the side of the cot and started to get up.

"No, no," said Padre Agostino. "No need to rise. I only came to say God does not approve of your practice of penance."

There was a long moment of silence. Padre Pio could hardly believe his ears. He stared hard at the dark-robed figure and the faintly illuminated face.

"If you are truly here at God's request, you must give me a sign. I ask you to say the name of Jesus."

Agostino's thin red lips parted and he started to laugh, his voice changing.

Padre Pio reached out to touch his brown robe, when his eyes suddenly could not focus. His hand was suspended in mid-air, touching nothing. The apparition had vanished, leaving behind the strong odor of sulphur.

There was a noise in the other room, and his mother appeared in the doorway, pulling an old shawl over her shoulders.

"How long have you been there?" asked Padre Pio uneasily.

"I thought I heard voices . . . and that smell . . . what is it?"

"Nothing, Mother, please go back to sleep."

"What is that smell?"

"Something from the street, coming through the window. Please go to sleep. I'm sorry you were disturbed."

Giuseppa felt a strange chill in the room. Her intense, dark eyes travelled around the kitchen area. "You have been praying?"

"I was meditating."

Padre Pio sat on the edge of his cot, leaned forward wearily, and clasped his hands under his chin. He closed his eyes. Giuseppa watched him a moment and then turned to go.

Prayer and meditation became Padre Pio's sole refuge from the apparitions that haunted him in the night. He couldn't escape them, and he didn't try. They came in the forms of his superiors, with the same request, that he give up his practice of penance. He even grew to expect the strange, terrifying night visitors, and he prayed constantly for strength to endure their assaults. He became so absorbed in prayer at mass that he would be unable to go on for an hour. Every day, as he offered mass, baptized, performed weddings, or conducted funerals, villagers became aware of the long lapses in his service.

"His mass is too long," complained an old peasant woman to Don Salvatore.

Don Salvatore was not surprised. It was the third complaint that day.

"It isn't that we do not like our young padre," the woman insisted. "But we must work in the fields. We cannot stay in church for long hours praying with him."

Before long the father superior of the Capuchins came for a visit. He held the devoted young padre in great esteem and Padre Pio's correspondence had already revealed to him the state of his union with God. So when Don Salvatore told him of the mounting complaints of the villagers, he wasn't surprised. He understood.

"You must order Padre Pio to continue Mass without long pauses," the superior advised Don Salvatore. The next morning Don Salvatore followed the superior's advice. Each time during a long pause he mentally prodded him to continue, and each time Padre Pio heeded the admonition and continued with the mass.

Padre Pio was following the lonely path of self-immolation, and that meant penance, blood and tears. It meant the destruction of something, in order that something else might live.

"I have felt a need to offer myself as a victim to the Lord for poor sinners," he wrote to Padre Agostino late that November.

His unceasing prayer brought him great comfort as he fought to continue on the rocky path he had chosen.

He was awake, kneeling beside his cot, meditating, one night when he lifted his head at the sound of the November wind whistling down Vico Storto Valla. From the corner of his eye he caught the movement of a dark shadow crossing the room toward him.

A harsh voice cut the silence of the night. "You will give up your penance, priest. I command it."

Padre Pio remained silent, waiting for the figure to step into the silver rays from the streetlight that shone through the tiny kitchen window.

"Priest, do you hear me?"

Padre Pio refused to reply, and braced himself as the shadow moved closer.

"Do you hear—"

"Leave this house," Padre Pio demanded suddenly, lifting himself to face the shadowy figure. "Go."

The harsh voice broke into spasms of laughter, and Padre Pio could feel a chilling hand clutch his gown. He could feel the cold penetrating and numbing his skin. The night visitor released his gown all at once and struck him full across the face. Padre Pio quickly folded his arms across his chest to shield himself from the blows that followed. Pain began to overtake him, and tears filled his dark eyes. He sank helplessly to his knees on the stone floor.

From somewhere in the night a voice called out, roused by the disturbance. It came from the house beside the kitchen window, but Padre Pio could not find his voice to cry for help. He couldn't even stand. He struggled to remain awake but something hard struck the side of his head and he felt his consciousness slipping away. When he opened his eyes again Giuseppa was shaking him. The grey light of dawn had obliterated the night shadows. He looked around fearfully, but only his mother was there.

Giuseppa was trembling, and Padre Pio moaned at her touch. Her dark eyes darted nervously over his pale bruised face, and her hands pushed back the hair high on his forehead to reveal three dark bruises.

"It's all right, Mother," he tried to assure her. "I am fine."

"Fine? How can you say that? What has happened? What were those terrible noises we heard?"

Padre Pio tried to smile. "Probably me falling over the chair."

"No, you must not hide this any more. We have heard the voices in the night, the strange sounds. Even our neighbors ask me who comes to our house so late in the night. I must know. This is our house, and I must know what is happening while we sleep." Her voice cracked, and she clasped her hands to control their shaking. "I demand that you tell me," she cried.

Padre Pio walked to the table and picked up a small mirror. His face was drained of color, and his cheeks looked hollow. His dark hair and beard hid most of the bruises around his head and face. He felt a sharp pain in his right side but refrained from examining himself while Giuseppa stared at him accusingly.

"I have asked you to tell me what has happened," she repeated insistently.

"It has nothing to do with you," he said, quietly dismissing the subject. He knew she would not understand the diabolic forces that tormented him—those "ugly gentlemen" and "Beelzebul and his equals," as he called them.

The more he was tormented, the stronger he became. "Jesus chooses souls," he wrote in another letter, "and among these, in spite of my shortcomings, He has also chosen mine to help Him in the great transaction of human salvation."

In March 1913 he wrote to his confessor, Padre Agostino:

"Friday morning I was still in bed when Jesus appeared to me. He was very sad and upset. He showed me a multitude of priests, regular and secular, among them various ecclesiastical dignitaries. Some were celebrating the Holy Sacrifice of the Mass. Others were putting on the sacred vestments; still others were taking them off.

"The sight of Jesus in distress gave me much pain, so I asked him why he was suffering so much. He did not reply, but kept looking towards those priests. When he became tired of looking, he glanced away. He raised his eyes towards me and two tears ran down his cheeks. He walked away from the crowd of priests with an expression of disgust and scorn, crying: 'Butchers!' Turning to me, He said: 'My son do not believe that my agony lasted only three hours. No, I shall be in agony until the end of the world because of those for whom I have done the most. During my agony, my son, we must not sleep. My soul seeks a few drops of human pity. But alas, they leave me alone under the weight of indifference. The ingratitude and the sleep of my ministers make my agony more difficult to bear. Alas, how they return my love. What pains me even more is that they add scorn and unbelief to their indifference. How many times I was ready to destroy them, but I was held back by the angels and the souls that love me. Write to your confessor and tell him what you have seen and what you have heard this morning. Tell him to show your letter to the Provincial.'

"Jesus continued speaking to me, but what He said I will never be able to reveal to anyone in this world."

For many days, this apparition physically affected Padre Pio. He was almost paralyzed, and it was some time before he felt all sensations returning.

## IV.

At the monastery of Our Lady of Grace in San Giovanni Rotondo, Padre Pio often went outside to the front of the small church after confession for a breath of air. A group of people had congregated, waiting for him.

"Padre Pio," said a young married woman from the village, "I live next door to the church and every morning after my husband has gone to work and the baby is still sleeping, I go into the church, hear mass, and receive Holy Communion. But fearing the baby might awaken while I am gone, I leave the church with the host in my mouth. Am I doing wrong?"

Padre Pio looked over and smiled at the concerned young woman. "No," he assured her, and watched the relief spread across her face.

"That woman," he told the small crowd later, "is more pleasing to God with her little time in church than you or I who would spend all day in church because she is taking time out of her duties in order to serve Him."

The people nodded, except for a fleshy, childlike peasant woman who was absorbed in her own thoughts. Padre Pio caught her eye and motioned her over.

Quietly, so no one else could hear, she explained, "I am ashamed to say this but I feel I must tell you. I love you more than I love God."

Padre Pio thought for a moment and then, with a straight face, asked her to go into the village and steal for him.

"Padre!" she exclaimed, totally shocked at him. "I would never do such a thing!"

"I command you," he insisted, with a stern, serious face, "do it under obedience."

She stared at him as if he had gone completely mad.

Padre Pio's seriousness gave way to a smile. "You see?" he asked. "You do love God more than me. Don't you see when I order a thing obviously contrary to the will of God that you do not obey. Are you convinced now?"

Her eyes met Padre Pio's and brightened as they exchanged a warm, silent message.

"Padre Pio, you are so good," said a woman nearby, overhearing them.

His smile quickly vanished. "I am not good," he replied brusquely. "Only Jesus is good. I don't know how this habit of Saint Francis that I wear doesn't run from my back."

An old man marvelled at his modesty. "You are a saint," he said.

"The saints stay only in heaven," Padre Pio replied, not the least impressed with the compliment.

It seemed to him that he had about enough fresh air for the time being and he turned to leave. Blocking his path, though was a pretty young woman in her early twenties. With wide blue eyes she looked adoringly at the handsome friar and handed him a bouquet of tiny yellow and white flowers.

"But what are these flowers for?" he asked. "Have you taken me for a gardener?"

Her face clouded at his indifference. He was clearly immune to the things of her world.

"Please tell me if this medicine is correct," begged a voice, and Padre Pio observed an arm sticking through the crowd. A short, bald man carefully pushed his way to Padre Pio's side and began detailing his illness.

"My good man," said Padre Pio, "you ask me? Go to a doctor."

It was too much. He looked for a path to escape, and left them as quickly as possible.

Inside the monastery he heard one of his brothers calling him. "Spiritual Father," the friar called. "Wait."

Padre Pio frowned at the title. It was becoming a habit among too many of them. "God sees the stains even among the angels," he told the friar. "Figure out what he sees on me."

He was gaining a reputation for being abrupt. His brothers liked to joke about the time a journalist from Milan begged him to reply to a woman who invoked strictly a particular blessing. "Tell her to get herself blessed by whomever she wishes," replied Padre Pio.

Or the time one of the padres asked him how he managed to say so many rosaries with the kind of schedule he had. Padre Pio, who loved to think of the rosary as "the weapon" cut him off without a smile. "You want to know too much."

It was only a matter of time before his comments were passed back and forth at the monastery and outside. His remarks on faith took on particular importance:

"Let us be especially grateful to God for the gift of faith, a gift which is given us at baptism. We must be especially grateful, because not everyone has the fortune to be born in a Christian country and a Christian family which sees to it that the Sacrament of Baptism is administered.

"We must remember that faith is the greatest gift that God has offered man on this earth, because from an earthly man he becomes a citizen of Heaven. Let us guard this great gift jealously. Woe to him who forgets himself, who forgets Heaven, whose faith grows weak, and worse still (may God preserve us all) who denies his faith. This is the greatest affront that man can offer to God.

"Pay attention. Pray God to preserve this gift in us as the most precious thing He has granted us. But faith, remember, must be exercised, because all of us have faith in one way or another, starting with Lucifer himself who is in hell with all the rebel angels. Scripture also tells us that they have no love, and therefore they hate. We must be sure not to fail in the faith which God has instilled in us at baptism and which is strengthened more and more by the sacraments.

"Let us pray to our most holy Lady, that if such a misfortune should befall us, she would pray to the Lord God to destroy us rather than make us monsters of ingratitude towards Heaven.

"A good heart is always strong. It suffers, but sheds its tears and finds consolation in sacrificing itself for its neighbor and for God.

"He who begins to love must be prepared to suffer.

"The field of battle with Satan is the human soul. In the soul a battle rages every moment of our life. The soul must give free access to the Lord so that it can be fortified by Him that His light may enlighten it, that it be clothed with Jesus Christ, with His justice, truth, the shield of faith and the word of God, to conquer the powerful enemies. To be clothed with Jesus Christ it is necessary to die to oneself.

"When one is with the good, one is good. When one is with the bad, one follows evil. This means having only half a conscience. It is like the behavior of those children who in the presence of strangers stuff themselves with all sorts of things only out of greediness because they are sure their parents will not dare to scold them in company."

Padre Pio felt strongly not only about faith and goodness, but about suffering—all kinds of suffering. He was sensitive to the slightest evidence of pain and abhorred violent acts of any kind.

It was noon, mealtime in the monastery, when someone asked Padre Pio if he saw a wounded bird that morning while walking in the garden.

Padre Pio shook his head, asking how the bird got hurt.

Between bites the friar explained: "Fra Vincenzo shot the bird and it fell in the garden with its wing bleeding."

Padre Pio looked up and stopped eating. He pushed his plate

aside. "But Saint Francis didn't do things like that!" he cried, shaking his head.

Silence fell around the table. At the far end an embarrassed young brother kept his eyes fixed to his plate until someone mercifully changed the subject. When Padre Pio got up to return to his room, the brothers quickly hurried to kiss his hand and wish him a good rest.

Shyly, the young hunter clasped his hand and kissed it.

Padre Pio patted his arm. "Excuse me," he said. "I didn't have anything against you."

But the incident provoked him to consider the pain and suffering of the world and his heart was heavy that day. In the evening Padre Mariano, before the Eucharistic benediction, spoke about the Holy Father, and Padre Pio was in the choir at the foot of his crucifix, listening attentively to every word.

When Padre Mariano hinted that some had offered their lives as victim souls, Padre Pio covered his eyes with trembling hands. After the sermon he wiped away the tears that were streaming from his sad dark eyes.

# War and Peace

*Padre Pio was twenty-eight years old* when Italy entered World War I on the side of England, France, and Russia, against Germany and Austria. In May 1915 all able-bodied men were called to report for military duty. Summer had withered into late fall when he was in Pietrelcina and a letter came addressed to Francis Forgione.

"What is it?" Giuseppa asked.

He recognized the official government stationery as he tore open the envelope. "By order of King Victor Emmanuel II," he told her, "I must report to Naples for a medical examination."

Orazio doubted that Padre Pio would get past the doctors. "He will never wear a uniform."

"Do not be so certain of that, Father," said Padre Pio. He was quietly resigned to the idea, thinking it was still another test—another trial to endure.

Before leaving, he wrote to Lucia Florentino, one of his spiritual subjects, asking her for prayers and remembrance in her daily Communion.

When the doctors finished with him in Naples, he waited patiently for the results in a small room with a dozen other young men, most in their late teens and early twenties. They were laughing and in high spirits, unconcerned that there was a war going on somewhere outside and that in a matter of days they would be carrying guns by day and sleeping on the cold ground by night. Padre Pio sat quietly on a hard wooden chair, his hands folded in his lap. The other young men looked at him occasionally, curiously eyeing his brown habit.

A harried doctor with his hands full of papers leaned through the doorway. "Francis Forgione?" he called. "Come in, please."

Padre Pio stepped into the adjoining office.

"Well," said the doctor with a broad smile. "Nothing wrong with you." Padre Pio managed a faint smile.

"These are your papers," said the doctor. "You can pick up your uniform on the way out."

Padre Pio shook hands with the doctor and thanked him. He walked slowly to the door, wondering what lay ahead.

"Oh—Forgione," the doctor called. He was looking at Padre Pio's sandals. "Guess you'll have to get used to boots. But don't worry about it. I've had three priests here in the last week. Keep your eyes open and you'll probably find one of your own kind marching right beside you."

Padre Pio looked back at him. "I do hope I recognize him without his sandals."

As Padre Pio went out the door, the doctor followed and nudged one of the young men waiting in the next room. "I hope he knows which end of the gun to point at the Germans." The recruits roared with laughter. Padre Pio paused in the hall outside, listening to them.

But he never entered combat. Instead, he was assigned to the Tenth Company of the Medical Corps in a hospital, Trinitá dei Monti, in Naples as an orderly. He lived in the nearby barracks, a large, plain, stone building with army cots for twenty to thirty soldiers. Along with his habit and sandals, the name of Padre Pio was carefully locked away, and he became Private Francis Forgione. Dressed in the grey-green Italian Army uniform, which was too large for him, and with his short hair and large brown eyes, he looked thin and sickly.

"Have a drink, Forgione?" asked a friendly, red-faced soldier. The young man was sprawled across his bunk, clutching a half-empty bottle of wine.

Francis shook his head. He was tired and wanted to be alone. The days were long and hard and left little time to meditate and pray.

Some of the men talked in low voices late into the night, recalling wild and undisciplined times. Their curses and blasphemies

rang painfully through Francis' mind. He tried to shut out the voices but they echoed relentlessly. His physical, psychic, and spiritual awareness heightened every impression, and the things he saw and heard robbed him of peace and sleep. There was little relief, not even during the day at the hospital. There, the sights and sounds of suffering penetrated like daggers into his heart. He began to live for the mornings when he could leave the hospital and go to the shrine of Caesarea on the Via Salvator Rosa to celebrate Mass at the altar of Our Lady of Patience, so venerated by him.

He endured only a few weeks of the daily harsh military routine and the lonely, sleepless nights, when exhaustion overtook him. He was eating poorly and growing weaker each day. A high fever had set in and he began speaking in a parched voice. The next day his commanding officer ordered him transferred to a military hospital.

Francis was half asleep in the hospital bed when he overheard his name being spoken.

"I don't understand it," a doctor was saying. He stood at the foot of Francis' bed and conferred with another doctor. "When I took his temperature, it went right off the scale. I had to have a special thermometer sent down, and it registered 125 degrees last night and 120 degrees this morning. He shouldn't even be alive."

"And you say he's not experiencing delirium?" asked his colleague.

"No." The doctor shook his head, looking totally baffled. "I've never seen anything like it."

"Nor I."

"Well, one thing we know. That cough of his is more than a bronchial infection."

"Tuberculosis?"

"Active tuberculosis. I'm recommending six month's leave of absence immediately. I've asked his father to come and get him."

"Why bother with a leave of absence? We both know he'll never be back. I doubt that he'll live out the six months."

Francis opened his eyes and listened to their footsteps grow faint as they walked away. Without making a sound he cried until his eyelids became heavy and he fell into a nightmarish sleep. When Orazio came, he listened to the doctors, but refused to accept their dark predictions. "He will not die. His mother will cure him." The doctors patted him on the shoulder and offered their sympathies.

## II.

"Did you sleep well?" his mother asked.

"Well enough to resume my duties," Francis said, and smiled. He felt his old self returning under Giuseppa's care and attention. It was good to be wearing his habit again, too, and for several more months he could forget about Private Forgione and start thinking about Padre Pio.

With his strength coming back he became busy again. He even built himself a straw hut near an old elm tree where he could go to read and pray. He chose a spot in the fields on the outskirts of the village in a place called Piana Romana, owned by the Forgione family. In this area there were several small houses and chapels which provided care and shelter for farmers.

He came home from his hut late one warm September day, a Friday, when the parish was commemorating the stigmata of Saint Francis. Giuseppa was sweeping around the fireplace in the kitchen when he walked in, shaking his hands strangely.

"What are you doing," she asked jokingly, "playing the guitar?"

Padre Pio wasn't smiling. "No," he said, "but I feel deep burning in the palms and backs of my hands." Giuseppa's smile disappeared. "What could it be?" she later asked Don Salvatore.

He listened in amazement. "I believe Francis has received the invisible stigmata," he concluded.

The stigmata were marks resembling the wounds of the crucified Christ, believed to have been supernaturally impressed on the bodies of certain persons, such as St. Francis of Assisi.

Giuseppa caught her breath. Her dark eyes grew wide as she tried to comprehend it all.

"Do not be frightened," Don Salvatore put his arm around her trembling shoulders. "Your son is on the right path. He has been chosen by God to suffer for others." She rubbed her eyes, brushing away the tears.

"Now, now," he soothed. "You must be thankful that Francis is one of the chosen."

Don Salvatore decided not to divulge the news to anyone except Padre Pio's superiors; later he wrote an account for the Vatican.

### III.

Wherever Padre Pio went, the reputation that he was very holy preceded him; some had started to call him the "little prophet."

He was assigned to the old monastery of St. Anna in Foggia early in 1916. At that time the monastery was in the suburbs surrounded by fields where he could walk. Sometimes he would stop to rest by the Chapel of the Seven Crosses nearby. He said mass in the little monastery church either at the main altar or at the altar of Our Lady of Pompei.

While in Foggia he received a letter from a young woman who questioned whether her brother should choose military or civilian life.

Padre Pio wrote to him: "It doesn't matter which career you choose, because you will succeed. The Lord will treat you as you treated your men."

His sister and her family, seeing the letter one day, were puzzled, until an enlisted man visiting them once commented that her brother treated his men as a father would treat his children. *How did the Padre know that?* she wondered. The brother returned to civilian life, and became successful.

The parish priest of Cagnano had observed such prophecies with interest. "Please have lunch with me," he said one day, anxious to know the young Capuchin better.

"I must speak with him," said the priest's servant. "He has a special gift for reading the heart . . . they say he's a saint."

The priest shook his head at her. "I'm afraid that's all the more reason why he won't have time for you."

Throughout lunch the servant waited patiently. When Padre Pio left she followed him downstairs.

Halfway down the stairs he turned, and said to her, "What is it you wish to say to me? You may tell me now." Before she could answer, he added, "You want to give yourself to Jesus of Nazareth."

The servant agreed she had been saying these very words to herself for many days. But she had other things on her mind, and explained, "I have an aunt who is very ill."

"We will pray," said Padre Pio, "and do God's will."

"I also have a niece who has a terrible abscess on her head, and two others on her arm and leg."

He nodded. "We will pray together for her."

It wasn't long before the servant's aunt died, but her niece, bedridden and unable to walk, felt the presence of someone near her who almost pushed her out of bed.

"Like a gust of wind," said the girl to her family, "compelling me to rise."

While everyone looked on in amazement she got up and walked. Later she confessed to Padre Pio, and when he came into the sacristy she wanted to speak to him again, but he left her abruptly and went out into the church. She burst into tears.

"Why are you crying?" asked a padre passing by. He tried to calm the distraught girl.

"Padre Pio will not listen to me," she sobbed, desperately unhappy. "He walked out on me."

"Perhaps you wanted to tell him that you wanted to become a nun."

Her eyes lifted. "Yes," she said.

The padre smiled, and joked. "That's why he left."

Padre Pio came back later and found the girl still waiting for him. She rushed over, kissed his hand and placed it on her head.

"Take it easy," he said gently. "Your head hurts you and my hand hurts me."

Her eyes widened. She was holding his hand over a wound in her head, carefully camouflaged by her dark hair so he couldn't see it. She was still struck with wonder as he softly stepped away.

Padre Pio walked some distance before he realized that he was becoming feverish. As the days passed, the warm and unstable climate around Foggia aggravated his old problem, and he began coughing again.

"Perhaps you should return to Pietrelcina," his superior remarked.

Padre Pio thought about it. He was glad he was being consulted this time because he somehow felt that Pietrelcina was not quite what he wanted. Something deep within him craved peace and quiet, and solitude for meditation.

Padre Paolino, superior of the monastery in San Giovanni Rotondo suggested that the climate at his monastery might help Padre Pio. Everyone was in agreement and on July 22, 1916 he made the move. The high mountain air did agree with him, and after two months he felt well enough to return to Foggia. But his superiors thought he should go back to San Giovanni Rotondo permanently. He was transferred under obedience in December.

"Welcome back," said Padre Paolino. He peered at Padre Pio through tiny round glasses perched on a long thin nose. His untrimmed grey beard fell nearly ten inches beneath his chin.

Padre Pio smiled at him. "I'm glad to be here again," he said.

He was introduced to Fra Agostino, Fra Fernando, Fra Gaudenzio, and Fra Archangelo. He had met Fra Nicola on his first visit.

"Yours will be room five," Padre Paolino told him.

His cell, next to that of his confessor, Padre Agostino, had an inscription over the door: "The cross is always ready and awaits you wherever." It was a simple room with only a cross on the yellow walls over the narrow bed. There was a chair and a small wood table filled with pictures of his family and one of the Madonna and Child. The father superior had ordered a heating system for his room so he wouldn't suffer from the cold, but Padre Pio had it taken out. He didn't want any privilege his brothers didn't have.

Padre Pio settled in and soon fell into a daily routine consisting of celebrating a long mass, and community prayers with other Capuchins. For long hours he would retire into the chapel, remaining in meditation and prayer before the large crucifix.

Our Lady of Grace Monastery was built in 1540. In 1624 an earthquake damaged it, and it was rebuilt in 1629. While it was being built, a drifter, Camillo DeLellis, arrived there. The friars were kind to him, and he responded to their kindness by helping them in their construction work. He made a shelter near the monastery and lived there for awhile. He was later canonized; Saint Camillus, the founder of many hospitals and tireless worker for the sick.

Twice the Capuchin fathers were forced to leave the monastery The first time was in 1810, following the suppression of religious orders by Joseph Bonaparte, but they returned in 1814. The second time was in 1867, after the laws of suppression by Prince Eugenio da Carignano. For forty years the monastery was used as a poor house, but was reopened as a monastery on October 4, 1909.

The monastery itself is a poor, small, and primitive beige stone building. The front entrance is through a small church. This consists of a nave and one aisle. Among its corridors are portraits of former Capuchin saints. Above the high altar is a beautiful painting of Mary of Grace, and below are Saint Michael and Saint Francis. The choir at the opposite end of the church is considerably raised above the entrance and hidden from the congregation.

One and a quarter miles from the monastery is the ancient-looking city of San Giovanni Rotondo, perched majestically on the ridge of Gargano Mountain. Its population of 20,000 was largely made up of shepherds and farmers. Their living conditions were primitive, because the town was cut off from the rest of the world through lack of roads and fast means of communication. Light and water, and even rudimentary plumbing, were nonexistent. Large families were forced to live in frightful hovels which were no more than dug-out caves below ground level. Sickness took its toll from dampness and poor living conditions, and the abilities of doctors were sorely tried when they had to perform urgent operations in the patients' homes under risky conditions. The name San Giovanni comes from ancient times when a circular temple was dedicated to Giano. This circular temple gave to the town the addition of "Rotondo," which means round, and the name of San Giovanni is from the first church built there.

A steep, winding road leads into the town from a huge plateau checkered with yellow wheat fields growing beneath a fierce southern sun. Century-old olive trees and almond trees give way to hills of rock near the summit, where nothing but scrub survives.

Padre Pio felt at ease here in this new home, so silent and calm.

"Is that all you're eating?" asked a brother at dinner. He stared across the table at a plate of boiled broccoli sprinkled with lemon juice. Broccoli, which could be found growing wild, cost nothing and was therefore the vegetable of the day almost every day.

Padre Pio nodded. "And this," he said, reaching for a small piece of bread.

"You would be stronger if you ate more," the brother advised.

Padre Pio looked up at him, trying not to show his irritation. He wished they would all occupy themselves with things other than his health.

The brother persisted "It's just that your fasts weaken you, and it would be better if you strengthened yourself between them" The others at the table agreed.

"Of course, it's your concern," said the brother.

Padre Pio let his fork fall with a clank on his plate. "You would do me a great kindness," he said coldly, "to keep that in mind." He snatched up the Breviary beside his plate and went to his room. There, he sat on the edge of his bed, asking himself, "Why must even my friends interfere with my duty to God? Isn't it enough that I must fight the devil and his hideous disciples?"

He slept fitfully again that night, tormenting himself over the scene. He knew very well what his twenty-day fasts were doing to his health, but he also knew that he must continue to do penance.

He had learned to put his sleepless nights to good use. He loved to write and spent his time late at night in his room writing long letters to those who needed help but couldn't come to the monastery. Often the letters were long, intimate, affectionate, and firm in their insistence on heroic courage and patience in carrying the cross.

"It is the divine mercy," he wrote, "which has placed us on the steps of Calvary to follow our divine Master. It is through the mercy of God that we live among so large a number of people. Do not let us lose sight of these souls, but keep close to them, unalarmed by the sight of the cross we must carry, or the length of the road we have to travel, or the steepness of the hill. We are encouraged by the consoling thought that after the ascent to Calvary there will be another road, leading up the mountain of God to the Heavenly Jerusalem, and the climb will be effortless!"

On another occasion he wrote: "There is one thing God cannot reject in his sinful creatures, and that is the sincere desire to love Him. . . . Stick to your daily communion, reject any irrational doubt, trust in cheerful and blind obedience, don't be afraid of evil. The weapon which is to lead you to victory is the submission of your own judgment to those who have the task of guiding you through the battles and perplexity of life."

Padre Pio took every letter he received seriously, and he always tried to give consolation and confidence as well as advice whenever he replied, as he did in this instance:

San Giovanni Rotondo
February 3, 1917

Dear Assunta,

"The Lord takes away even the recollection of the consolation received so that the shadows shall be complete. Be calm, and feel sure that these shadows and temptations are not a punishment to fit your iniquity, you are neither impious nor blinded by your malice, but one of the many elect who are tried by fire like gold. This is the truth and if I spoke otherwise I should be betraying my sincerity. I can discover no sin in your soul that can legitimize your fears, and so your anxieties and agitations are only a cross. But my daughter, what are the feverish searchings for God that your heart feels itself incessantly making? A consequence of the love that attracts and the love that urges. Love takes flight? To love and to stimulate love.

"You know well, my good child, that Mary was petrified before her Son crucified, but you cannot say that she was abandoned by Him. On the contrary, how much better did He love her from then on, when she suffered and couldn't even cry? Take heart then, defend yourself as well as you are able and if you don't succeed, resign yourself to seeing night fall, without feeling afraid.... In the meantime, practice David's saying: Lift your hands in the direction of the Holy Place during the night, and bless the Lord. Yes, my child, let us bless Him with all our hearts and bless Him always, and pray to Him to be our guide, our ship and our port."

Your humble servant,
Padre Pio

## V.

During World War I, General Luigi Cadorna found that the Libyan War and his battles against the Austrian Army had exhausted his troops. His soldiers were pushed back at Caporetto, and he was held responsible for the defeat. Now, camped in Libya, Africa, his spirit was near collapse.

"Do not disturb me, under any circumstances," he told the sentries as he disappeared into his tent. He was a brusque man of average build, with olive skin, dark eyes, and a black mustache.

He removed a revolver from the holster at his side. For a long agonizing moment he stood there, his arm hanging limp, the weapon in his lifeless hand. Slowly then his arm raised, and the short barrel leveled above his right ear.

"Such an act is foolish."

The general wheeled about, staring into the sensitive dark eyes of Padre Pio.

"How did you get in here?"

Padre Pio didn't reply. He removed the gun from the general's hand, placed it on a small table, and left as quietly as he came.

The general rushed from the tent, losing sight of Padre Pio in the night. "I told you to let no one disturb me," he shouted angrily at the sentries. They looked bewildered. None of them had seen the young Capuchin.

General Cadorna relentlessly searched for the young padre who had stopped him from taking his life. After endless days he was directed to the Monastery of Our Lady of Grace at San Giovanni Rotondo, where Padre Pio had been sent. There he immediately recognized the youthful padre in the chapel.

"I must speak with him," he told a friar. He explained the debt he owed.

"That is impossible," said the friar, listening to the story. "Padre Pio never left San Giovanni Rotondo."

The general went away, confused, leaving the friars to speculate on the similarity of this to other reports they had received. They knew that Padre Pio was seen on two occasions in Rome, once by a bishop at the beatification of St. Therese de Lisieux, and at the tomb of St. Pius X, whom he venerated above all popes for his simple, Christ-like meekness. At both of these times, the friars had seen him also—following his daily routine at the monastery.

The possibility of bilocation was raised, as reports continued to reveal that the young priest had been present in two different locations at the same time. It was not a new concept. In the history of the Church a number of saints are on record as having possessed this gift, such as St. Anthony of Padua, St. Alphonsus of Liguori, and St. Martin de Porres.

Padre Pio ignored the speculation about himself and kept silent, going about his duties as usual. The six months of sick leave were over, but he did not return to his army post. He was completely involved with his work.

"I can't get over how much better you look," said a Capuchin. He shook his head in amazement at Padre Pio's trim, dark figure. He looked less than his thirty years. The sickly palor had left his face, and his dark brown beard had thickened, making him look heavier.

"I can't get over how much better I *feel*," Padre Pio replied.

In spite of his rigorous penances, his health had improved so much that he was able to take care of the spiritual direction of the friar's school. His health was even sufficient for him to accompany his sister Grazia on a trip to Rome when she joined a religious order.

His family came to see him each month, and he always looked forward to their visits. The girls were young women now, and Michael a settled, married man. Time had taken its toll of Giuseppa and Orazio and the wrinkles that creased their hands and faces made them look old before their time. Whenever any of them sought his advice he eagerly tried to direct them.

Padre Pio made a good reputation for himself as spiritual director. Looking back, a Capuchin padre said: "The Padre worked with all his heart for the glory of God and the sanctification of the youth under his care. We students respected and appreciated his gentleness and his honesty. We venerated him for his deep piety. To see him celebrate mass was enough to persuade us that his was a soul lived only for God."

His work as spiritual director was not limited to the students of the seminary either, but extended also to the inhabitants of the town. His first group of intimate friends were formed this way—known as "spiritual children." Soon a group of Franciscan tertiaries, members of the Third Order of St. Francis, formed about him and spread his teachings.

Padre Pio became known to the residents of San Giovanni Rotondo through his sympathy and interest in their conditions. From the beginning he seemed to have a thirst for ministering to people through the Sacrament of Penance. His genius in knowing how to comfort penitents was a magnet. The poor, the sick, and the needy found their way to the monastery of Our Lady of Grace.

He had a kind word or a word of advice for everyone. "He has a patience that never ends," said a villager. They all insisted that he loved everyone.

## VI.

Private Francis Forgione was listed as a deserter. When his six months of sick leave were over and he didn't return, his commanding officer wrote to the marshall of Pietrelcina, ordering an investigation. The marshall obeyed and wrote back that there was no one in town by the name of Francis Forgione.

Seeing Padre Pio's married sister, Felicia Masone, in Pietrelcina one day, the marshall asked, "Do you know a Francis Forgione?"

Felicia's oval face broke into a smile. "Of course. He is my brother, Padre Pio. He is now stationed at the monastery near San Giovanni Rotondo."

The marshall of Pietrelcina quickly wrote to the marshall of San Giovanni Rotondo to tell him an army deserter was in the area, but he neglected to mention the name Padre Pio.

The marshall of San Giovanni Rotondo began a thorough search for Private Francis Forgione.

"I never heard of him," said a villager, echoing the conclusions of everyone the marshall asked.

It was a cold, windy day when a friar from the monastery saw the marshall turning up his collar and marching up and down the deserted streets. His ruddy complexion had turned blue from the biting wind. "Why are you out in this weather?" he asked.

"I'm looking for an army deserter—Francis Forgione." The friar was aghast.

"But surely there is a mistake. Francis Forgione is Padre Pio's secular name."

"Then he's here?"

"At the monastery, but there must be a mistake," the friar insisted, looking worried.

The marshall shook his head, breathing heavily in the stiff wind. "No, he's a deserter. No question about it."

The friar stood speechless, not knowing what to do, while the marshall hurried off.

Dusk had fallen when the marshall reached the monastery. "Are you Francis Forgione?" he asked the good-looking padre who was pointed out to him.

Padre Pio turned and looked at the marshall's blue face. "Yes," he said, "I'm called Padre Pio now."

The marshall's dark eyes shifted nervously as he met Padre Pio's disarming gaze. "But you *are* Francis Forgione?"

"Yes." Padre Pio saw his discomfort and tried to put him at ease with a smile. "Is there something you want to tell me?"

The marshall took a deep breath, and said, "I have orders to see that you're returned at once to your army post."

"Will tomorrow be satisfactory?" asked Padre Pio agreeably.

The marshall nodded with surprise. "I'll leave you on your own, if I have your word you'll return—you being a man of God."

Padre Pio looked puzzled. "Why wouldn't I?"

The marshall shrugged his shoulders and left. There was something about men of the cloth that he just couldn't understand.

Padre Pio left the next morning for Naples. He was wearing his army uniform and carried a small bag with his habit.

"You're in big trouble, Forgione," said the tall stern officer who met him. "Big trouble."

They went to the officer's quarters. "I'm afraid I don't understand," Francis said, searching for a clue in the officer's hard expression.

"Don't understand?" snapped the officer. He whirled about and paced back and forth behind his desk. Francis shook his head, not understanding.

"Do you think being a priest gives you the right to come and go as you please? Sit safely in your little church while brave men go out and die?"

The words stung Francis like a slap in the face. He could feel the warmth creep across his cheeks. His teeth clenched and his dark eyes narrowed. With controlled effort, he reached into his pocket and calmly displayed the document he had received when sent home for convalescence. He began to read: "To await further instructions at the expiration of leave of absence." He paused and looked openly at the officer. "Instructions to come to Naples were received yesterday, so here I am."

The officer stared at him, his jaw starting to droop. He pointed at Francis. "You thought—?" Francis held out the paper.

"No, no." The officer shook his head, feeling embarrased. He smiled and gestured awkwardly. "I never did think you were a deserter. But I have a job to do, you understand." Francis nodded solemnly and put the paper away.

"I see no reason to keep these charges against you. But I want you to report to the hospital for some tests before you settle in at the barracks."

Francis startled the doctors when he walked into the examination room.

"Well, well," said the doctor who had insisted he wouldn't live out the six months' leave. "Look who has come back. We were wondering when you would return."

Francis stripped down and waited patiently while two men examined him. "What is the verdict?" he asked when they had finished.

One of the doctors helped Francis back into his uniform. He reached out, putting an arm over his shoulders. "Padre, we are going to recommend an immediate discharge for you."

"Why?" Francis looked up, surprised.

"You still have tuberculosis."

Francis looked away and fell silent for a moment, and then, with a smile on his lips, turned back to the doctor. "Thank you," he said softly.

They watched him walk away. Somehow he looked terribly sad and alone.

"If you'll sign here," said a cheerful young officer, just before

Francis left, "you'll be all set."

Francis studied the paper and shot a disapproving glance at the smiling young man. "But this is a pension. I've done nothing to deserve it."

The young officer laughed. "So who will know?"

Francis was appalled. "God will know and so will I."

"Look," argued the officer, "You have to take it. Do you realize how much paper work is involved in this? It would cost more to take it away than the entire pension is worth."

Francis thought for a moment. "May I request that it be sent to the monastery—for the poor of the town?"

"Suit yourself," said the young officer, unimpressed. "We'll send it to whatever address you give."

Francis consented. Now all that remained was to change into his habit once more and return to the monastery as Padre Pio, leaving the life of Private Francis Forgione behind him forever. He stopped at Pietrelcina on the way and visited with Giuseppa and Orazio.

"You have no more need of this," said his father, anxiously admiring the clean, pressed grey-green uniform.

Padre Pio sighed, knowing what was in Orazio's mind. He shook his head. "That is government property. It would not be right to keep it."

"But it is good strong cloth," Orazio persisted, "and would stand up well in the flelds."

Padre Pio turned away to hide a smile. "Please see that my uniform is returned to headquarters," he said to his mother.

She started to laugh, but Orazio didn't think it was very funny. There were times, he thought, when his son carried this business of right and wrong too far.

# The Stigmata

*The stillness of evening* settled upon the monastery as Padre Pio heard the confessions of students. It was August 5, 1918, a day he would long remember as the beginning of his own special agony.

He was suddenly struck with terror as a strange being wielding a long thin blade confronted him without warning. He couldn't move and his eyes were helplessly fixed upon the tip of the menacing object from which flashing tongues of fire evaded the dimness around him. A cry escaped his lips when all at once he felt the iron blade being thrust into his very soul. Somehow he recovered his voice and quickly dismissed the students. Throughout the night and into still another day and night his body grew weak from the constant sensation of iron and fire ripping and tearing him apart.

More than a month passed, when after mass one Friday morning, on September 20, his terror and agony reached a pinnacle beyond human comprehension. The nightmare began, however, in a moment of complete peace and quiet. He felt drowsy, almost as if he had fallen into a deep sleep that numbed his senses. The strange sensation penetrated every fibre of his body and nearly anesthetized him.

Then, into this sweet dream came the mysterious visitor, only this time drops of blood were falling from its hands and feet and side, collecting in pools on the floor. Padre Pio's calm was instantly shattered and his heart began beating with uncontrolled spasms erupting inside the prison of his motionless body. Mercifully, it all began to fade as suddenly as it appeared, and his weak body slid limply into a huddle on the floor.

He opened his eyes, letting the tears escape. Sensation was returning to his limbs and he felt his hands quivering. He moved his legs and noticed that a dull ache was quickly changing into a sharp pain that stabbed repeatedly at his hands, his feet, and his side. He raised himself on an elbow and looked at his trembling hands. They were soaked with blood. Glancing down he saw that a portion of his brown habit on one side was damp. His eyes travelled over the long robe to his feet. They, too, were red with blood. His entire body began to quake in horror. He tried to speak but the words choked in his throat, and he gasped for breath.

The nightmare went on. Something drove him to try and move, to reach his room before the other priests returned to the monastery and saw him. He pulled himself over, shuddering with agony at every move. Somehow he dragged himself down the long corridor and into his room. He pulled himself onto his bed and collapsed in fear and pain.

"Help me," he pleaded softly. "Please, God, help me to understand."

He began to breathe easier, but the pain throbbed fiercely. His hand gently moved toward his side. He could feel that the blood-soaked spot on his habit was growing larger. Something was hemorrhaging inside. With terrified eyes he raised himself and studied the dark spot on his habit, wondering if he would die from internal bleeding.

"Please," he prayed. "Take away my fear."

The minutes dragged by. Slowly he pulled himself together and examined his wounds. There was no way to escape it—they were real. It had not been a nightmare or an hallucination. The truth sank into his consciousness. He had received the stigmata—real wounds of skin and tissue which by shape and location correspond to the five wounds of Christ.

His mind groped with the reality of his condition, and relief swept over him when he realized that the wounds weren't fatal. He began to cry, and he thanked God.

For a week he stayed out of sight as much as possible and kept his hands hidden by gloves. But at weeks end a brother cleaning the rooms saw the blood-stained sheets. He nearly flew to Padre Paolino and nervously reported his finding.

"What is the meaning of this?" Padre Paolino later asked Padre Pio.

Padre Pio hesitated for a moment. But he knew it was useless to try and hide the wounds. Those on his hands and feet were too obvious, and they simply weren't healing. He stripped off the gloves from his hands and held them out to show the torn, bleeding tissue.

Padre Paolino recoiled at the sight. He fumbled for words and finally just stared at Padre Pio, totally speechless.

"Be at peace," Padre Pio assured him. "It is not a thing of the devil. After mass last Friday," he explained, "A strange personage appeared before me, and I was struck in my hands, my feet, and my side."

Padre Paolino shook his head incredulously. He examined the wounds then, ordered immediate attention to them, and reported the phenomenon to the provincial in Foggia and the general superior in Rome.

The Church had recorded only about 290 persons who were granted the stigmata by God. The most popular stigmatist of the ages was St. Francis of Assisi, the founder of the Franciscan order. St. Francis, who was a deacon, received the stigmata on September 17, 1224, on Mount Alvernia in the Appenines, two years before he died. So now this news of a stigmatized priest served as a magnet to draw great crowds of people, including the sensation seekers.

Since Orazio and Giuseppa couldn't read, a relative wrote to Don Salvatore Panullo, the parish priest of Pietrelcina, and asked if he would break the news to them. At the time this relative was attending boarding school in Foggia.

Giuseppa was alone in the kitchen when she heard that Don Salvatore had a letter he wanted to read. Her heart jumped. A flu epidemic had taken Felicia's life on the twenty-fifth. Had something terrible happened to someone else? Her thoughts flew to her other children. Pellegrina, a seamstress, was married and living in Pietrelcina; Grazia was now Sister Pia, in Rome; Michael was working in America; and Francis was now Padre Pio, in San Giovanni Rotondo. She cried when Don Salvatore told her what happened.

"You must not cry," he said. "It is for his sanctification."

The tears stopped, but she thought about it for a long time. "We must no longer call him Francis," she told Orazio. "He is Padre Pio."

Michael was working in Flushing, New York when he heard the news. "Oh, God," he cried, "what an injustice that Francis, so good, has to suffer so much!" He took the next ship back to Italy. When he found out it was the stigmata, though, he cried for joy, instead.

They all rushed to see him and in the days that followed spent long hours visiting him. Through it all Padre Pio was glad to see them, but often, especially just after his stigmata, he wondered who was consoling whom.

Just after it happened, the news spread in spite of the father provincial's attempts to delay public announcement until doctors could examine and treat the wounds, and report to the Holy Office.

The wounds were showing complete independence of any physiological law. The four wounds on his hands and feet bled continuously, drop by drop, with live red arterial blood. The fifth lesion, a chest wound near his heart, drained—separately and not at the same time— arterial blood and a living watery substance.

Although the father provincial tried to keep the lid on everything, the news simply couldn't be contained.

"It is the will of God," Don Salvatore said to the villagers.

"I don't believe it," mumbled an incredulous peasant. "These things don't happen."

Don Salvatore shook a finger at him. "Then you don't believe that Saint Francis of Assisi was stigmatized."

"Of course I do," said the peasant stubbornly. "But that is different."

"Why is it different?"

"Saint Francis lived long ago when strange things happened. These things don't happen anymore."

Don Salvatore threw up his hands. "Very well. I urge you to go to San Giovanni Rotondo and see for yourself."

The peasant went, and so did half of the village of Pietrelcina.

Although Padre Pio tried to hide his wounds while saying mass, the people were soon whispering about his bleeding hands. Soon the news spread to all the village of San Giovanni Rotondo, a few miles away, and then to nearby Foggia. Suddenly it picked up momentum and spread all over Italy and from there to every place in the world. Some priests began to attack Padre Pio and the stigmata through sermons and the press; others defended him and attacked the press. San Giovanni Rotondo became the mecca of a religious explosion made of faith, hope, credulity, skepticism, and devotion. And the legend of Padre Pio was born.

## II.

"Look what has come for you," said a brother to Padre Pio. "A present from Switzerland."

Padre Pio's dark eyes turned to the small brown box. "A gift for me?" He opened it and started to smile, holding out a pair of soft, cloth shoes. "This is very thoughtful."

The brother nodded. "Yes, indeed. Perhaps now your feet will not give you so much pain."

Padre Pio was pleased. He went to his room and found some socks. He carefully pulled them over his swollen feet, trying not to disturb the open wounds. Then he slipped on the cloth shoes. His feet and ankles were continually swollen, particularly the right one. He stood, testing the shoes. They threw the weight off the wounds, and he could tell they would help alleviate the pain somewhat, although he still couldn't walk without shuffling and scraping his feet, and his gait was slow, uncertain, and hesitating.

He found a small hand mirror and studied himself. *I am thirty-one*, he thought. *Already a crippled old man.* He ran his hand over his beard and across his forehead, pushing back the closely-cropped fringe of hair. His dark eyes were clear and bright, and he really didn't look afflicted in any way—so long as he didn't walk or stand too long. His long brown habit hid the wound in his side and brown fingerless gloves hid the open and bleeding wounds in his hands. Lately he had gained weight and now weighed 165 pounds. He was still slight, though, only five feet ten inches tall, but the bulky habit made him look taller and heavier.

He stared at himself a while longer. There was something hauntingly sad and mysterious in his solemn face. Even he could see it. It was almost the face of a complete stranger looking back at him. "You," he whispered to the solemn image in the mirror, "shall never again know freedom from pain."

He turned away and stared at the closed door before going out. *He who begins to love must be prepared to suffer,* he reminded himself.

Outside, there seemed to be a lot of commotion. "They are coming by the thousands," said a brother, meeting him in the hall.

Padre Pio nodded. "I know." He began to look worried. "Do you think it will get out of control?"

The brother shrugged his shoulders. "Some say it already is. The police are outside every day now, watching the crowds. Did you know that?"

Padre Pio raised his eyebrows in surprise and reluctantly ventured on. He really didn't understand all this attention. Slowly and laboriously he walked through the crowds gathering in the corridors. He managed to keep smiling, and paused to speak tenderly to an old woman, bent over with age and illness. He began to feel a new happiness and warmth, and he blessed the crowd.

Fall deepened and the brisk winds of winter blew over the monastery of Our Lady of Grace. But each day it was the same. "These crowds are a public annoyance," mumbled the short, balding police commissioner to himself. He pointed to one of the policemen lingering outside his door. "You, there. It is time we put a stop to this. I want that priest arrested."

The policeman was aghast. "Padre Pio?"

"Yes. That's the one."

The policeman unhappily left for the monastery. He found the road jammed with carts, private cars, and even strange vehicles that looked like gypsy wagons. Near the entrance men, women, and children were crowding around a young-looking, dark-haired priest in a brown habit. The policeman watched them reach for his hands and kiss them while the young padre blessed each person.

"Is that Padre Pio?" he asked.

"Yes," replied a woman in front of him. She glanced back over her shoulder. "Isn't he wonderful? To think God has placed him right here among us."

The policeman left. "He was not doing anything wrong," he explained to the Commissioner.

The policeman was abruptly dismissed, and someone else was sent in his place. But it was the same. He returned without Padre Pio too.

"I shall have to do it myself," said the commissioner with a sigh. He stuffed a pair of handcuffs in his pocket.

Dark, heavy storm clouds were hanging low in the winter sky when the police commissioner arrived at the monastery. Everyone had gone to lunch except Padre Pio who was painfully shuffling over to a woman and child. She threw herself at his feet, clutching the child in her arms.

"Padre Pio," she pleaded, "help my child. He is deaf and cannot speak."

He looked at the small little body snuggled in the woman's arms. "What is my name?" he asked.

The boy turned his tiny face toward him. "Padre Pio," he answered softly.

The police commissioner's mouth fell open, and he watched the deliriously happy woman whisk the little boy away.

"What do you want?" Padre Pio asked the commissioner.

"I want to confess," he said meekly.

"All right," said Padre Pio, "come with me." He gestured toward the commissioner's coat, and said dryly, "Be careful you don't hurt yourself with those handcuffs in your pocket."

## III.

By 1919 the clamor over Padre Pio of Pietrelcina and the stigmata grew so intense that the poor friars of San Giovanni Rotondo were suffering battle shock, but they did not stand alone. Support for Padre Pio came from priests in Ireland, France, Spain, England, and Poland. There were also a large number of Italian priests who believed that Padre Pio had the stigmata by divine gift.

Among the many doctors, psychiatrists, psychologists, and neurologists who examined Padre Pio's stigmata, the first was Dr. Luigi Romanelli, a handsome, noted doctor in Barletta; his study included five examinations.

Summoned by the Capuchins, Dr. Romanelli visited Padre Pio in June, 1919. In his medical report he described the wounds in Padre Pio's hands as anatomic lesions of tissues near the third metacarpus, almost circular in shape, with clean-cut borders, having a diameter of little more than two centimeters. These lesions were covered by red-brown scabs, and there was no bleeding point, no edema, and no inflammatory reaction in the surrounding tissue.

"The wounds in his hands are not superficial," said the doctor, "because by exercising a certain pressure with my fingers, squeezing the thickness of his hands, I had a feeling of emptiness between my fingers. The wounds in Padre Pio's hands," he concluded, "are real transfixions or perforating wounds. This may be why Padre Pio can not completely close his hands." Dr. Romanelli repeated the barbarous experiment many times during the night, even though he realized it caused Padre Pio a great deal of pain. He did it again in the morning and always had the same assurance of emptiness or perforated wounds.

"The wounds in his feet," said Romanelli "present identical

characteristics to those in his hands, but are wider at the tip. The feet are more difficult to examine, because of their thickness. The slightest pressure on his feet causes Padre Pio to wince with pain. Tears fill his eyes, and it is obvious that his physical agony is very real."

The red-brown radiating scabs were produced by the progressive drying of blood that flowed from them, and these scabs, from time to time, fell off and revealed the wounds in all their details. Their contours were so clean that even under a magnifying glass they produced no edema or reddening. When soft, the scabs detached themselves first from the edges, then from the center, until they fell off completely and gave way for the formation of new scabs.

Dr. Romanelli examined the wound of the chest one day. He could see that the lesion there was two and three-quarter inches in length with a tapering line not appreciably deep, but it was bloody and had the shape of an inverted cross. It was located about one inch below the left *papilla mammaria* (nipple) clear to the border of the heart and offered the same characteristics as the other wounds, with a flow of arterial blood. The edge of the lesion showed it was not superficial. The tissue that surrounded the lesion was not inflamed, but it was painful at the slightest touch.

When a Capuchin from Milan visited one day, the others at the monastery told him about the location of Padre Pio's wound in his side being to the left, in the region of the heart.

"The wound of Christ was at the right," the Capuchin priest pointed out. "Surely the strike of the lance came from below, entered the right, and went to pass the heart without coming out of the other side of his chest."

The friars found Padre Pio. Asked one, "Is your wound situated at the opposite side of the Savior's?"

Padre Pio met their probing eyes. "It would be too much," he said quietly, "if it were exactly like the Lord's."

What puzzled Dr. Romanelli, though, was the fact that wounds heal if they are treated well, but complications set in if they are treated badly—but Padre Pio was proving to be an exception to this.

"I want you to wash your hands in unsterilized water and cover them with common wool gloves and handkerchiefs, without using a disinfectant," he instructed Padre Pio.

Padre Pio willingly but wearily did everything he was told. The long, often painful examinations were beginning to tire him. When nothing happened by mistreating the wounds, Dr. Romanelli had Padre Pio wash with a soap of the worst quality. Still all this did not aggravate, infect, or cause any complications. He applied ointments that should have healed the strange wounds. Finally, he tried to medicate them in every conceivable way, but the wounds remained unchanged.

Dr. Romanelli shook his head hopelessly. "I do not find clinical evidence which would allow me to classify the five wounds medically." He submitted his conclusions in a long, detailed report, along with photographs, to the Holy Office in the Vatican.

"I cannot explain it," Dr. Romanelli told Padre Pio's superior, Padre Paolino. "The wounds or his perfume."

"His what?" asked Padre Paolino.

"The perfume. Isn't it strange that a friar like Padre Pio would use perfume?"

The superior was astonished and agreed it was rather peculiar.

"It happened again," Dr. Romanelli wrote to the superior of the Capuchins some time later. He explained how he noticed the same sweet smell while going up the steps of his house when he was preparing to return for another visit with Padre Pio. It was not auto-suggestion, he insisted, because no one had told him anything about this before. Each time the odor was identical.

Padre Paolino thought he had better look into this before it got out of hand too. He stopped two young Capuchins on their way to the chapel. "Do either of you know if Padre Pio uses perfume?" he asked them.

The two young brothers grinned broadly. "Perfume, Padre?" asked one. He tried to stifle a giggle.

Padre Paolino frowned disapprovingly. "I don't believe I said anything funny."

"No, Padre, nothing," the young Capuchin hastily agreed. "Shall we ask him for you?"

Padre Paolino wiped away the perspiration collecting on his forehead. "Certainly not." He sighed, and hurried away.

Padre Pio pretended not to notice the brothers talking in low voices, and he avoided the curious eyes that followed him as he laboriously shuffled down the corridors. When he talked to anyone he tried to keep the conversation on other matters.

"We need a hospital," he told the friars one day.

"Yes," said a brother. "I have to agree with you there."

Padre Pio thought more and more about it and became almost obsessed with the idea. He tried to convince everyone he talked with, although no one really needed convincing. "From the first days of my arrival in San Giovanni Rotondo," he said, "the conditions of health assistance on the Gargano have been so wretched that when a poor man was seriously injured, he had to be taken from the Gargano to Foggia on a cart. This meant a journey of at least six hours, during which time the injured man could die of loss of blood."

It was true, they all agreed. The hygiene and health of the growing population had long been neglected. The name "hospital" was applied to a group of small rooms in a building in the town, and they were inadequately supplied with beds. The local practitioner was called for emergencies but was forced to supply his own surgical facilities. For serious operations the patients had to go to nearby Foggia, San Severe, or Monte Santangelo, and there, operations were sometimes delayed through lack of means of communication to summon medical help in time to aid the patient.

"I am going to do something about it," Padre Pio exclaimed suddenly at lunch one day.

Everyone looked up. They were all seated at rows of narrow wood tables placed along the walls, forming a ring around the dining room.

There was a moment of silence. A young friar at the other side of Padre Pio's table smiled and looked at his beaming face. "Would you pass the bread, please?" he asked.

## IV.

The General Curia of the Capuchins, their international headquarters in Rome, deemed it necessary to have additional reports on the wounds. The father general, therefore, asked the Vatican to recommend a doctor. The Holy See sent Dr. Amico Bignami, a distinguished-looking, balding man who was an eminent professor of pathology at the University of Rome. As he was an atheist, it was expected that his views would be objective and scientific. He arrived at the monastery of San Giovanni Rotondo on a hot and humid summer day in July, 1919.

Dr. Bignami noticed the size and location of the lesion and the scab in the palm of Padre Pio's right hand. The scab, he said later in his report, was round and almost black, loosened in part from skin underneath. The skin surrounding the wounds was normal, however, and not broken, but it was colored with iodine.

"What have you been doing?" he asked.

Padre Pio explained how he had tried time and again to cure the wounds by using iodine, and to reduce the hemorrhage. But the blood continued to flow, and he even had to change the linen coverings twice a day.

The doctor found an identical scab, more superficial, in the back of Padre Pio's hand, in the region corresponding to the palm. Even this scab and the surrounding skin were conspicuously colored with iodine. Dr. Bignami noticed similar symmetrical lesions in Padre Pio's left hand as well.

On top of the right foot, over the second metatarsus, the doctor observed a lesion of tissue and a small superficial scab, dark brown, again with the surrounding skin colored with iodine. On the sole of his foot he found a small area of skin rounded and strongly tinted with iodine.

"More iodine," said the doctor. "Is there any left in Italy?"

Padre Pio smiled faintly. "I had to do something," he said. He found a spot on the wall and fixed his eyes on it while Dr. Bignami examined his left foot.

The lesion was perfectly identical to the right foot in extension, position, and character.

Padre Pio removed his brown habit and hung it over a chair. The doctor studied the wound in the left of Padre Pio's chest. It extended from his armpit to the middle of his chest, in the figure of a cross, from five to nine centimeters across, then tapered off. The skin was dry, red-brown, with a superficial abrasion. No blood was flowing. Dr. Bignami noticed that this lesion was not deep and the skin was not harmed.

"I'm going to apply a remedy to heal the wounds," Dr. Bignami said. As a precaution against fraud he sealed the dressing covering the wounds.

When the time came to break the seal, he removed the dressing, and stared in amazement at the wounds. They were completely unaffected by the remedy he had used.

"I just do not understand the symmetrical position of the wounds in both hands, feet, and side," he said. "Nor do I understand how these wounds have persisted for nearly a year now without getting better or worse."

Padre Pio shook his head. "I don't know."

"Why do you have these wounds in these particular five parts of your body, and not elsewhere?" Bignami suddenly asked.

Padre Pio pulled his habit down and adjusted the rope around his waist. "This you must tell me," he replied. "You are the man of science." Dr. Bignami looked at him skeptically.

The essence of Dr. Bignami's report to the Capuchins was that he attributed the stigmata of Padre Pio to a necrosis of the dermis and epidermis, such as the death of the surface and subsurface tissues. This was his famous theory of necrobiosis, but he maintained he could not find an explanation for the position of the five wounds.

Speculation continued in spite of all examinations. Some visitors questioned Padre Pio openly. One asked him about the sixty-two persons who had borne the stigmata in the course of the history of the church and had been canonized.

"The wounds of our Savior are an eternal marvel," he snapped brusquely, "But those of men are nothing more than the corruption of tissues."

Padre Pio began to wonder where it would all end. He prayed and meditated for long hours, and during these hours he found that the pain and bewilderment would leave him, and a deep feeling of peace would bring him welcome relief.

Dr. Bignami's report, meanwhile, had not satisfied the Capuchins. Summer had given way to fall when the same General Curia of the Capuchins summoned Dr. Giorgio Festa, a renowned doctor and surgeon from Rome. He was an older man with greying hair and a neatly trimmed beard. Dr. Festa, a Catholic, was highly esteemed and considered to be strictly objective. He first stopped at Foggia to see the Provincial of the Capuchins, and to examine all the documents available on Padre Pio. Then he and the provincial drove to San Giovanni Rotondo and met Padre Pio.

Dr. Festa remained in the monastery long enough to get a good idea of the life and character of Padre Pio before he began his examinations. He watched the young priest humbly and unobtrusively go about his daily tasks. All the attention paid to him seemed to embarrass him.

Padre Pio submitted to more long and tedious examinations without complaint. Dr. Festa's conclusions confirmed those of his two colleagues. He was concerned with the regularity of Padre Pio's respiration and circulation, and with his lungs, the tone of the heart valves, and his blood pressure. He also agreed on the regularity of the digestive system, the abdominal organs, and the perfect balance among the functions of the nervous system and the mind. He confirmed the findings of his colleagues on the skin in the region around the stigmata. Then, Dr. Festa joined Dr. Romanelli in contradicting Dr. Bignami's description of the wounds.

"I want to take home a sample of your blood," he told Padre Pio, "to examine under microscope."

He took a piece of bandage soaked with blood from Padre Pio's side and put it in a small case. When he left the monastery, he shared a taxi on the way to the train station with a well-tailored man and two women.

"I smell something wonderful," said one of the women.

The others sniffed about and, in spite of the strong draft from the speeding taxi, they agreed. "It's a beautiful fragrance," said the man. Dr. Festa listened to them with interest, but said nothing.

He kept the cloth for a long time in one of the dark drawers in his Rome office. The blood-soaked cloth perfumed the atmosphere so noticeably that many patients asked where the fragrance came from. It gave an aroma the combination of violets, lilies, and roses.

"I have to admit it puzzles me," Dr. Festa said. He knew that the smell of blood which comes from the veins is normally repulsive. He concluded that this odor was contrary to any natural or scientific law. "It defies the possibility of logical discussion," he said, "but I have to admit to its reality."

The Capuchins listened eagerly to his reports. "Padre Pio wears stockings at night and fingerless white gloves, of cotton or wool, depending on the season," he told them. "During the day he wears brown gloves, placing them directly over his wounds. In the morning when he takes them off, the bloodstains correspond to his wounds. I examined many pairs of these stockings and half-gloves, and my analysis reveals that the stains are products exclusively of arterial blood." The Capuchins shook their heads in wonder.

"Once," said Dr. Festa, "when he took off the stockings, I found that the red-brown scab had fallen, and I could see a well-defined scar that contrasted strangely with the pale color of his surrounding skin. The actual wound was in the center of this rose-shaped scab. The wound was as large as a pea, with an irregular red-brown border. It seemed to extend into the foot as though produced by a pointed instrument. The scar on the back of the foot presented a lesion which matched perfectly the lesion of the sole of the foot."

One of the Capuchin priests, a provincial, Padre Pietro da Ischiatella, who had been with Padre Pio during one examination, said: "I witnessed the stigmatist place his open hands on a table,

4

covered by a newspaper. When he took off his half-gloves, the scab covering the wounds fell off. I saw the hole which passed clear through the hands. I could even see the large printed letters of the newspaper through the wounds in his hands. The wounds are real holes!"

## V.

In the history of the saints a perfumed odor is not new. St. Dominic's hands gave off a perfume when people kissed them, and St. Helena had the gift of perfume when she received Holy Communion. Some saints' bodies gave the perfumed odor after death, such as in the cases of St. Coletta, St. Joseph Cupertino, and St. Martin de Porres. Whenever any one was in the state of grievous sin, St. Philip of Rome would experience a foul odor when approached by him, even though he was immaculately clean physically.

In Padre Pio's case, the perfumed odor was called the consolation of his presence. It was said to encourage, focus attention to an immediate danger, or recall his presence, advice, or guidance. Many persons began to remark about it independently, as not everyone noticed it at the same time.

The friars at the monastery of Our Lady of Grace listened to the visitors fervently discuss the perfume.

"Some claim it is carbolic acid," said a priest, talking to two other friars. "Even oriental incense or tobacco has been suggested."

"No," said a friar. "That is nonsense. He uses no disinfectant." The other two nodded. "I have heard some say it all depends on the state of your soul. They say persons who are in the state of grace get the sweet smelling odor, while those in mortal sin get nothing. But I think it is being proved that non-believers and grave sinners receive the odor of sweet perfume as the first sign, and this influences their conversion."

They stood for a long time, debating the issue. Across the room, from a shadowed doorway, Padre Pio watched them for a moment before going about his business.

"I have experienced it," said Grazia Formicelli, the godmother of Padre Pio, to a friar. "I was on the mountain picking berries and was walking backwards. Suddenly I smelled the perfumed odor of Padre Pio. I lifted my head, turned around, and saw behind me a steep precipice. Another step and I would have fallen into it."

Later, when she went to San Giovanni Rotondo to thank Padre Pio for saving her life, he waved the thanks away, saying sharply, "That will teach you not to walk backwards like a little girl."

A biographer of Padre Pio, Gian Carlo Pedriali, wrote a book called *I Have Seen Padre Pio* and told how he went out of curiosity to see the stigmatist. "I was standing in the church," he said, "with my young son, when I first saw him being greeted by a crowd of people. I was some distance away when all at once a sharp and pleasant odor invaded my nostrils. At the same time my son pulled at my sleeve, asking what this perfume was."

Josephine Marchetti of Bologna documented an account of a miracle: "Before I recovered the use of a withered arm," she said, "I first had the sweet perfumed odor of Padre Pio. From that moment on I began to feel life in my right arm, although several doctors had said I would never have the use of it again."

Signor Domenico Tognola, of Zurich, Switzerland wrote to the monastery in San Giovanni Rotondo, and told the friars: "One morning I awoke and had a strong odor of violets, roses, and lilies. I recognized it as being associated with Padre Pio and wondered what it could mean. I understood its meaning when a postman brought me a letter from my brother whom I had not seen in thirty-two years and had presumed dead. I had been praying to Padre Pio for any kind of news concerning my brother, and this was an answer to my prayer."

A seminarian from America, James Bulmann, visiting the monastery of Our Lady of Grace one morning had the privilege of serving Padre Pio's mass. Afterwards, he said to the friars: "While answering the prayers at the foot of the altar, I noticed a beautiful perfume, the likes of which I have never smelled before. I had come with little knowledge of Padre Pio and did not know of this phenomenon."

The friars smiled. Said one, "This is generally a sign that God has bestowed some particular grace through Padre Pio."

"Yes," said a friar, "and many of those who know Padre Pio recognize this perfume as proof that he has heard their prayers, or as a warning to proceed or desist from some action, or an encouragement to pray or to hope. They say it is his way of telling the persons that he was praying and taking an interest in their problems and of indicating that he was morally present though physically far away."

"What does Padre Pio say about all of it?" asked the seminarian.

"He doesn't," said a friar. "He doesn't like to talk about any of it."

"Well," said the seminarian, "I can see that it is a strange mysterious phenomenon, regardless."

One of the friars prepared to leave. "Do you want to know what I think?" They all looked at him.

"I think it is all an enormous case of overactive imagination!"

The friars were shocked, but the seminarian started to laugh. "What would life be without a little controversy now and then, right?" The others eyed him suspiciously, and walked away.

Controversy continued in medical circles as well. Summer had turned the land green when Dr. Romanelli met Dr. Festa in July 1920 and they ended an initial disagreement on the wounds. A year ago, Dr. Romanelli had seen only one deep chest wound which extended seven or eight centimeters. Dr. Festa, on the other hand, had seen a double lesion just as Dr. Bignami had, which was superficial and in the form of an inverted cross. Now they agreed—it was an inverted cross.

This figure of the inverted cross was superficial and barely affected the epidermis. More strange was the condition of the derma. A narrow, short scar covered the central part of the wound. The surrounding tissue did not present any redness, infiltration, or edema.

But the scar's appearance was deceiving, for it caused great pain when it was touched and was more extended than the scar tissue which bordered the other lesions.

Although this chest wound was superficial in appearance, Dr. Festa said he witnessed drops of blood trickling in greater quantity than from the other wounds. "In my first examination," he said, "toward nine o'clock in the evening I removed a small cloth from the surface of the wounds, the size of a common handkerchief, all impregnated with a liquid-like red lead, so I placed a new white handkerchief on the wound. The next morning at seven o'clock the cloth I placed on the wound the previous evening, together with another cloth of equal size added in the night by Padre Pio, were completely soaked with the same secretion, indicating a real hemorrhage."

Padre Pio kept handkerchief-size cloths on a night table beside his bed. Before the superior of the monastery received orders from the Vatican to preserve these cloths, he wanted to burn them.

"Keep them and distribute them among the faithful," Dr. Festa suggested to him. Padre Pio thought about it, and finally agreed.

"I collected a number of them," said Dr. Festa, "and the blood and watery substance which impregnated the small cloths appeared always in the same proportion and had the same characteristics, though the total quantity of the fluids varied. During my year of examinations Padre Pio used at least three of these cloths a day, some of which were totally saturated."

The doctor also noticed that the blood and water would come out separately from the tapered wound of the side. The cloths showed a fusion of the blood and water. When they remained for a period of time, they turned into dried blood.

Over the years, Dr. Festa kept a record of these small cloths and from time to time he reported to the Capuchins. "In no case," he said, "was the fusion of these liquids complete. There was no corruption or presence of microbes or bad smell." In every case, he told them, the spots of blood became brown with the years, but by looking at the small cloth in a clear light, they appeared more red than brown.

Explained Dr. Festa: "In the palm of his left hand, about the middle of the metacarpus, there was an anatomic lesion of the tissue, nearly round, clean-cut, and having a diameter of little more than two centimeters. This was covered with a red-brown scab. This scab was hardened from the blood that trickled from the center of the wound."

The lesion in the palm, even when observed with a magnifying glass, did not present any edema or inflammation. It was clean-cut skin. And the lesion in the right hand, said Festa, was the same as that of the left hand. During the examinations he saw drops of blood trickling from the surrounding area.

All of the doctors noted that Padre Pio's pain continued, and he couldn't walk without dragging his feet. Before an elevator could be installed for him, it was an agonizing climb up the stairs each day.

"The steps are really a calvary for you," said his assistant one day.

"Not only are the steps my calvary," he replied.

He tried to remain apart from the controversies and disputes over his stigmata and the supernatural powers ascribed to him. But he couldn't help hearing and seeing, and when he was ordered by the Vatican to submit to questions and examinations there wasn't much he could do.

The controversy over his wounds was mounting daily. One dissenter was Padre Agostino Gemelli, priest, doctor, psychologist, rector of the Catholic University of Milan, adviser to Pope Pius XI, and consultant to the Holy Office. He was considered to be a priest of great religious and scientific authority.

Padre Gemelli unexpectedly arrived at the monastery of Our Lady of Grace late one evening.

"I've come to see Padre Pio," he told the young Capuchin who welcomed him.

"I'm sorry," said the youth, "but Padre Pio is praying in the chapel. Please stay the night and see him in the morning."

Padre Gemelli did, and he was waiting in the corridor the next morning. Dawn was barely breaking when he saw the shuffling form of Padre Pio coming his way. He looked hard at the gentle sensitive face when he drew near. He thought he saw a grimace forming on Padre Pio's lips each time his weight shifted on his feet.

"Padre Pio" he asked, catching his arm. "I've come for a clinical examination of your wounds." He cast a broad smile at Padre Pio, showing a mouthful of white teeth, and pushed his thick-rimmed glasses up on his nose.

Padre Pio stopped. He could feel his muscles tense. "Do you have written authority?"

Padre Gemelli stopped smiling and stiffened. "Written authority?"

"Yes."

Padre Gemelli looked away. "No," he said hesitantly. "I—" He changed his mind and left the word hanging in silence.

Padre Pio met his shifting eyes and, without a word, continued on his way to celebrate Mass.

"We'll talk about it later," Padre Gemelli called after him. But he left the monastery without seeing Padre Pio again.

Later, Padre Gemelli stated in private and in public that he had conducted a series of examinations on the stigmata of Padre Pio and he found they did not present any spot formation of the flesh as did the stigmata of Saint Francis. He continued that the stigmata of Padre Pio appeared to him instead to be a characteristic destruction of the tissue which came to him or rather was induced in effect by a true and precise deception. Word of his remarks got back to the monastery.

"Do you know what he said?" a friar asked Padre Pio. "Do you know?"

Padre Pio nodded, looking quite unconcerned. "Everyone has made it his solemn duty to tell me."

"But—" the friar sputtered. "How can you just stand there? That man has even convinced the Pope that your wounds are merely auto-lesions of a hysterical person."

Padre Pio shrugged his shoulders. "He is entitled to his opinion."

"No, no," the friar argued. "This is not a simple matter of opinion. He is writing articles that are stirring up all kinds of things. Why, even the religious orders are having fights. Take the English

Jesuits, for example. They're being attacked for defending you!"

Padre Pio let his gaze fall to his feet. They were throbbing and aching from standing even these few minutes.

"Don't you understand how serious his attack is," cried the friar. "Are you not going to answer such charges?"

Padre Pio looked up and shook his head. "No."

# Troubled Times

## I.

*A year and a half* had passed since the stigmata, and his wounds hadn't healed. Padre Pio was still at the monastery in San Giovanni Rotondo. The heavy snows and fierce winds from the Adriatic Sea and the Gulf of Manfredonia had run out. March's moderating temperatures had arrived and with them the almond blossoms. Great flocks of pink blossoms decorated the dwarfed trees scattered among the ancient cypresses and pines in the monastery garden. Padre Pio liked to stroll down the narrow avenues created by rows of tall slim cypress trees, but sometimes his swollen feet and the intense pain discouraged him. Then he would sit by one of the monastery windows and gaze out over the peaceful green hillside beyond the monastery. Not far away was a crude shelter for sheep, and sometimes he could see them grazing nearby. It was all very still and beautiful, and he enjoyed these quiet, reflective moments—while they lasted.

His own affliction was the least of his concerns, though. There were times when even the three hours' sleep he allowed himself after midnight were impossible, as deep, unsettling thoughts weighed heavily on his mind. His assistant couldn't help but notice and made a point of checking in occasionally.

"Padre," he said one night, "you surely have some thought that does not allow you to sleep."

Padre Pio's eyes were fixed on the ceiling which was dimly lit by moonlight coming through his cell window. "Yes." He sighed unhappily. "But what thoughts? The troubles of humanity. These are the thoughts for everyone."

It was a hard spring and even a harder summer for Padre Pio. There were ever-increasing crowds waiting for a glimpse of the

young priest with the five Christ-like wounds; and then there were the wounds themselves—they just wouldn't heal. He tried to keep his pain and discomfort to himself, but one of the brothers caught him wincing as he shuffled along the corridor.

"Do your wounds pain you today?" he asked.

Padre Pio lifted his dark eyes and nodded. "Yes. Today my legs are swollen from my ankles to my knees."

The brother shook his head sympathetically and tried to think of something to say.

Padre Pio caught his expression and quickly smiled. He nudged the concerned brother. "What a shame I can't walk on my hands!"

The wide-eyed brother just looked back at him with an "I don't see how you can joke about it" stare.

Padre Pio managed to keep most of the others at the monastery from falling into some depressed state over his condition, but he couldn't keep them from thinking, talking, and watching. Several brothers coming from choir noticed him facing the window of a small reception room the next day.

"I absolve you . . ." Padre Pio was saying.

"What is he saying?" asked a short, rather chubby brother, trying to elevate himself to see over the shoulders of his friends.

"Shhhh." someone whispered, looking down at him. "Do you want him to hear?"

"But what is he saying?" the brother whispered back, leaning close.

"He's obviously hearing someone's confession."

The short young man tugged at his friend's arm. "Whose?"

One of the brothers shrugged. "How should we know?"

"But—"

The friend looked at him impatiently. "What is it?"

"I just wanted to point out to you that there's no one else in the room with Padre Pio."

The friend nodded, straight-faced. "I know."

"But you just said he was hearing someone's confession."

"I know." It was too much for the young brother. He left them.

One of them muffled a snicker, and it became the joke of the day, the joke of the week, in fact, until three days later a letter came saying that Padre Pio had been in another town hearing the confession of a sick man that day.

"So that's who he was talking to," said one of the brothers.

Another hastily glanced at him to be certain he wasn't being facetious. "I think you're quite right," he said soberly.

One of the brothers, Fra Ornato, put a finger to his lips. He motioned toward the far end of the corridor where the door to Padre Pio's room was opening. Padre Pio stepped out and started toward them, keeping his eyes on the floor where each foot slowly and painfully fell. Everyone rushed over to say hello and wish him well.

Fra Ornato grasped Padre Pio's hand, kissed it lightly below the brown, fingerless gloves. "Madonna mia!" he exclaimed suddenly, and his head snapped back.

Padre Pio frowned and stroked his dark beard. "What is the matter, my boy?"

Fra Ornato got up and stared at him. "Nothing, nothing," he stammered, and rushed away.

"What is it?" asked a friend, catching up with him.

"It was roses," he said. "I smelled roses. Didn't you smell it?"

The brother looked skeptically at Fra Ornato and put a hand on his shoulder. "If you say so."

II.

Pope Benedict XV supported Padre Pio. In 1921 he said to a group of lawyers: "Padre Pio is indeed an extraordinary man. He is one of those whom God sends from time to time to convert mankind. Take on the task of making him better known. He is not appreciated as he deserves."

Many of the faithful shared this sentiment, but not all. One skeptic was a bishop who was a member of the pope's advisory staff.

"You've been badly informed about Padre Pio," he told the pope.

But the pope wasn't convinced and asked him to go to San Giovanni Rotondo and see the stigmatist for himself.

The bishop did not have his heart in the trip, but he went. When he arrived at the railway station in Foggia, he was greeted by two young Capuchins. "Who told you that I was coming?" he asked. He was utterly amazed.

"Padre Pio," they answered.

"This is incredible!" the bishop exclaimed. "No one except His Holiness knew I was coming."

"I only know," said one of the friars, "that Padre Pio told us to go to the railway station and greet the bishop who was coming to San Giovanni Rotondo, sent by the Holy Father."

The bishop was still dumbfounded. He threw up his hands, and said, "Please tell Padre Pio that I'm not coming to San Giovanni Rotondo, that I'm taking the next train back to Rome, because if he knew of this, then he knows how bitterly I've felt about him and all the damaging things I have done against him with my tongue."

The Capuchins went back and told Padre Pio. He nodded, not the least surprised. He was getting used to the controversies centered about him. But he was surprised when things took a serious turn. The new superior, Padre Ignazio da Lelsi, wanted to see him one day.

"You are temporarily forbidden to say Mass in public or hear confessions," said Ignazio.

Padre Pio listened to the words falling like a guillotine. His dark eyes held fast to the floor and sadness masked every inch of his face.

"I'm sorry," the superior said softly. He peered sympathetically at Padre Pio and patted his arm apologetically. "Truly, I am, but I hope you'll remember your own philosophy now."

Padre Pio looked up. "Philosophy?"

Padre Ignazio smiled. "Obey, promptly. Do not . . . how does it go?"

"Obey promptly," Padre Pio repeated. His voice was barely audible. "Obey promptly. Do not consider the age or merit of the person. In order to succeed, imagine you are obeying our Lord."

He returned to his cell and began to write: "Jesus wants my

sufferings. He needs them for souls." He gripped the pen tightly for a moment and then, feeling a shiver of pain, put it down. He quickly pulled back the brown, fingerless gloves to see if he had opened the tender wound. He stared at the dark scab that had formed on top. He began to write long letters to his confessors, opening his heart. And when he wasn't writing he was praying. Just when his doubts seemed to be getting the best of him and he felt abandoned by God and a prey to desperation, he would sense God's presence, coming to him almost with flashes of blazing light and an embrace of infinite tenderness.

But he couldn't escape the restrictions imposed on him. After Pope Benedict XV had died, Achille Ratti, Pope Pius XI, was elected, and was soon faced with the bitter opposition that had grown up against Padre Pio, so he had quickly placed even more stringent restrictions on him. Loneliness and despair had closed in on Padre Pio.

### III.

Padre Pio met an American named Mary Pyle on a sunny, warm October day in 1923. She too was in her mid-thirties, a tall and slim young woman with blue eyes and fair skin. She had a sensitive, interesting face that he liked. There wasn't any doubt in his mind that he was going to see a good deal more of her in the years ahead. The idea pleased him.

She was born Adelia McAlpin Pyle on April 17, 1888, in Morristown, New Jersey, one of six children. Her parents were wealthy, and her maternal grandparents were the owners of the McAlpin Hotel in New York City. Sometime later the family moved from New Jersey to New York. Adelia's parents were staunch New England Presbyterians, and Adelia was reared in that atmosphere; her education was accomplished chiefly through private tutors, but she attended the Chapin School and the Masters School in Dobbs Ferry, New York.

During her adolescent years she was often taken to Europe. On one occasion she met the famous Italian educator, Dr. Maria Montessori. Some time later Dr. Montessori went to New York and asked Adelia to go with her and work as her interpreter. Adelia by then spoke English, French, Italian, Spanish, and German fluently. But she was undecided.

"I think you should go," her brother James urged.

So she kept thinking about it and finally accepted the position. She wrote a letter to her mother, who was travelling at the time. When the letter caught up with Mrs. Pyle she hastily wrote back and said she wasn't in favor of Adelia doing this kind of work because it would keep her away from home too often. But her letter arrived too late. Adelia was gone.

During one of Dr. Montessori's lecture tours in 1918, in Barcelona, Spain, Adelia converted to Catholicism. She chose Mary for her baptismal name, and from that time on she became known as Mary Pyle.

At Capri, where she was still employed by Dr. Montessori, a girlfriend, Rina d'Ergin, an Orthodox Romanian, asked her to go along to San Giovanni Rotondo to meet Padre Pio. They attended his mass when they arrived and went to confession to him. Afterwards they both met him personally.

"What do you think?" Rina asked excitedly.

Mary was beaming. "He's going to be my spiritual director," she exclaimed happily.

But for the time being she had to go back to Capri and continue her services as interpreter to Dr. Montessori, and she travelled with her from Capri to London to Amsterdam. She couldn't keep her mind on her work though and finally told Dr. Montessori, "After seeing Padre Pio I feel restless. I can't find any peace. You know, I can even visualize his stigmatized hand raised in blessing."

Dr. Montessori listened patiently.

"There is a saint living in this world," Mary said with a sigh, "and I am not near him."

Dr. Montessori smiled understandingly and reached for Mary's hand. "I can see we're going to have to pay a visit to your Padre Pio."

Mary's eyes opened wide with excitement. For days she couldn't

talk about anything else, and in every free moment she worked the
conversation around to Padre Pio and the meaning of his stigmata.

All this time, the Church itself had not really done anything
to cast doubt on his stigmata. Nor had there been an official Church
condemnation of him. In 1923, all that the Holy Office would say was
that the stigmata could not be "confirmed with certainty to be of
supernatural origin."

This caution with cases of stigmatists dated back to the time
when science was much less advanced in these phenomena. But both
science and theology were unanimous in confirming that the wounds
cause great suffering, whether related to natural law or the sacred
and profane, and that they almost completely take away any desire
for food and sleep. One way or another they were considered true
lesions of soft tissues, with frequent loss of blood, even real hemor-
rrhage.

In the history of the Church, cases of only about seventy stigmatists were well attested. In the case of beatifications of stigmatists,
with the exception of St. Francis of Assisi, the Church was careful
not to state positively that the stigmata had been divinely imposed,
and usually was not even considered to be a proof of sanctity. Even
if the stigmata was definitely established in a preternatural order, then,
the phenomena was still no guarantee or proof of holiness. The Church
never thought it opportune to make a declaration on these phenomena, except for St. Francis of Assisi who had a feast sanctioned in
honor of his stigmata.

While Mary Pyle was impatiently waiting for plans to go to the
monastery to materialize, everything again took a turn for the worse
for Padre Pio. Fall had withered into an icy winter, but the controversy over his stigmata had grown warmer. By the time the snows
had melted and the land had colored, Padre Agostino Gemelli's
controversial attacks had created a furor.

"Look at this!" said one of the priests at the monastery, a stout,
easily-agitated man. He tossed an open letter on the small wooden
table in Padre Pio's cell.

Padre Pio lifted the long skirt of his habit and tried to slide sideways on his chair. He could see the shifting, nervous eyes of the unhappy priest. He pushed the letter aside. "I already know what it says. I am to be transferred to some remote place in Spain."

"Well," said the priest, "then you also know that if there is much more publicity over your . . . your problem . . . this monastery may as well close its doors or sell tickets to curiosity seekers. Do you know how many buses are here today? Do you know how long the line is at the church door? They're coming from all over Europe, from America, everywhere."

Padre Pio hid the hurt in his dark eyes. He leaned an elbow wearily on the small table and shook his head sadly. "I am sorry that my . . . problem . . . has become . . . your problem, too. But I did not put these holes in my hands and feet or in my side myself."

The priest mopped his brow with a large white cloth. He breathed deeply and picked up the letter. "It is I who am sorry. Of course, it's not your fault. You are suffering enough. Forgive me, Padre."

Padre Pio scratched his bearded chin and let a smile form on his lips. "There's nothing to forgive."

A sandy-haired novice poked his head through the doorway. "Excuse me, padres," he said, out-of-breath, "but there is trouble in San Giovanni Rotondo."

Padre Pio pulled himself onto his feet with a grimace. "Trouble? What do you mean?"

"They know, Padre, about your being transferred to Spain."

"But that is pure rumor, only speculation at this point."

"I know, Padre, but they are not waiting to find out. They have taken up weapons to defend you."

"Oh, no," murmured the horrified priest, still clutching the letter. He grasped Padre Pio's arm. "What shall we do?"

Padre Pio thought carefully a moment, and said, "Whatever is necessary to prevent pain and sorrow from befalling the town. I know the people mean well, but they must be stopped."

"I agree," said the priest.

Outside the monastery the marshall was rushing toward the

crowd along with a few policemen. "Please," he was pleading, "please go back. Leave." But his voice was drowned out by angry shouts. "The idea," the people screamed, "going to send him to Spain! Over our dead bodies! He is a saint; he is the glory of our country!"

The marshall tried to get a look at things. They had posted armed sentries at the doors, along the garden wall, and behind the church.

One of the policemen whispered to the marshall, "They are saying that if he is sent to a foreign country it will look like the people of Italy don't believe in him."

The marshall's ruddy cheeks were flushed with annoyance. "We'll out-wait them," he said, clenching his teeth with determination.

But for three days and nights the crowd grew till the courtyard, the parking lot, and the garden were packed solid. Reluctantly the marshall rounded up his policemen and went home.

Padre Pio was kept inside. Not knowing what else to do he went about his work as usual. But even inside, trouble popped up unexpectedly. He was at the altar, saying Mass one day, when a ragged unshaven man rushed up to him, jerked out a revolver, and pushed the cold steel against Padre Pio's temple.

"If you leave San Giovanni, you'll leave in a box," the man said angrily.

Padre Pio caught his breath and stared into the man's threatening eyes. Carefully and slowly he continued the sacrifice. All at once two Capuchins appeared behind the man. They snatched the gun and whisked him away. For a long time Padre Pio's dark eyes stayed glued to the door where the desperate, struggling man had disappeared. In his heart he knew that his life was completely in God's hands. He seemed to have no control over it at all. He could feel a terrible helplessness sinking around him.

The next day Padre Pio wrote to Francesco Morcaldi, mayor of San Giovanni Rotondo:

"The facts that happened in these days have moved me deeply and I am immensely concerned because they have made me fear

I am able to be involuntarily the cause of mournful happenings in this my dear city.

"I pray God that He wishes to remove such loss rather He would let fall on me some mortification. But it has been communicated to me that a decision was made for my transfer. I pray to employ every measure to comply, because the will of God and of my superiors I obey without ceasing.

"I will always remember these generous people in my poor and assiduous prayers imploring peace and prosperity for them and as a sign of my predilection, being unable to do anything else, I express the desire, that if my superiors are not opposed, my bones be placed in a tranquil corner of this land.

"With respect I have said all in the sweet Lord."

Padre Pio of Pietrelcina

The Holy Office soon sent several visitors to report the behavior and actions of Padre Pio. The first to appear at the monastery was Monsignor Benevenuto Cerretti.

"He is a man of God," he told Pope Benedict XV.

While at Rome, Signor DeBono, minister of interior, went to Secretary of State Cardinal Merry del Val and asked him to withhold the transfer of Padre Pio from the town of San Giovanni Rotondo.

It was finally over. When Padre Pio got the news he rushed to the open window of the small church, blessed the people waiting outside and with a broad smile, called out to them: "I am not going anywhere! I shall stay here!"

Cheers went up, and a few began to gather their belongings to leave. But to make sure there was no other plot to take him away, they regularly sent men to act as guards. After a week it was proved that Padre Pio was really going to stay in San Giovanni Rotondo at the church of Our Lady of Grace. The people had won, and the matter was dropped. Padre Pio felt a new sense of relief, but he stayed inside the monastery, only going out on rare occasions to assist the dying and to vote.

The number of faithful around him increased daily, however,

and the ecclesiastical authority feared that the religious fervor would turn into fanaticism. So on July 24, 1924, the Holy Office took an official stand, and said they were not certain of the supernatural origin of Padre Pio's stigmata, and therefore requested that the faithful refrain from visiting him.

The troubled times were still casting dark shadows over Padre Pio when Mary Pyle came back.

"I want to stay near the monastery, near you," she told him.

Padre Pio listened and although she had never told him that her mother had objected to her work with Dr. Montessori, he said simply, "Obey your mother."

Dr. Montessori was there when Mary's courage lifted. "I'm going to stay in San Giovanni Rotondo," she announced. She quickly looked to Dr. Montessori for approval.

The older woman smiled. "What can I say?"

Mary flung her arms about her neck and kissed her. "Thank you. You're so good."

Dr. Montessori said nothing, until she was alone with Mary later. "You've been employed by me for ten years," she reminded Mary.

"Yes, they were wonderful years."

"If it weren't for the influence of your Padre Pio, it might have been many more years."

Mary's sparkling eyes clouded, and she saw the irritation in Dr. Montessori's face. "I'm sorry. Believe me, please. I must stay, but it's my decision. He certainly has done nothing to encourage me to leave you."

Dr. Montessori sighed. She resigned herself to the fact that nothing was going to change Mary's mind. "I wish you well, my dear," she said, managing a faint smile. "Let me know if ever you need me."

When Mary was alone, the first thing she did was to purchase a plot of land at the bottom of the hill near the monastery. There she had a rose-colored villa built among the almond trees, very

Franciscan in style, and there she began the work of making a home for herself under the spiritual guidance of Padre Pio.

Not satisfied at being an average Christian she wanted to ascend higher in virtue, and asked Padre Pio if she should enter a Franciscan convent.

"The convent is not suitable for you," he said. "Enroll in the Third Order."

Padre Pio invested her in the Franciscan habit on September 6, 1925.

"I adopted the Capuchin habit but without a cowl," she said, "and I have now cut all the bridges between me and the world."

After accepting this rule of life she decided to sell all her expensive jewelry and give it to Padre Pio's charities. She wrote to Dr. Montessori who had custody of the jewelry, and asked her to mail it. Dr. Montessori, however, thinking the jewels were too valuable to mail, presented them to the Capuchins in Rome.

"We don't believe in all this devotion to Padre Pio," they told her. "I don't feel we should accept these." After repeated attempts, they finally consented.

The villagers of San Giovanni Rotondo began calling her *"Maria l'Americana"* (Mary the American), because she didn't relinquish her American citizenship. She soon made a name for herself. When the poor came to see Padre Pio and had no place to stay, she put them up. She generously gave young people financial help to study for the priesthood, and had no objections to helping young married couples financially. The word travelled far and wide, and she became known about as well as Padre Pio.

"She's quite a marvel, isn't she?" said a priest one day to Padre Pio.

He shook his head in wonder. "The world is so much better because of her."

Mary was a skilled musician, too. Besides tending to the needs of the poor, she established a *"Scuola Cantorum,"* for Padre Pio's Our Lady of Grace church, and she played the organ for the daily masses and the afternoon Benediction services. She also directed groups of Tertiary Franciscans.

She always kept open house for visitors, and people came to her simply-furnished home from all classes of life and from all parts of the world, including famous names in the theatrical world of both Europe and America. Mary even had a large brown book where some of her visitors registered their names. Some of these signatures belonged to American movieland personalities such as Loretta Young and Ramon Navarro, while others belonged to ordinary people who were attracted to Padre Pio.

But during the years that Padre Pio was in confinement while his case was being investigated by the Church, the villagers, unable to contact him, claimed that Mary was the cause of his troubles.

"She told stories and cases of miracles and described his supernatural powers to the journalists," they insisted, "and the journalists made sensational headlines out of the stories." And that, they thought, was why Padre Pio was under investigation.

So for a while the villagers ostracized her. No one would speak to her outside of her household. For days and months she couldn't even take a walk without facing the stony, accusing stares. She suffered terribly, not only from the outside rejection but from being kept away from Padre Pio's confession. Even when she attended daily mass and received Holy Communion, the villagers would all leave the altar rail and allow her to receive alone. Often times, the women especially would light candles for the dead and recite the litany for deceased persons in her presence.

She told a friend later: "When my white angora cat had a beautiful litter of kittens, I wanted so much to share the news with the people at the church, but there was no one who would listen to me."

Mary prayed long and hard for the restriction to be lifted from Padre Pio. One day she walked the twenty-five miles to and from Saint Michael's shrine in Monte Santangelo, and a year later she walked again to the shrine, but this time spent the night in the village and walked back the next day. These were troubled times for her too.

When the ban on him lifted, she celebrated along with the villagers. As time passed they began to throw a friendly smile her way. Finally the icy glares gave way, and she knew she had been accepted. A group of citizens from Pietrelcina contacted her then and asked if she would build a monastery in their little town for the Capuchin fathers of the Province. It seemed like a good idea to her, but she wouldn't think of consenting without giving Padre Pio a chance to comment.

The next day she asked him, "May I build a monastery in Pietrelcina?"

He folded his arms and tried to look very solemn. "Yes," he replied, "do it quickly, and let it be dedicated to the Holy Family."

Then their eyes met, and they both began to laugh, deliriously happy.

## IV.

Dr. Giorgio Festa was exhausted and decided to take a vacation and visit Padre Pio. The ecclesiastical authorities had forbidden any more examinations of the wounds, so it was strictly a social call.

Padre Pio started grinning when he opened the door and saw the friendly bearded face. "I'm glad to see you again."

Dr. Festa returned his smile and put his hand on Padre Pio's arm. "How are you?"

Padre Pio crossed his arms and pretended to be very serious. "I don't know if I should answer that."

Dr. Festa laughed. "It was a personal question. I'm aware of the orders that further medical examinations are forbidden."

"To tell you the truth, I haven't been feeling well lately."

"I shouldn't wonder."

"No, no, not my wounds or the recent trouble with the villagers. I've been having abdominal pain."

Dr. Festa grew solemn. "Hmmmmm. Better let me have a look." He pointed to the bed for Padre Pio to lie down. It didn't take long for him to discover a large hernia in the region of the right groin. When he detected peritonitis, he decided something had to be done right away. He sat on the edge of the bed and looked into Padre Pio's worried eyes. "Don't be alarmed, but you do have a hernia and there is some inflammation. Under the circumstances an immediate operation is advisable."

Padre Pio pulled himself up and leaned back on his elbows. "I'm still restricted to the monastery, you realize."

Dr. Festa nodded. "Yes, but I don't see any problems. I can take care of it here."

Padre Pio smiled and sighed. "I was afraid you would say that."

After his usual offering of the Sacrifice of the Mass, and having heard confessions, Padre Pio went back to his room and calmly waited for two hours before Dr. Festa came for him.

"I have found some assistants," Dr. Festa said. "Dr. Angelo Merla, the Mayor of San Giovanni Rotondo, and Dr. Leandro Giuva. And I've found a freshly whitewashed room that will serve nicely as our operating room. Now that I'm ready, what about you?"

"I am ready," said Padre Pio, "but let's understand each other. I do not want any chloroform."

Dr. Festa shook his head. "That's out of the question. It will be a long operation and any movement could be dangerous."

"Do not fear," Padre Pio persisted. "At the end of the operation you will find me exactly where you put me in the beginning." He started to follow the doctor. "Tell me," he asked, "do you intend perhaps to observe my wounds if I should be chloroformed?"

"Why not?" answered the doctor with a laugh.

Padre Pio caught his arm and frowned. "Because I am forbidden by my superiors, and I am bound to obedience. Therefore, I refuse the chloroform."

Dr. Festa nodded without commenting. They arrived at the room and Padre Pio shed his brown habit, slipped into a white gown, and sat on the edge of the table.

"Here," said the doctor, holding out a brown bottle. "If you refuse the chloroform at least take a sip of Benedictine."

Padre Pio started to drink in small sips, closing his eyes and grimacing.

"Take a little more," the doctor urged.

Padre Pio shook his head and handed him the bottle. "No, no. There will be an internal battle between the Benedictine and the Capuchin."

The operation lasted one and three-quarters hours. It had barely started when Padre Pio began to feel intense pain, and he couldn't stop a loud moan from escaping his lips. His face contracted as the pain became excruciating, and he started to pray. When the tightly-joined adhesions were detached, two large tears rolled down his cheeks and disappeared in his beard.

"Jesus, pardon me," he murmured, "if I do not know how to suffer as I should."

When the surgeon was putting nine stitches in the suture, Padre Pio turned to Dr. Guiva, and said, "Leandro, if you wish to take my place you can come. The table is still warm."

Dr. Guiva's face reddened. He, too, was in need of a hernia operation but had said nothing to anyone about it.

After being carried to his room, Padre Pio was unconscious and remained in this condition for several hours. Dr. Festa took advantage of the opportunity to re-examine the five wounds. He wondered if there would be any change in them. To his amazement he found them exactly as they were during his first examination in 1919. There was no further decomposition, or any unhealthy change in the tissues, and no offensive odor.

Since the wound of the side was not covered during the hernia operation, Dr. Festa had examined it, too, and noticed that there was a small but evident radiation that surrounded it in the form of a cross. Later Dr. Merla and Dr. Guiva agreed and told the superior of the monastery about it. In his original report to the superiors,

Padre Pio had said that the wound on his left side bled more pro-
fusely from Thursday to Saturday. However, it still bled every day
as did the other wounds.

When Dr. Merla removed the stitches four days later Padre Pio
had recovered sufficiently from the hernia operation to resume his
activities.

"You know," said Dr. Merla, "the incisions from the operation
are healing perfectly."

Dr. Festa nodded. "And that lets out any possibility that the
other wounds haven't healed because he's a hemophiliac."

Except when the Church ordered it, Padre Pio refused to discuss his wounds at any great length.

"Do they pain you?" a curious visitor asked.

Padre Pio laughed. "Do you think the Lord gave them to me
for decorations?"

A scholarly-looking friend with thick eyeglasses, just as curious,
overheard him. "Seriously, Padre Pio, how *do* your wounds pain?"

"The same as if you would take a nail, drive it into the hands,
and turn it around." The visitor gasped.

"It's true, isn't it, that the wound in your side is always open?"
asked his friend.

Padre Pio shrugged his shoulders. "It is a small thing," he said,
trying to dismiss the subject, "in comparison to that which the Lord
suffered."

"Is it true you suffer more during Mass and in Passion Week?"
the friend persisted.

Padre Pio sighed. "Yes," he practically snapped, and walked off.

The visitor who had lingered to hear the discussion glanced at
Padre Pio's friend. "Is he angry because of the pain?"

The friend shook his head. "No, he just doesn't like to be questioned about it all the time. I don't really blame him."

"He's a good man, said the visitor. "My wife says he's a saint."

The friend smiled. "So do several million other people."

The millions of people from every social class who entrusted themselves to Padre Pio felt that his stigmatization was the fruit of a great union with God, the fruit of intense and loving meditation of Christ's suffering and death. So people gave him their burdens and cares, and he tried to give them hope and courage, and the feeling that he shared their burdens. To the many faithful and those who received benefits through his blessings, the stigmata created no problem. As far as they were concerned Padre Pio was a saintly priest and, therefore, his wounds had a mystical meaning.

Not everyone accepted the stigmata so easily, though. One man, Dr. Riccardo Valente of San Giovanni Rotondo, was a Communist and was violently opposed to priests, Padre Pio in particular. When he became seriously ill he shocked the community by insisting that he would confess only to Padre Pio.

It was evening on a snowy, cold winter day in 1925 when someone appeared at the monastery to tell Padre Pio that Valente was dying.

Padre Pio stood in the doorway, pulling up the hood of his habit as the cold wind tossed snowflurries into his face. "Are you certain he wants me?"

"Yes, Padre. Will you come? It's two miles to his house, and I'm sorry there is no transportation. We'll have to walk."

Padre Pio went for his outer garment and trudged into the wintry evening. The cold numbed his face and legs, and bit into his feet and hands, aggravating his wounds. The land was all white except for the tall green pines, and the shadows of early evening were sinking from the dark overcast sky. His breath was short and his body chilled to the bone when he reached Valente's house. There he heard his confession, anointed him, and gave him his blessing. By the time he left, he knew the doctor would recover—spiritually as well as physically. He was feeling happy but the long hard walk back nearly did him in. When he finally got to his room, he collapsed in bed, pulled the covers tightly around his neck, closed his eyes, and shivered for almost an hour.

He knew it was late when he opened his eyes again. The light was off in his room but the door to the corridor was open and let in a path of light alongside his bed. He suddenly realized someone was leaning over him. He squinted and sat up.

"Please don't move," said the soft, gentle voice of a woman. She put her hands on his shoulders. "Lie back. You've had a cold walk tonight, and you must keep warm."

"Who are you?" he asked. "What are you doing in my room at this hour?"

"I saw you returning and you looked chilled and tired. I was worried about you, and followed you in to be certain you were all right."

He could see she was in her early twenties with long black hair falling over her shoulders, wide dark eyes, and smiling coral lips. She was wearing a red dress that fit snugly over her full body. She sat on the edge of his bed then, her hips pressing against his side. He tried to move over but her right arm reached across him and locked him close to her. With her left hand she stroked his forehead and ran a finger through his short chestnut hair.

He reached up and put her hand aside. It was as if he clutched empty air, and he snatched his hand back. "The devil has sent you," he gasped, becoming alarmed. "Get away from me. Don't touch me."

"Now, now," she soothed. "Do I look like an evil spirit?" She ran her hands over her hips and across her full breasts.

"Jesus," he cried out, "take away the evil that tempts me on this dark night! Cleanse my heart!" The unearthly hands were massaging his shoulders and neck now.

"Jesus, please." he cried again, as loudly as he could.

"What is it?" came a voice from the corridor, and his assistant raced to his side.

The apparition of the beautiful young woman evaporated in an instant.

Huge tears were bursting from Padre Pio's eyes, and a sob erupted from deep in his throat.

"What is it?" the assistant repeated.

Padre Pio shook his head and moaned. "I don't know. If I had not called out for Jesus, I just don't know."

He cried for a long time, until every fibre in his body ached.

## V.

Suffering struck Padre Pio deeply. For a long time he had been saying that San Giovanni Rotondo needed a hospital. As a result of his appeal to his followers, in the winter of 1925 a little hospital of St. Francis came into being, using the rooms of a former convent. Two wards were furnished with twenty beds. Treatment was free. Dr. Angelo Merla was the director of the institution, and a famous surgeon, Dr. Bucci of Foggia, was the head surgeon.

Padre Pio was overjoyed. He talked about it constantly. "It's small, I know," he told the brothers, "but it's a beginning."

The days moved along, one pretty much the same as another, for a while, though a brother predicted quite accurately that it wouldn't last. He caught up with Padre Pio in the corridor one evening.

"I told you it wouldn't last," he said.

Padre Pio turned around at the sound of the high nasal voice. He smiled at the young, baby-faced brother who had not much more than a stubble on his chin. "How's the beard coming?" he asked.

"What? Oh, poorly, Padre, poorly. Someone told me at dinner tonight that I probably have a gland problem."

Padre Pio patted him on the shoulder reassuringly. "They were just having fun with you. It hasn't been that long since you started it, has it?"

The brother rubbed his soft, flushed cheeks. "Well, I started to grow it a year ago."

Padre Pio nodded. "Oh." He decided not to pursue the subject. "I wondered if you had heard the news about the books?" the brother asked.

"Books?"

"Yes. They banned your books ... the books about you, I mean." Padre Pio looked surprised. "Why?"

"The writers didn't get ecclesiastical approbation, so the church condemned the books."

"I see."

"Aren't you upset?"

"It's not for me to question the church."

The brother hesitated. "I just thought you would be upset."

Padre Pio smiled. "As you can see, I'm not." He excused himself and went on to his cell.

"I don't understand him," the young brother told the next person he saw.

Once again, the days moved along without any crushing catastrophe. Padre Pio had learned to pace himself. By now he knew about how far he could walk or stand before the pain from his wounds would overcome him. He had long ago resigned himself to all the controversies, and he was managing to cope with the ever increasing masses of people who came to see him and confess to him.

It was a warm September day a year later when Dr. Festa returned again to see Padre Pio. This time he came to remove a cyst, a little larger than a bird's egg, from the region of the mastoid.

"What will it be this time," he asked Padre Pio. "Benedictine or chloroform?"

Padre Pio smiled. "Benedictine, of course."

Dr. Festa shook his head. He really didn't approve, but, with the aid of Dr. Merla, once again he performed the surgery without anesthetics. Seven days later he removed the stitches. In the meantime, Padre Pio had not skipped a day in his ministry.

"No change," Dr. Festa told Dr. Merla when they were alone.

"In the wounds?" Dr. Merla asked. "No change in the controversies over them either, I understand."

Dr. Festa took off his glasses and cleaned them. "No, I'm afraid you're right. Dr. Bignami insists the wounds are dead tissue covered with iodine; Dr. Romanelli found one deep lesion on his chest; and I found two superficial ones. So there you have it. It just defies analysis."

Dr. Merla scratched his head. "For us, yes. To his faithful followers, the wounds are a mysterious conversation between a man and God, and their manifestation is a measure of the faith of the observer."

"Faith has no bounds or need for explanation," said Dr. Festa. "That reminds me of the story I heard about the socialite, Mrs. Luisa Vairo. Did you hear it?" Dr. Merla shook his head no.

"Well," said Dr. Festa, putting his glasses back on, "she apparently confessed to Padre Pio and he exposed all her sins as if he were reading from a diary . . . except one. But he didn't give her absolution, so she couldn't decide whether to reveal the one yast sin or not. Finally, she did, and he said that's what he was waiting for, and then he gave her absolution."

Dr. Merla smiled and nodded. "There have been some interesting stories indeed."

Festa agreed. "Take this one. Frederick Abresch, the photographer in San Giovanni Rotondo, was a convert to Catholicism, but he wasn't convinced that Jesus had instituted the Sacrament of Penance. He accepted it only as good psychologically. Padre Pio, it seems, told him his communions had been sacrileges and he had to make a general confession and try to remember his last sincere confession. Finally, Padre Pio had to point out to him that it was after his return from his wedding trip. So then he was absolved and given a penance. Later, his wife was told she should have a tumor removed to avoid natural childbirth. Padre Pio, though, advised against the operation and predicted she would have a son. Two years later, when she was pregnant, she woke one morning and saw Padre Pio at the foot of her bed holding a pillow with a baby boy on it. Supposedly he asked her, 'Do you believe it now?' Then he disappeared, and lo and behold, later they had a son ... named Pio, of course."

Dr. Merla held up his hands and laughed. "Please, no more. If word gets around, all my patients will leave me and go to him!"

Padre Pio dismissed all such accounts of his work with a simple "it was nothing," when he bothered to comment at all, that is. He continued to guide others, though, including his own family.

Giuseppa and Orazio visited him often, and Michael, Pellegrina, and Sister Pia came at least once a month. Giuseppa had grown old before his eyes. She was seventy now, and her face was thin and heavily wrinkled. Her dark eyebrows were close to her eyes and seemed always to mask her face with a troubled frown. Even her voice sounded weary and old to him.

Mary Pyle went with Giuseppa to meet Padre Pio, in the church one day when suddenly Giuseppa dropped to her knees at his feet, her arms hanging down, and her hands outspread.

Looking up at him, she asked, "How can we know that in God's sight we are not great sinners? We try to confess all of our sins. We confess all we remember, but how can we be sure that God does not see many sins which we have forgotten, or which we have not even recognized as sin?"

At other times, Padre Pio wouldn't even let her kiss his hand. He felt a son should kiss his mother's hand, not the other way around. But this time he let her stay at his feet.

He looked long into her dark, worried eyes, and said, "If we have good will and try to confess all our sins, confessing those which we remember, God's mercy is so great that it will wipe out every fault and sin, even those which we have forgotten."

Mary Pyle helped Giuseppa up. The next time the family came, winter had settled on the monastery. In spite of a raging snowstorm on Christmas eve in 1928, Giuseppa insisted that they visit Padre Pio and attend his mass. The next day she was sneezing and came down with a high fever. The family gathered at her bedside in Mary Pyle's villa.

"She is dying," Orazio said through his tears, and the others felt a state of shock and sadness.

Four days later Padre Pio administered the last rites, and she died. It was a bitterly cold day when the sombre cortege, including the mayors of San Giovanni Rotondo and Pietrelcina, followed the bier to the little cemetery at the monastery. Orazio and his family said a long, lonely goodbye, and left.

For days Padre Pio was heard whispering, "Mother . . . my Mother."

# The Verdict

## I.

*Winter had weakened* when Maria Ghislieri went to San Giovanni Rotondo to confess to Padre Pio and attend his daily mass. She was a slender young woman with a long, thin face, from Castelnuovo in the province of Piedmont in northern Italy. Just about the time the first buds began to appear on the almond branches, she became ill and the local doctor diagnosed her case as pneumonia. Two weeks later he discovered a complication: there was pleurisy and an abundance of liquid in her lungs. A cousin came immediately and stayed with her for two months.

"I'm worried about Maria," the cousin told Padre Pio after mass. "Will you pray for her?"

Padre Pio smiled reassuringly and nodded. "Of course." He watched her sigh with relief. "The illness will be long," he added, "but Maria will be cured."

"Do you think so?" she asked, grasping for hope.

"You may be certain of it," he said.

When Maria was strong enough she returned to her home in Castelnuovo, but a doctor there said she had tuberculosis in both lungs and sent her to the Sanatorium of Alessandria.

"There is nothing to be done for her," the doctor at the sanatorium insisted. The family gathered to talk it over.

"Padre Pio said she would be cured," the cousin reminded them.

Maria's father shook his head hopelessly. "I don't see how. You heard the doctors."

"But Padre Pio knows what God will do. The doctor doesn't. Don't you see?"

"I don't know. Perhaps if I talked to this padre myself."

It was agreed, and he went to the monastery. There, he waited for Padre Pio outside the chapel. As soon as he saw the bearded, brown-robed figure shuffling along, he rushed over and began to question him anxiously.

"Your daughter is not lost," Padre Pio told him with a decisive tone.

"Can you be sure?" asked the girl's father. "The doctors say—"

Padre Pio cut him off. "Let science deny the cure, and I tell you she *will* be cured."

The man's worried expression began to fade, and he smiled at Padre Pio.

Padre Pio smiled back tenderly. "Tell Maria to remain calm and she will see."

At the hospital Maria suffered at first and couldn't find a position to give her any relief. Then the nurses noticed she was fresh and rested in the mornings.

"I see you're sleeping well," a heavy, fleshy nurse remarked one morning.

"I am now that he helps me at night," Maria explained.

The nurse, who was fluffing the pillows, stopped and stared at the thin, pale face. "Who helps you?"

"Padre Pio, I mean."

"Who is that? A relative?"

Maria smiled happily and sighed. "I think he's a saint."

The nurse shook her head and frowned. "Well, saint or not, no one is permitted in here after hours. You know that."

Maria giggled. "I'll tell him."

"Please do, and please tell me how he got past the desk outside?"

"He doesn't come in that way. He . . . he just appears . . . from nowhere."

The nurse put her hands on her hips. "Oh, now, really, Maria!"

"No, it's the truth," Maria insisted, sitting up.

"Lie back," said the nurse.

"It's the truth," Maria insisted again.

The nurse shook her head. "I think your temperature is up."

She snatched a tray from the bed table and waddled out, mumbling, "A saint! Really, now!"

"It's the truth," Maria called after her.

Maria's father went back to see Padre Pio. "They say her days are numbered," the man said, holding back his tears. "They say she is the most gravely ill person in the sanatorium."

Padre Pio put his hand on the man's trembling arm. "She is not lost; she is cured," he said quietly, and left him.

By the time Maria's father returned, her condition had reversed. Soon she gained thirteen pounds. In a short time she was completely well and showed no sign of ever having been ill.

Her doctor was amazed. "I don't understand it," he said. "I cannot explain it."

"I can," said Maria.

Maria's family wanted to have the story printed in the newspapers, making a public declaration to give glory to God.

Padre Pio looked annoyed at the suggestion when they told him. "No," he said, "none of that. Live good Christian lives and that will be enough."

Another young woman came from northern Italy to see Padre Pio. She was slender and tall, with sparkling hazel eyes and long brown hair that glowed like amber in the sunlight. For days the others at the monastery would see her going to confess to Padre Pio, and they wondered who she was. She walked about as if in a daze and waited daily with a wide smile and adoring eyes for a glimpse of the handsome priest.

"He tells me beautiful heavenly and inspirational things," she told someone once while waiting for Padre Pio. Then one day she was gone.

"She was a lovely girl," Mary Pyle told Padre Pio. "Where did she go?"

Padre Pio looked distressed at the mention of her. "She returned to her home."

"I wonder if she is a chosen soul. Someone whom the Lord will use to work his wonders."

Padre Pio looked hard at Mary. "No," he said firmly. "The Lord has not chosen her."

Two months passed and she was forgotten until one of the priests at the monastery came across something in a newspaper. He hurried to Padre Pio's cell, where he found him writing a letter.

"The mystery girl has made herself known," said the priest. He ran a hand over his balding head and adjusted his glasses nervously. He placed the newspaper on Padre Pio's table and tapped his finger on the bottom of the page.

Padre Pio put his letter aside. "What is this?"

"According to this story, you made quite an impression on that attractive young woman who used to be so taken with you. She was the one—"

"I know which one," Padre Pio interrupted.

"She seems to have misunderstood something. According to a statement she made to a reporter, she thinks you made a pass at her." Padre Pio glanced at the article, expressionless.

"Of course," said the nervous priest, "everyone here knows it's ridiculous, but what about strangers who don't know you? What will they think?"

Padre Pio shrugged his shoulders. "What would you have me do?"

The priest hesitated. "I don't know. I hadn't thought about it. Nothing, I guess."

Padre Pio nodded and dropped the newspaper in a wastebasket by his table. "Good, because nothing is precisely what I intend to do."

"You'll deny it, though, of course."

Padre Pio looked up at him. "You just told me everyone here knows it is ridiculous."

"Oh, yes, of course, but—"

Padre Pio let his eyes meet the gaze of the priest. It was a curious, probing gaze. "Is there something you want to ask me?"

"It's just that you're not at all surprised." The remark provoked Padre Pio, but he didn't reply.

The priest glanced about the room, beginning to feel embarrassed. "I guess it's not the first libelous article you've read." He laughed weakly and excused himself.

Padre Pio's dark eyebrows drew together in a frown. Unfortunately, there had been other accusing articles. Only an hour ago he had been talking with Alberto Del Fante, a journalist who once wrote a libelous piece in a Florence newspaper. At that time Del Fante was an atheist and Freemason, and he despised all priests, nuns, and saints.

Then, in November 1930 he went with his brother-in-law to San Giovanni Rotondo, primarily out of curiosity. Just before the visit his doctors had looked at his nephew who was critically ill. They had discovered a high fever in the boy caused by an internal abscess in the kidneys. Del Fante's brother-in-law asked Padre Pio for prayers.

"Have faith," Padre Pio told him, and he predicted a cure on a certain day.

Padre Pio's prediction was correct, and Del Fante was impressed. He became not only a convert but an ardent supporter of Padre Pio, and he began to write several books about him.

"Before I start to write," he told Padre Pio, "I will bless myself and say a prayer."

One night he forgot and started to write. Suddenly the room was filled with a sweet, delicate scent.

"Come quickly!" he shouted to his wife, his son, and their maid.

Before he could comment, they all began talking excitedly about the perfumed scent throughout the room. "What is it?" they asked.

Del Fante smiled. "I'm not sure, but I think Padre Pio is reminding me that I forgot to make the sign of the cross and say a prayer before starting to write."

## II.

After Giuseppa died, Orazio went to San Giovanni Rotondo to spend the rest of his life near Padre Pio. Mary Pyle made a place for him in her villa. He spent most of his time sitting in the shade of an old elm tree in front of the monastery. There he would exchange tales about Padre Pio with visitors.

Padre Pio went to say hello after mass on a clear spring morning. He stopped before his father and looked down. Orazio's hair was white now, and age was shrinking the features on his beardless face.

"What would you do without your elm tree?" Padre Pio asked.

Orazio's wrinkled face broke into a grin. He was bursting with pride for his son. His eyes settled on Padre Pio's brown fingerless gloves and all at once he reached out to kiss his hand.

Padre Pio quickly raised his hands. "I have already said this to my Mother, that the children should kiss the hands of the parents and not vice versa."

Orazio stood and reached out for Padre Pio. "I do not want your hand as a son, but as a priest."

Padre Pio felt a shiver go through him, and his eyes grew misty. "Oh, Father," he murmured, and opened his arms. He kissed Orazio on the cheeks, and held out his hand and left him then. He had to meet Abbot Benoit who was the secretary general of the Catholic Institute of Lille, France. Abbot Benoit was coming with a group of pilgrims. Padre Pio limped and shuffled as quickly as he could to a small reception room inside the monastery. His wounds were particularly painful today.

"It's good to have you," Padre Pio said. There were about a half dozen men in the room standing near a short, dark man with a ruddy complexion who introduced himself as Abbot Benoit.

They soon fell into relaxed conversation and after debating theology for some hours decided it was time to leave.

"Will you autograph these cards?" Abbot Benoit asked.

Padre Pio smiled. "Of course." He hesitated a second and glanced at Abbot Benoit. "May I have your breviary?"

Abbot Benoit handed it to him and curiously watched him start to write at great length on a blank page.

Padre Pio finished and handed it back to him. He said good-bye to each person, and went off in another direction.

Abbot Benoit was standing motionless, his mouth gaping, as he stared at Padre Pio's writing.

"What is it?" someone asked.

"I don't believe it."

"What's that?"

Benoit shook his head. "He wrote a precise and clear solution to a problem I've been trying to solve for years."

"Yes," said one of the men. "I'm not surprised. He has a good mind."

Abbot Benoit shook his head. "You don't understand. I never told him about the problem. How did he know?"

Silence fell about the small room. A tall, bony man scratched his head. "What do you make of someone who can pick things right out of your mind? Right out of nowhere?"

"I'm not certain I like the idea of someone looking into my mind," said the man behind him. "I'm not at all certain of that."

Abbot Benoit led them out before it went any further. He glanced to his right while leaving and noticed Padre Pio shaking hands with someone. *It's strange,* he thought. *He looks like an ordinary priest.*

"He looks like an ordinary priest," one of the men echoed his thoughts.

Said another: "Ordinary priests don't have holes in their hands and feet."

Padre Pio caught a glimpse of them going out the door and raised his hand to wave good-bye to Abbot Benoit. Then he turned back to the man who was standing with him. He was talking to Nino Salvaneschi, a journalist from Brussels, who was recently stricken with blindness.

"I don't understand why," he was telling Padre Pio. "There must be a reason. Why does a man just become blind?"

Padre Pio shook his head. "The Lord gave, and the Lord hath taken away. Go in peace; I shall pray for you."

Salvaneschi thanked him. He stayed to listen to Padre Pio talk to others who were waiting to see him.

"Never allow your soul to be disturbed by the sad spectacle

of human injustice," he was telling a ragged peasant. "In the general plan of God you will see the inevitable triumph of divine justice."

A woman wearing a white kerchief and a brown cotton dress was staring at his hands. Padre Pio's dark eyes focused on her horrified expression. "Spiritual and physical pains are a test of Divine Will," he said softly. "All souls who love Christ must conform to their eternal Model. The Redeemer experiences these incomprehensible pains as He sees Himself again abandoned. Those who have chosen to be a part of divine service must experience all the pains of Christ to some degree. We must thank God for the sufferings that enrich us."

The woman with the kerchief relaxed a little. Padre Pio smiled understandingly.

"Padre," said a skeletal old man who was leaning heavily on the arm of his daughter. "Is it possible that saints are not aware of being in two places at once . . . what do you call it?" His daughter whispered something to him.

"You are referring to bilocation," said Padre Pio. "And they are indeed aware of it. They may be uncertain whether the body or the soul goes, but they are certainly aware of what is happening and where they are going."

"How do you know that, Padre?" asked the man's daughter.

Padre Pio rubbed his bearded chin and smiled. "I have been told it is so."

"Is it possible," she persisted, "that you have experienced bilocation yourself?"

He laughed and dismissed her question. "Many things are possible in God's world." Before she could continue he shuffled into the crowd.

Some people near the old man and his daughter pressed close and began to question her.

"Well," she said, "there is this one story that I hear members of the church hierarchy confirmed. Monsignor Fernando Damiani was vicar general of Salto, Uruguay, and a brother of the famous baritone, Victor Damiani, of the Colon Opera House in Buenos Aires. The monsignor had been cured of cancer of the stomach through Padre Pio, and they became friends over the years. The monsignor, it seems, asked Padre Pio to assist him before he died, and Padre Pio promised he would. A year later, then, Monsignor Damiani joined some distinguished ecclesiastics from South America who were celebrating the twenty-fifth anniversary of the ordination of Bishop Alfred Viola of Salto, Uruguay, and the laying of a cornerstone for his minor seminary. On the vigil of the jubilee, about midnight, Archbishop Antonio Maria Barbieri of Montevideo, Uruguay, was awakened by a knock at his door. The door was open about a foot. He saw a Capuchin pass by and heard a voice: 'Go to the room of Monsignor Damiani who is dying.' The archbishop dressed, hurried to get the holy oils, and in turn alerted the others. Ten bishops went to the bedside of Monsignor Damiani and they raised their hands in the blessing for the dying. Well, there, assisting them was Padre Pio himself. He had kept his promise to be there. They say Monsignor Damiani was able to scribble a note with the words: 'Padre Pio came,' and then he died. But at this same time when he was in South America the friars here say he never left the monastery." A murmur went through the crowd that had gathered.

"There is another story," said the woman, "that Signor Pietro Calice of Corsica heard wonderful stories about Padre Pio and went to see him because his son, Giacomo, had joined the Foreign Legion and was reported by the government as missing in the desert. The father begged Padre Pio to bring him back. The padre promised him that the sheep would return to the fold if he would pray to God with love and faith. Giacomo, meanwhile, truly was lost in the desert, wandering about aimlessly. Then, he later told how a man appeared to him and told him to follow him. Together they reached the coast where they found a raft, and Giacomo used this to go to Marseilles. From there he reached Corsica. When the boy arrived home and told his story, the father quickly showed his son a picture of Padre Pio, and the boy said it was the same man who led him out of the desert." The people shook their heads in wonder.

"A man couldn't do such things," said the skeletal old man. "Only saints do that."

"But if he's a saint," someone asked, "why doesn't he admit it?"

"Yes," agreed a plump woman who was wrestling with four grimy children, "it's nothing to be ashamed of."


### III.

Padre Raffaele da S. Elia a Piansi, superior at Our Lady of Grace, received an official communique from the Vatican on June 11, 1931. He called Padre Pio into his office.

Padre Pio's feet and ankles were badly swollen, and he dragged his feet slowly and painfully as he struggled down the corridor, unable to quicken his pace. He felt old and tired. Only last month he had celebrated his forty-fourth birthday with his family. Though they all told him he looked ten years younger, he knew that youth was far behind him, and lately he remembered it as if it were a story he once heard about some stranger. He looked different, too. The pain from his wounds caused him to walk slowly and stiffly, slightly bent over. During the past years he had put on some weight, and his short hair had thinned a little and had receded about his hairline, though his beard was longer and fuller, with the first signs of grey. His deep brown eyes, though, were still clear and intense, and his face, as handsome as ever, was completely devoid of wrinkles except for a few creases at the corners of his eyes. His feet were aching by the time he reached the superior's office, and Padre Raffaele could see the discomfort on his unsmiling face.

"May I help you?" he asked, getting up.

Padre Pio raised a hand. "No, thank you. I am fine."

The superior studied him before sitting down. "I did not know your wounds were troubling you more than usual today or I would have gone to your cell to see you."

Padre Pio managed a faint smile. "I'm glad for a chance to get some air. It's a perfect day, isn't it?"

"It's my duty," said Padre Raffaele, "to advise you that while the Holy Office is investigating the phenomenon of your wounds, the public shall not have access to you."

Padre Pio didn't reply. He folded his hands in the lap of his brown habit and let the words digest in his mind.

"I'm certain it is only temporary," the superior hastened to add.

Padre Pio glanced at him. "Do they say how long?" Padre Raffaele shook his head no. For some reason he couldn't find the right words today.

Padre Pio nodded. "I understand."

"I'm truly sorry."

"Shall I say Mass?"

The superior hesitated. "Privately," he said then. Unable to offer any consolation, he let Padre Pio return to his room.

Padre Pio didn't notice the pain in his feet during the walk back. After he reached his room he couldn't even remember walking back. He collapsed wearily into a chair and stared across the room to the crucifix on the wall above his bed. There was nothing to be done. The Church had commanded, and it was his duty to obey. But he knew that there would be widespread suffering and concern as untold numbers of bewildered persons would be turned away at the door. His eyes dropped to his hands. He pulled off the fingerless gloves and stared at the loosened scab on the wound in his left hand. He touched it with a finger and it slid into his lap. He watched it until his eyes filled with tears and he couldn't see it any more.

He was still sitting in his chair, trying to focus his eyes on the crusty scab in his lap, when there was a knock at the door, and two brothers entered.

"Forgive us, Padre," said a handsome, sandy-haired young man with a gentle face. "The superior has asked us to assist you."

Padre Pio stared at them. "Assist me?"

"Yes, Padre. Are you ready?" Padre Pio continued to stare at them until they both looked flustered.

"Didn't Padre Raffaele tell you we were coming?" asked the other brother. He was a lean, colorless youth with a short pointed beard. Padre Pio shook his head.

"He didn't tell you?"

"No."

"Well," stammered the youth, glancing at his companion, "we
... we are to move your bed to the library and take down the crucifix
from the gallery where you were stigmatized." Padre Pio looked away.

"I'm sorry," the boy said softly, sounding genuinely distressed.
"With your permission, Padre—."

Padre Pio motioned to the bed. "You have your instructions.
Obey them."

He sat motionless, saying nothing, and waited until they were
gone. Then he pulled himself to his feet and slowly shuffled down
the corridor after them.

The long, lonely hours began, and the days turned into weeks.
No one contacted him except Padre Raffaele, who suffered almost as
much as Padre Pio. He lived as though in the shadows, moving
quietly in the early hours to the second floor chapel where he would
celebrate mass alone, and then returning to his quarters before anyone would see him. He ate his meals alone, like a prisoner in solitary
confinement, and spent his hours praying, meditating, reading, and
writing letters to his family. Out of his despair he drew closer to God.
He eventually discovered a new feeling of peace, and his sense of
abandonment no longer seemed totally without purpose.

Then Padre Gemelli and some of his followers urged the Holy
Office to take even greater measures. They sent a message to Pope
Pius XI: "He must be unfrocked and expelled from the Capuchin
order."

"No," the pope declared, "the present restrictions are justifiable
and sufficient."

A group of Capuchin superiors met with Padre Gemelli soon
after that. His large face was all smiles when he sat down at a long
table with them, and his eyes were dancing behind his thick-rimmed
glasses. He was so certain that his cause was in a position of strength
that he nearly fell from his chair when one of the Capuchins accusingly
demanded that he publish the *true* account of his visit to Padre Pio.

"True?" he asked, clearly taken aback. "You doubt the account
of my examinations of his wounds?"

"Yes," a Capuchin flatly stated. "I am convinced that Padre Pio, obeying orders, did *not* let you examine him, and that your theory disproving the origin and purpose of his stigmatization is pure speculation and no more than your own personal bias against this man."

Padre Gemelli fell silent. He knew when the game was over. Within a matter of days he mended his reports.

When Padre Raffaele brought the news, Padre Pio listened carefully and thanked the superior quietly. He was glad to have the record set straight but in his estimation there was no cause for joy in another man's defeat, for whatever the reason.

Not long after that Padre Pio wanted to talk to the superior about something else. Padre Raffaele asked him to come to his office.

"You say it is urgent?" he said, pointing to the chair in front of his desk. "Sit down."

Padre Pio started talking while sitting down and adjusting his long habit. "The pope has lost a document of great importance concerning Catholic Action in France, and I know where it is."

The superior sat forward and frowned. "Where did you hear that? And how do you know where it is?"

"God revealed it to me while I was celebrating Mass. He instructed me to notify the pope."

Padre Raffaele stared at him incredulously. "That's out of the question, Padre."

Padre Pio shook his head. "I don't understand. The document is of extreme importance."

"No." The superior raised his hands and gestured emphatically. "Please understand, Padre Pio, I am not doubting your word, but I could not possibly go to the Holy Office with such a story when you are already within an inch of being expelled for creating a furor over your supernatural powers."

Padre Pio sat forward on his chair, searching for some opening in the superior's response.

"I'm sorry," said Padre Raffaele, kindly but firmly. He closed the discussion by standing and thanking Padre Pio for his concern.

Padre Pio left, completely dismayed. When time and again he received the mental impression while saying Mass, he went back to Padre Raffaele, insisting that he sensed precisely where the pope's lost document could be found and that it was God's will that he get the message through to the Holy Office.

The superior finally consented. He shook his head and smiled. "If I don't notify them you won't let me rest, will you?"

Padre Pio smiled back, feeling very relieved. "I did not mean—"

"No, no," Padre Raffaele interrupted. "It is nothing. I have concluded that if you are right it may open some eyes in Rome."

And it did. The lost document was found where Padre Pio said it would be, and it was returned to a grateful Pope.

Nothing happened, though the amended report of Padre Gemelli and the recovered document both worked in Padre Pio's favor. But he still lived day and night in the monastery library. He fasted, prayed long hours, and looked at the lonely Gargano Mountain from a small window. The rocky hills had been transformed into a deep forest green, and a summer sun now burned intensely on the thick stone walls of the monastery.

During this time Padre Luigi Orione, a worker for derelicts, wanted to pray at the tomb of Pope Pius X. He asked to have the gate of the crypt opened for him, and there, to his astonishment, he found Padre Pio praying inside the enclosure. He spoke to him just as he started to walk out of sight, and then rushed to tell Pope Pius XI.

The pope listened, and said, "I have faith in what you say, Padre Orione, but up to this moment I have been assured that Padre Pio has never left the monastery. From what you tell me, what good are restrictions?"

He quickly contacted the monastery, but Padre Raffaele assured him that Padre Pio had never left, and the pope was left to ponder Padre Orione's report.

As suddenly as the gates had closed for Padre Pio, they swung open again. On July 16, 1933 Pope Pius XI sent word that all his priestly rights were to be restored.

Said the pope later: "I have not been badly disposed toward Padre Pio, but I have been badly informed about him."

"The verdict is in," Padre Raffaele said, smiling broadly. "Your captivity is ended!"

Long lines formed at the monastery, and Padre Pio opened the outside door and smiled into the hot summer wind.

"Padre Pio," a woman cried, grasping his hand, "we have waited two long years for this day."

He laughed with the cheering throng as it pressed against him from all sides. "I was waiting with you," he told the woman. He took a deep breath and tasted the sweet flavor of freedom.

## IV

In prophecy Padre Pio was very prudent. He knew much more than he said, and he restrained himself when he didn't think it was wise to speak. However, a short time after the restrictions were lifted, newspapers started to publish details and elaborate texts of his alleged prophecies about wars, days of darkness, and other disturbances coming to the world and the catastrophies which would follow. Many people believed them because of Padre Pio's well-known power of prophecy.

The superior called a meeting of some of the friars at the monastery, and told them: "Considering the difficulties we have encountered before, I have concluded that we must stop this rash of press reports about Padre Pio's prophecies."

"Some of them are true," an oval-faced, middle-aged priest volunteered.

Padre Raffaele nodded. "Our task is to halt the publicity, not evaluate the individual accounts."

"Shouldn't Padre Pio be at this meeting?" someone asked.

"No." Padre Raffaele snapped, and then quickly tried to change his tone. "He has suffered enough."

"But he could tell us which stories are true."

"No." The oval-faced priest shook his head. "No, he doesn't like to talk about these things. He's very ... well ..."

"Evasive?" someone asked.

"Something like that."

The superior tapped on the table with a pencil. "Please, let us get down to the business at hand."

"Did you hear about Padre Pio and the King of England?" asked a large man with several chins.

Padre Raffaele sighed. "Is the King of England pertinent to our task here?"

"Then you haven't heard about Padre Pio and the King."

"No."

"I don't want to take up time now if everyone has heard about it."

Padre Raffaele impatiently twisted a finger around the cord of his habit. "No one has heard it. Please tell us . . . quickly."

"No, I've heard it," someone remarked. Padre Raffaele threw up his hands and looked away.

"But," the man hastily added, "I'd like to hear it again."

The heavy priest with several chins told them that one evening in January Dr. William Sanguinetti and two laymen were in Padre Pio's room.

Unexpectedly Padre Pio said: "Let us kneel and pray for a soul that is soon to appear before the tribunal of God." When they finished Padre Pio asked them if they knew for whom they prayed.

"No," they all replied.

"It was for the King of England," he explained.

"But only this morning," said Dr. Sanguinetti, "I read in the newspaper that he had only a slight attack of influenza, and he is not seriously ill."

"It is as I say," Padre Pio answered.

The priest paused in his story to catch the eye of Padre Raffaele, but he was busy untangling the twisted cord.

"And on January 20," the priest concluded, "the King died." The others nodded.

"You heard about Savino Greco, didn't you?" asked the oval-faced priest.

Padre Raffaele glanced up and grabbed for his pencil to pound on the table, but the oval-faced priest was already off and running.

"Savino Greco of Cernignola," said the priest, "lived with his wife and five children in two poor rooms. He was a farmer who was paid a salary. Until recently he followed the theory of Marx and was an active worker for the Communist party. He had even forbidden his wife to baptize the children or to take them to church. However, without his knowledge his wife had the children baptized. One day Savino became very ill and went to a doctor. Here other doctors came to see him, too, and their verdict was clear and terrible: a brain tumor and another tumor in the back of his right eye. There was no hope for him or at the most very little.

"Savino went to the hospital at Bari then and here also the doctors did not hesitate to confirm what he had already been told. So full of fear he turned to God for the first time since he was a child.

"He was transferred to a Milan hospital then and the doctor who examined him there said that it was necessary to take out the right eye and this kind of operation was extremely difficult and the results were dubious.

"One night he saw Padre Pio in a dream, and Padre Pio touched his head, and said: 'You will see that with time you will be cured.' The next morning he felt much better and the same doctor was amazed at what he saw; nevertheless, the doctor still believed an operation was necessary. But Savino was so upset that before entering the operating room he ran away from the hospital.

"He sought refuge in the home of a cousin who lived in Milan where his wife was staying, but after a few days the pains began again and became so acute that, in spite of the fear of the operation, he was forced to return to the hospital. The doctors, provoked with him, at first did not want to operate but their professional conscience superceded and it was decided to operate. First, however, they decided to conduct new examinations.

"When the doctors finished their examinations, they were completely amazed because they did not succeed in finding a trace of any tumor! Even Savino was surprised, but not at what the doctors had said. Before, you see, while they were examining him, he had received an intense perfumed scent of violets, roses, and lilies, and he knew that such perfume often announced the presence, visible or invisible, of Padre Pio.

"Before he left the hospital then, he asked the doctor how much he owed him. 'Nothing,' the doctor told him, 'because I did not do anything to cure you'!"

Silence had fallen around the table, and even the superior was completely absorbed in the priest's story. It took him a moment to collect his thoughts.

"None of us here doubts the powers of Padre Pio," he said, "but we have another obligation—to control the release of such accounts so that the results are not damaging to the public or to Padre Pio. Can you understand what I'm saying?" They nodded solemnly.

"I believe we should issue a formal denial in Padre Pio's name stating that he has made no such statements as have been publicized recently in the press, and that the many prophecies attributed to him have no foundation."

One of the friars scratched his head and frowned. "If this statement is going to be issued in his name," he asked, "shouldn't Padre Pio have something to say about it?"

Padre Raffaele glared at him. For some reason they were all rather troublesome this morning. "Rest assured," he told all of them, "that I will . . . advise . . . Padre Pio of our decision."

# A New Era

## I.

*World War II broke out* and Padre Pio predicted that Italy would be the first nation to seek an armistice.

"It's not the war I fear, but the post war," he said.

Everything intensified then, and he remembered World War I. He could still recall the terrible suffering he saw as an orderly in the hospital in Naples where he was stationed. The painful memories would bring tears to his eyes.

"Why do you cry?" one of the brothers asked, catching him rubbing his eyes one day.

"Why should I not cry," he wondered aloud, "seeing humanity damning itself at all cost."

The war interrupted the life of everyone, and it interrupted the university studies of Ezio Saltamerenda, a handsome young medical student in Genoa. His life was one trial after another; when fighting at the front lines he saw the face of death many times, and was seriously wounded in Tobruk, Africa; finally he was captured and experienced the horrors of a German concentration camp. Through it all and later when he was married, he still defended and propagated his atheism.

Through a chance meeting with Mario Cavaliere, a spiritual son of Padre Pio, Dr. Saltamerenda saw a large photograph of Padre Pio on Cavaliere's desk. When he saw the photo, a strange look came over his face, and he felt a knot in his throat. Cavaliere noticed this and proceeded to tell him about Padre Pio. That same evening Dr. Saltamerenda left Genoa for Rome. To his surprise he finished in one day the business that he had calculated would require many days. The following night he kept hearing an inner voice, imperative and insistent, calling him to San Giovanni Rotondo. It was simply impossible to resist. He left that night for Foggia where he arrived too early to continue to San Giovanni Rotondo by bus, so he found a taxi in front of the station and continued that way.

Dr. Saltamerenda entered the church of Our Lady of Grace and went into the sacristy where only a few persons were present to await the arrival of Padre Pio for mass. Little by little the crowd increased. The shuffling, bearded figure of Padre Pio darkened a doorway, then, and a murmur went through the crowd. Dr Saltamerenda felt the strange knot in his throat again, and suddenly he felt like crying. When Padre Pio walked past, the devotees knelt and tried to grasp his hands.

But Dr. Saltamerenda remained standing in an angle of the sacristy, rigid in a force of tension that dominated all his senses. He asked himself *Why am I here? What did I come here to do?* He remained there, immobile during the entire mass. He couldn't take his eyes off Padre Pio.

After mass, Padre Pio returned to the sacristy, flanked by the usual crowds, for thanksgiving. Dr. Saltamerenda followed him but he was disturbed by the priest's appearance. Physically exhausted, Padre Pio's face was pale and drawn. An hour and a half later Padre Pio returned to the church to hear confessions, and Dr. Saltamerenda finally made his move. He knelt at Padre Pio's feet and asked him to bless a sick relative.

Padre Pio looked down at him with a scowl on his face. "He is blessed," he said dryly.

Dr. Saltamerenda caught the tone and his head snapped back; he quickly struggled to his feet. It seemed there was something he should say.

Suddenly Padre Pio exploded: "Tell me, young man, about your soul. Don't you even think about it?"

Dr. Saltamerenda's mouth fell open. He tried to avoid Padre Pio's piercing brown eyes. "Certainly, Padre," he mumbled. "Otherwise a person would not be alive."

"And what is the purpose of life?"

Dr. Saltamerenda was confounded. "The preservation of the species!"

Padre Pio's face flushed with annoyance. "Wretched one!" He nearly bellowed at him. "Don't you see that your soul is going to ruin?" After a pause Padre Pio calmed himself and placed his hand firmly on Saltamerenda's mouth. "Get out of here," he said quietly, nodding his head toward the door.

The touch of his hand deeply disturbed Saltamerenda. When he recovered from the outraged remarks of Padre Pio, he felt it was imperative that he see him again. That afternoon he followed a group of men into the sacristy.

Padre Pio saw him from the corner of his eye and felt another sense of outrage building up inside. Then he couldn't restrain himself any longer. He whirled around and looked squarely at Saltamerenda's puzzled expression. "Genovese!" he shouted at him. "You have a dirty face and you have not washed. You live near the sea, but you don't know how to wash." Then after taking a deep breath, he added, somewhat more softly, "A strong boat without a pilot."

Saltamerenda's hand unconsciously raised and he rubbed his face. More confounded than ever, he tried to kneel beside Padre Pio, who again, pointing, indicated for him to leave. The severity of the rebuff only tended to increase his attachment to the friar. The more he was humiliated, the more he genuinely loved him.

"Padre," he wanted to cry out, "now that the ice in me is melted, forgive me." But he knew that Padre Pio didn't want to hear another word from him—ever. He left with overwhelming despair in his heart. Perhaps, he thought, he would return some day when he would be more composed.

He went for a walk in the nearby fields. It was a cool, fall afternoon, and the land had gone brown. As he walked, he felt as if a dog were on his heels, and all at once he sensed the perfume of violets.

He went back to the monastery and met Fra Francis. The young brother comforted him and induced him to remain. He even accompanied him to Padre Pio's room. Fra Francis knocked on the door, and when it opened, a wave of perfume of violets met them.

"What do you want?" Padre Pio asked gruffly. "Don't let me waste time. Go to the church where I will hear your confession."

Saltamerenda stared at the angry, bearded face a moment and then wheeled about and left. In the confessional, he started to cry. His head was leaning on Padre Pio's perforated hand. "Those were the most beautiful moments of my life," he later told Fra Francis.

The act of contrition was dictated word by word by the Capuchin. "Padre," said the doctor, "I wish that this my sorrow for sins, the salvation of my soul, would bring you a little consolation."

"What do you say, my son?" said Padre Pio. "It is a *great* consolation that you received absolution."

That night Dr. Saltamerenda collapsed wearily, though happily, on his bed. Moments later, though, he heard a mysterious, formidable pounding on the walls of his bedroom and against the bed. He had never been afraid at the front lines during the war and had even defied death in the German concentration camp, but he felt his limbs trembling like a baby now. He invoked Padre Pio, and the room was instantly flooded with perfume.

Dr. Saltamerenda shot out of bed, threw his clothes on, and raced to the monastery Padre Pio calmed him and confirmed that he had had some·undesirable visitors.

"My son," he said, "we do not know what happens down there." Saltamerenda was still shaking.

"You now hold wonderful bread in your hands," Padre Pio told him, "and around you are the hungry "

"What shall I do?" asked the doctor, his voice pleading.

"Cut it in slices, and distribute it to satisfy the hungry. In this way you will serve the Lord. And I shall always be with you."

Padre Pio's serious expression softened, and he smiled warmly. Saltamerenda stopped shaking long enough to smile back and meekly thank him before leaving.

Padre Pio regularly exhorted his spiritual children: "Be good Christians, or your journey will serve you no good purpose. Only by good example can you change the world."

A man from Vincennes once became acquainted with Padre Pio's spiritual children through his mother. The idea intrigued him. A friend told them that he had heard Padre Pio say he would like to put his spiritual children in his pocket and take them to heaven with him, but if they didn't behave, he'd slap them. When the man heard this he was no longer so sure about the idea. But finally he found the courage and went to see Padre Pio.

"Could I become one of your spiritual children?" he asked. Padre Pio hid a smile. "Yes," he said, "but aren't you afraid?"

## II.

Mario San Vico, a clean-shaved, smiling doctor from Perugia, went to see Padre Pio out of curiosity. He hoped to examine his wounds.

At the monastery Padre Pio took one look at him, and said, "You will collaborate with me in the construction of a hospital."

Dr. San Vico, completely caught off guard, was speechless. He stared at Padre Pio who was looking back at him in all seriousness. He started to say something but changed his mind and began to smile. *Why not?* he thought.

Padre Pio had never let go of his dream to have a good hospital in the area. At the monastery he had talked constantly about the need of one. And as far as he was concerned it was time to do something about it. Padre Pio soon found another collaborator, Dr. Carlo Kisvarday.

Dr. Kisvarday, a heavy-set man with a grey moustache, was a wealthy pharmacist living in Zadar, Yugoslavia. One day he and his wife intended to drive to Bavaria, in Konnersreuth, to visit Teresa Newmann, a stigmatized girl.

They travelled from Zadar to Trieste and from there to Bressanone, where he made a short stop. By chance he met a poor woman with two children who had both been stricken with polio. He was interested in them and was surprised to hear that they, too, were going to Konnersreuth to visit Teresa Newmann. He was about to suggest to the woman that she and her two crippled children accept a lift in his car, when she told him that she had been to visit Padre Pio, who was also stigmatized.

He suddenly changed his mind, and said to his wife, "We are going to San Giovanni Rotondo."

He didn't linger a moment and they immediately set out for San Giovanni Rotondo to meet Padre Pio. A year later on an icy, silver day in January he went back to San Giovanni Rotondo.

Padre Pio was glad to see him. "I want you here beside me," he said. "Make your home here."

Dr. Kisvarday didn't utter a word of objection. He settled his affairs in Yugoslavia and built himself a home not far from the monastery.

Padre Pio's collaborators frequently visited him to talk about the hospital project. One evening Dr. San Vico, who was appointed secretary, stopped by his room, and asked, "Padre, what name do you want to give this hospital?"

Padre Pio had already thought about it. "*Casa Sollievo Della Sofferenza* (Home for the Relief of Suffering)," he said.

San Vico repeated it. "I like that," he said. "How did you decide on it?"

Padre Pio smiled. "It was easy. I just don't like the word *hospital* because it evokes ideas of pain, suffering, and loneliness. But *home* reflects a family atmosphere. It will free the patients from a feeling of isolation, and give them confidence. Don't you agree?"

San Vico nodded. "I certainly do."

Funds began to trickle into the treasury lira by lira. Then one day Padre Pio said, "We have seventeen thousand liras (about $30.00) in the treasury. Are we able to begin construction? The amount is small, I know. I don't want this hospital to be a depressing home for the cure of suffering, but I want it to look like a large home of relief, a place to study all things well. I want my hospital to be one in which a person does not experience any bad odors, a house free of the smell of ether and medicine."

Hospital odors reminded him of his own suffering as a patient and his army service in the Naples hospital as an orderly during World War I.

Dr. Kisvarday was appointed treasurer of the hospital fund, which was not going to be an easy task. The impoverished villagers had little to offer in donations for the hospital. The value of the lira had shrunk, and fund-raising campaigns had to be set up.

The question of finances continued to harass the doctor. Once in desperation he went to Padre Pio, and said, "I'm afraid I have no money to pay the workers."

Padre Pio listened solemnly, and nodded. "Pick up the handkerchief on the small table," he said.

There was some money in it. Kisvarday started to smile as he counted it.

"Is it enough?" Padre Pio asked.

Dr. Kisvarday shook his head and started laughing. "Yes, just right—by some coincidence."

Padre Pio's brown eyes lit up. "Are we back in business?"

Kisvarday patted him on he shoulder. "We're back in business."

Dr. San Vico began to keep a diary. In 1940 he wrote:

"I cannot remember if between the ninth and fourteenth of January it was raining or snowing. Not many people were thinking about fulfilling the desire of the friar. The Capuchin was dreaming about caring for people's bodies as well as their souls.

"The Gargano is a strange world. It is cut off geographically from the great march of events. In the past, the sick people of the area went down to the plains for medical care. But the friar is dreaming about assisting not only the people of the Gargano. Crowds come from other parts of Italy and from other countries.

"They have no more faith in the science of men. They turn to God, asking Him either to cure them or help them to accept their suffering in peace. The Gargano is full of sorrowing pilgrims. They come, they pray, they weep, and then they go off with a small shred of hope."

Padre Pio had a third collaborator, Dr. William Sanguinetti, a serious-faced, balding man who supervised the construction of the hospital and became director of the project. Padre Pio especially liked Dr. Sanguinetti and looked upon him as a brother.

The doctor and his wife, Emilia, had previously lived in northern Italy in a small community, Parma, in the province of Boro San Lorenzo. He was a medical practitioner and had a thriving practice there. Through friends, his wife learned that Padre Pio had received the stigmata like St. Francis and was reputed to have unusual powers and could give wise counsel. Since Mrs. Sanguinetti was perplexed with a personal problem, she decided to pay a visit to Padre Pio, and she asked her husband to go along. At the time he was strongly anticlerical but he consented to accompany her. As a doctor he wanted to ascertain the facts anyway.

As soon as they reached San Giovanni Rotondo they tried to get into the monastery, but were unceremoniously sent away by a brother who told them to come the next day. The next morning they saw Padre Pio and he told them to wait. They were both told it would be possible for them to confess the next morning. Mrs. Sanguinetti went to confession and was so pleased that the doctor decided he, too, would go to confession that afternoon. When he confessed to Padre Pio he felt that this priest had been a genuine brother to him, rather than an inquisitor. As a result he decided to bury the past and become a new man. Later that day Padre Pio talked to him and his wife, and they were so impressed with his warm cordiality and simplicity that they promised to come again and visit him. The result was that Dr. and Mrs. Sanguinetti spent a few days of their vacation every year in San Giovanni Rotondo, near Padre Pio. During one of those yearly visits, Padre Pio asked him to come and work for him.

Sanguinetti remembered the first meeting he had with all the collaborators: Padre Pio, Kisvarday, and San Vico. It was a cold, damp January night when they gathered in Padre Pio's small room. During the conversation, Padre Pio clearly had the suffering of mankind on his mind.

He told them: "In every poor man it is Jesus Himself who is languishing; in every man who is both sick and poor, Jesus is doubly present. We must do something for the sick. We must build a hospital." He had reached into his pocket then and pulled out a gold coin that had been given to him for his work of charity. Offering it to the three men, he said: "I want to give you the first donation towards the hospital fund. It is for the first stone of a large hospital that we shall construct here." The three men had looked at one another in utter amazement.

"But Padre Pio," Dr. Sanguinetti had said, "this isn't the time for such an undertaking. With the world at war, with storm clouds hovering over Italy, and with Italy threatened, it is an absolute impossibility!"

But Padre Pio had calmed their fears and assured them that nothing would be done at the present time; however, he felt that the solicitation of funds should get underway as soon as possible. He simply wasn't going to take "no" for an answer either.

When spring settled on the monastery the three men and Padre Pio decided to launch an appeal for funds throughout Italy and abroad, based on the words of Sacred Scripture: "He who has pity on the poor, loans to God." The appeal was answered with moving generosity.

"It's going exceptionally well," Padre Pio told his brothers at the monastery, who followed his work with considerable interest.

Then an administrative committee was created, comprised of a president, vice president, treasurer, and eight advisors, including a mayor, engineer, doctor, banker, and lawyer. This committee served at a nominal fee of one dollar a year.

When the directors of the hospital overcame obstacles of construction, they still had to face the lack of funds. Whenever there was no money in the treasury for either the workers or materials, the construction stopped. Dr. Kisvarday, as treasurer, was worried.

Though contributions had been made by housewives, who even made door-to-door collections throughout Italy and many parts of Europe, the amounts were not very large.

"It will come," Padre Pio told the friars at lunch one day. "It will come."

Everyone looked at him skeptically, and someone said, "Even if it doesn't, at least you tried."

## III.

Padre Pio's health was holding up reasonably well in spite of his busy schedule. Although the hospital occupied him daily, he still had all his priestly duties to attend to. He had to say Mass each day, hear confessions, direct his spiritual children, and receive as many visitors as possible. And he still spent long hours in prayer and meditation. The pain from his wounds didn't allow him much sleep at night, but somehow he managed to work it all in.

During the war, in 1940, he gave the original impetus to a movement called Prayer Groups. It was his answer to an appeal by Pope Pius XII for groups of faithful to unite in prayer for the purpose of renewing Christian life, the love of God, and the love of neighbor.

In an address to a large gathering, he said: "Groups of faithful will live full and open Christian lives, if they follow the desire of his Holiness. First of all, they should pray together." Padre Pio asked that these prayer groups unite their intention with his and pray for all people, especially those who requested his prayers. He also appealed to the groups to pray not only according to the intentions of the pope, but for the intentions of bishops and priests as well. "Prayer is the best armor that we have," he said. "It is a key which opens the heart of God."

The groups were not an association or a confraternity, but merely faithful—spiritual children—who followed Padre Pio's example and invitation to pray together. The prayer would generally culminate in Mass, and have a follow up in works of charity. In many parishes the prayer groups became cultural and social centers.

Each prayer group would meet once a month in the church, under the spiritual guidance of a priest. The members would have no other pledge than to invite friends to join, and no group would be formed without the permission of the local bishop. At the meetings Mass would be celebrated, Benediction given, and prayers recited, the ultimate aim being the spiritual perfection of each member through a prayer-life.

Many who organized such groups said it was hard to find priests to be spiritual directors. When Padre Pio heard that his groups were not well attended and hence did not fulfill their purpose, he felt sad, and he urged those who promoted them to work towards their own sanctification through a more intense life of prayer. But with time the movement gained strength and soon it spread throughout Europe and the world. Padre Pio began to feel considerably better about all of it.

He was fifty-three years old now. Sometimes he didn't know where the years had gone. His face did not show the years, though his tense expression often betrayed the pain that constantly tormented him. It was more than two decades since he had fallen in a pool of blood before the crucifix, and in all the years since, his wounds had never changed. He knew they would never heal. Walking was becoming more painful each year, but at the same time he was learning how to manage a little better each year. Sometimes the pain and weariness would cloud his otherwise clear and sharp brown eyes. But even on those days he made certain that his face would be wearing a smile for everyone he met. His bulky brown habit and his slightly stooped position when he walked made him look heavier nowadays, though he had put on weight over the years, too. And his face was fuller, while his greying hair and beard had softened his features to give him a gentle and kindly, fatherly appearance.

"He looks lovable," said a novice, and the others agreed. Padre Pio really never understood why everyone fussed over him so much. He accepted it but there were times when he thought he could do nicely with a little less concern and attention.

Sometimes he would stand by a window and look sadly at the hundreds of people below who were waiting patiently in line to see him.

"What is troubling you?" one of the priests asked him, stepping over to look out the window with him.

Padre Pio shook his head unhappily. "Some are curiosity seekers but most are genuinely disturbed over something. Can you imagine how many millions of people all over the world need help? How can I begin to reach even a small number?"

"Let's face it," said the priest, "you can't."

Padre Pio turned to look at him, and as he did his hand banged into the windowsill. He winced as the pain flashed through him.

"Are you all right?" asked the priest.

Padre Pio's eyes had filled with tears and he kept his hand lowered. "Yes," he said softly, and excused himself. He went to hear confessions, and that rapidly took his mind off his throbbing hand.

He recognized a rather homely young woman who had told him a month ago that she wanted to enter the convent.

"First take a vacation at the seashore," he had told her, "and then talk about taking the veil."

She was wide-eyed and smiling today, and said, "Padre, I do not want to become a nun any longer. I met a young man at the seashore and we are going to get married."

Padre Pio laughed. "You see," he said, "I told you to go to the seashore first!"

There was a corridor from the monastery to the confessional where people waited for him to pass each day going to and from confessions. Often those who had pressing problems and couldn't confess in Italian would seek out his advice for either spiritual or material requests through a Capuchin priest who acted as interpreter. Even those who did succeed in confessing to him and had a request to make would wait until later. Padre Pio first wanted to administer the Sacrament of Penance and then take care of their other needs.

Padre Pio had this advice to give about sin: "The demon is

like a mad dog on a chain. He cannot seize anyone beyond the reach of the chain. Therefore, keep your distance. If you go too close he will get you. Remember that the demon has only one door through which to enter your soul, the will. There are no hidden doors. Nothing is a sin if it isn't committed wilfully.

"Take heed of the temptation that says to you: you can never return to the love of God if you have offended Him. This is an insinuation of the devil. Didn't St. Peter, the Apostle of Jesus, on whom the Lord conferred authority over the other Apostles, deny his Master? But afterwards he repented and loved the Savior to the point of becoming a saint."

Padre Pio didn't ask incomprehensible sacrifice of men; he didn't impose rigorous penances or demand heroic self-denial; nor did he ignore individual ideals. He appreciated everyone's talents and never dissuaded anyone from cultivating them, if only they followed the path of Christian honesty.

One of Padre Pio's spiritual sons went to see him in the fall. "Are they going to bomb Genoa?" he asked.

"I fear," Padre Pio answered.

"Your fear serves nothing," said the visitor sadly. "Then Genoa will be bombed."

Padre Pio's face suddenly paled and his eyes misted. "Oh, how they will bomb that poor city," he cried. "How many houses, how many mansions, and how many churches will crumble!" The visitor looked stricken.

"Be calm; your house will not be touched," Padre Pio quickly added.

Somehow his prophecy ended up in the newspapers, and just as he predicted, when the bombs rained inhumanely on the city of Genoa, numerous houses, mansions, and churches crumbled. From the ruins of the heaped-up masses of debris, it was hardly possible to distinguish what had remained standing.

His spiritual son came back later and told him that his own home had remained miraculously safe, just as Padre Pio had prophesied. Numerous fragments of incendiary bombs were stuck in the vases on his terrace, and there were a few broken windows, but otherwise no damage.

The war went on, and fall had deepened when, in the town of Monte Santangelo, the whole family of Luigi Gatta were gathered around the bedside of a little girl named Graziella. She had been at death's door for many hours. No one entered apart from the family, and no one spoke except to utter a prayer. The little girl had typhus, and her uncle, a doctor, left without giving much hope. Since morning her tiny body had been rigid, her eyes closed, and her breathing labored.

"What if we should go to see Padre Pio," murmured the mother. Everyone in the room stared at each other, filled with new hope all at once.

An aunt said, "I'll go, but don't expect me back before late tomorrow."

At San Giovanni Rotondo, Padre Pio received the woman kindly. She revealed the purpose of her visit and waited for the friar to confirm the inevitable, or at most, to give her comfort.

Instead, Padre Pio looked at her, and said, "This one will not die." Happily the aunt rushed back to Monte Santangelo to convey the good news to the family.

Before long Graziella opened her eyes, whispered a word, and little by little recovered her color and strength. Within a few days she was well on the road to recovery. Everyone prepared to celebrate, but all at once Maria, Graziella's sister, was stricken by the fever.

"Oh, no," cried the girl's aunt. "That's what Padre Pio meant when he said *this one* will not die." Maria died unexpectedly on November 7, 1940.

On a chilly, damp day not long after that, when the sky was dark with the purple storm clouds that carry the first breath of winter, a captain in the Italian army asked Major Teseo Isani to help save an English major who had escaped from a prison camp. He didn't hesitate to give his assistance, and the captain and Major

Isani hid him in a wagon of hay. But just when success seemed certain, the trick was discovered at one of the control points.

There they met not only Italian soldiers but the German S.S. The captain was immediately imprisoned, and Major Isani was shut up in a room of the town hall. After a court martial both were condemned to death.

On the day of the execution, the major, a slight man with receding black hair, was seated solemnly at a table, thinking about his end. He was a believer and not a coward, and he was prepared to meet his death. He loved his religion and wanted to die in the main square of the city, with an emblem of a cross pinned on his clothing, to make amends for the scandals of his youth.

While he was leaning wearily on the table, thinking about all of it, a voice loudly and distinctly said: "Run for it! Run for it!"

The major thought he had gone out of his mind. Without attracting attention he pinched himself on the arm. *No, he thought. I'm not mad yet.*

The same voice echoed in his ear more loudly and clearly: "Run for it! Run for it!"

The major thought it must be his father who was dead and wanted to save him. *But how can I escape?* he wondered. *There are two mastiffs here ready to tear me to pieces.*

A third time the voice insisted: "Run for it! Run for it!"

*Well,* thought the major, *it is only too clear; I must run for it. After all, they are going to shoot me anyway. Whether a bullet gets me standing still or running doesn't really matter.*

He knew he had to remain calm. Like a child, asking a teacher for permission, he asked the guard to allow him to go out. To his surprise the guard appeared indifferent and agreed without a second thought.

The condemned major passed by the officer on guard outside. When he reached the outer steps of the building he made a dash for it and began to run, winding across the street. He nearly flew, not paying attention anymore even to the possibility of being noticed.

His salvation was in the voice that kept ringing in his ears, urging him to flee.

A guard terrorized him suddenly by calling his name, and ordering: "Stop or I'll shoot!"

But he didn't shoot, and the major didn't stop. He saw a path between two buildings and bounded over a stone wall at the end. Days later he managed to reach Switzerland.

The captain, he learned, had been executed immediately, and posters had been sent to all parts of Italy and Switzerland with his own picture and a price on his head.

When it was finally safe for him to return to Italy, he went to Bari, and from there, having heard about Padre Pio, he went to San Giovanni Rotondo.

When Padre Pio saw him, he smiled warmly and listened to his confession. Then the major got up to leave and Padre Pio called after him: "Run for it!"

"My God!" cried the major, wheeling around. "It was *your* voice!"

Padre Pio folded his arms, and smiled mysteriously. "Goodbye," he called, just as the major started back toward him.


## IV.

Padre Pio followed the war closely. In 1942 the Italian Army stopped the Allied attacks which had penetrated into Egypt nearly as far as Alexandria. Then came the capture of Alamein, and it appeared the war would end in total victory for the Italians. The people of Italy were jubilant.

It was a hot and humid summer day when the news reached the monastery. Padre Pio was strolling in the monastery garden and he stopped to talk with Dr. Sanguinetti and several visitors.

"We are going to lose the war," he told them. "Yes, we have

some victories, but we will not last. The English are landing in Italy. They will wage war in all parts of the country, and it will be a good thing that they do this."

The men were shocked, and they stared at Padre Pio as if he had lost all his senses. Dr. Sanguinetti was shaking his head in disagreement. "Padre, how can you say the ruin of our country will be a good thing?" he asked.

Padre Pio shrugged. "To win the war would not mean that *we* would win it, but that *Germany would* win it. Then we would fall under Nazi slavery, which is the most diabolical slavery that one can imagine."

"But, Padre Pio," argued a visitor, "don't you think that between nazism and communism, it would be better that nazism should triumph?"

Padre Pio shook his head emphatically. "It is quite different. Nazism attacks all religions, attacks the very idea of God. It would substitute for the religion of God the exaltation of the race and the deification of a greater Germany. And that is an idea which could capture the imagination of all, especially the youth. On the contrary, the negative materialism of the Soviets will never succeed in satisfying the mysticism which is part of the Russian soul. Russia will return to religion and to God!"

Everyone stood stiffly without responding. Padre Peo decided not to pursue the subject and turned back toward the monastery.

Summer was firmly entrenched when the Americans occupied the air base at Foggia, thirteen miles away. The people of San Giovanni Rotondo feared that bombs might fall on their town, and a group of men went to Padre Pio and told him they were worried.

"Not one bomb will fall on San Giovanni Rotondo," he assured them. Though they heard the guns echoing on the plains, and they suffered from lack of food, they had faith in his words. And as the days passed, not one bomb fell on the town.

"He's been right all along," said one of the priests at the monastery. He was talking with a clean-shaven, well dressed businessman who was standing in the shade of a tree, waiting for his wife. The businessman nodded but looked generally unconvinced.

"Only yesterday," said the priest, anxious to persuade him, "I was talking with an army major stationed at the air base in Foggia. He comes to the monastery every Sunday afternoon and visits with Padre Pio in the monastery gardens. Last Sunday he made plans to accompany a pilot friend on a scouting expedition in the surrounding area, but when the friend came for him, the major remembered he had promised to see Padre Pio again that Sunday. No amount of coaxing could convince him to change his mind, so his pilot friend left and the major went to the monastery. Later we all learned that for an unexplained reason, the plane of his pilot friend exploded in mid-air, and the pilot was killed. The major might have gone along had it not been for Padre Pio." The businessman looked into the priest's open, unquestioning eyes.

The priest sighed and looked at the white wisps of clouds in the summer sky. "It was truly . . . truly . . ." He laughed and glanced back at the businessman. "I can't even find the right word."

"I believe," said the businessman, "it's called coincidence." He left the priest standing under the tree.

"I believe it's also called prophecy," the priest called after him. "I believe—" He stopped, the man was already out of sight.

The war went on, and Padre Pio urged Dr. Kisvarday to transfer his personal effects from Yugoslavia to San Giovanni Rotondo as soon as possible. Dr. Kisvarday succeeded in reaching San Giovanni Rotondo with a sickly wife and a faithful servant. Had he delayed his journey for even a short while, his move would not have been possible. He took the last boat leaving his country for Italy.

Word soon spread that Dr. Kisvarday had left his wealth in Yugoslavia and had built a house in San Giovanni Rotondo, and people said that Padre Pio had surely made a mistake this time in giving such advice. But while Dr. Kisvarday and his wife were safely in San Giovanni Rotondo, the Nazis invaded Zadar, Yugoslavia. All Dr. Kisvarday's property was destroyed and his brother killed when the family home was demolished. His nephew, together with a group accused of resistance, were lined up against a wall and shot. All Dr. Kisvarday had left now was his wife, their servant, the home he built in San Giovanni Rotondo—and his dedication to raising funds for Padre Pio's hospital.

Padre Pio was torn from all sides these days—the war, the hospital, the people, his work. No one was the same during a war. They all tried to pretend nothing had changed, but Padre Pio could sense the difference, particularly during confessions.

"What about the stolen purse you do not want to confess?" he asked a nervous, jumpy little man.

"What purse?" asked the man, wondering how Padre Pio had found out.

"You don't seem to think of it any more. Don't you remember? It was in the French campaign. You entered a house and found a purse. There were 75,000 francs in it. Although you had no title to take that purse, you took it without any remorse."

The man's dark eyes darted about, avoiding Padre Pio's penetrating gaze. "I did not know," he said, "to whom the purse belonged."

"Strange," replied Padre Pio, "you did not know to whom the house belonged either. Why didn't you take the house too?" The man flushed and lowered his eyes.

Padre Pio asked him to do charitable acts for the amount, a little at a time. "You are in a position to do so," he said.

The man stood and shook his head. "I do not want to do that, Padre."

"Then," said Padre Pio, "I will not absolve you." He slammed shut the little slide in the confessional right in the man's face. With time, the man reconsidered and returned. He promised to atone for the theft, and repent.

Padre Pio smiled and absolved him. When he left Padre Pio greeted a smiling young man.

"I would like to become a priest," said the young man.

Padre Pio nodded. "Yes, the Lord has called you. Do as you like, but you will not become a diocesan priest, but a priest of some religious order." The young man looked surprised. He had intended to do just that.

Another youth also entered the confessional that day, and asked: "Padre, shall I marry or become a priest?"

"Marry," Padre Pio replied without hesitation. "It is better not to be a priest than to be a bad priest."

The days began passing then, one much the same as another. Summer died, and then fall. The snows were heavy that winter and in many places the huge white drifts hid the country's battle scars. The monastery had somehow escaped the worst thus far, and for many it served as a refuge. Days of sadness and thanksgiving mingled erratically. Suddenly on February 19, Pellegrina developed a high fever and died. But for Padre Pio the demands of each day left little time for mourning. And for everyone the war went on.

Because of her American citizenship, Mary Pyle was not interned by the Italian authorities. They recognized her as a spiritual daughter of Padre Pio. But one snowy evening she was summoned to the Italian police marshall's office.

"I want you to leave San Giovanni Rotondo," he told her, "now that this area is a war zone."

She obeyed and fled to Pietrelcina, living in exile in the Forgione homestead as a guest of Padre Pio's family. For Mary Pyle, like Padre Pio, the years had slipped away. She was now in her fifties, and the slender young woman who had first come to San Giovanni Rotondo had turned into a grey-haired, plump, pleasant-faced and matronly middle-aged woman.

Pietrelcina was never bombed, but life there was hard, as it was everywhere in Italy. She used her time well, though, working with the architects on plans to build a new monastery in the area. Whenever she ran into a snag and wanted Padre Pio's advice, she contacted him through Orazio. And so the Capuchin monastery had its beginning, just as Padre Pio had predicted when he was a seminarian many years ago. Mary made the bulk of the financial contributions herself, though funds were augmented by the Pietrelcina villagers and by donations from outside. The monastery and church

soon became her favorite charity, and she worked at it as hard as
Padre Pio worked at his hospital project.

When the war shifted and she could go back to San Giovanni
Rotondo, she became a hostess to thousands of American soldiers
who were stationed at an air base near Foggia. When these soldiers
went to see Padre Pio she acted as interpreter. Once they had a roll
call of American states, and there was a soldier present from each
of the states.

Sometimes the soldiers came in groups, and Padre Pio would
place his hands on each one who knelt before him. Some of them
were sons of emigrant Italians, and of other nations. When Padre Pio
learned of their national backgrounds, he commented on how great
a country America must be to act as a melting pot for so many
different nationalities.

Padre Pio felt a warm glow whenever he talked with the soldiers,
and they loved him. Many of them took back to America the story
of his desire to build a hospital, and this resulted in donations of
thousands of dollars for his charity. Mary Pyle even took charge of
aid sent to Padre Pio from America.

Numerous soldiers wrote letters home telling about Padre Pio.
The press got word of him, and soon reporters arrived from *Life*
magazine to document the latest of the great religious stories of
the century.

"I don't think all this publicity is good," a priest commented
to Padre Pio after the reporters were gone. "Particularly your war
views. Not everyone appreciates your prophecy—such as the Germans."

Padre Pio looked unconcerned and preoccupied with something
else. "The life of a Christian," he said, "is nothing but a constant
struggle against self, and its beauty does not manifest itself except
at the price of suffering."

He simply didn't believe that Germany would win the war.
Soon, when the Germans were retreating from Foggia, two German
officers went to the monastery and asked for Padre Pio. As he was
coming from the chapel, they met him with two revolvers drawn.

One of them spoke Italian fluently, and said: "Padre Pio, who is going to win the war?"

Padre Pio shrugged his shoulders. "Someone will win," he said. The two stern faces looked back at him suspiciously.

He began to feel uneasy. "Look," he said, "I am unarmed. Why do you come with revolvers pointing at me?"

The two men looked at each other and finally put their revolvers in their holsters. They gave him one last hard look, turned and walked away.

The next Sunday an ardent Communist from San Giovanni Rotondo returned from a Communist rally in the nearby town of San Marco. He was so exhilarated with the meeting that he stood on a box and started to make a speech. A number of persons gathered to listen. He was denouncing Padre Pio.

"Down with Padre Pio!" he screamed at the startled faces around him. "We will cut off his head!"

All at once his hand froze in mid-air and his eyes went blank. While bystanders gasped, he toppled from the box. A local doctor pushed his way through the crowd and carried him to his office. Shortly afterwards the man died of a stroke.

## V.

When Padre Pio was urging Dr. Sanguinetti to come and work for him on the hospital project, he predicted that through a ticket the doctor would be able to leave Parma and settle in San Giovanni Rotondo.

Years later, Dr. Sanguinetti was called to the home of a wealthy gentleman, Don John Sacchetti, to treat his son who was quite ill. The boy recovered, and his parents were so grateful that they became personal friends of the doctor and his wife. Once while visiting Don Sacchetti, Dr. Sanguinetti spoke of Padre Pio's plans for the hospital and he mentioned the mysterious ticket. The Sacchetti's were interested, but made no move to make any contribution.

As the doctor and his wife were leaving, Don Sacchetti jokingly said, "Be sure to let me know about the ticket, when you find out what it means."

A few weeks later Dr. Sanguinetti returned triumphantly to Don Sacchetti's house, waving a letter.

"I have found out what ticket Padre Pio meant," he said. "Once I bought a government bond and received a ticket as a receipt. I have just received news that the bond won a prize and I will receive a small fortune. This means that I am now free to leave my practice completely and go to help Padre Pio build his hospital."

The doctor began the serious business of helping Padre Pio then. His work was the beginning of a career that launched him on to new fame. He became the business manager of the whole project, and he kept in contact with everyone, from the high society of Rome and luminaries of medical science to the more modest Apulian world to obtain aid for Padre Pio's hospital.

It was Dr. Sanguinetti to whom Padre Pio confided his sufferings over the wounds in his hands, his feet, and side. Once the doctor told a friend, "If you or I would suffer one-tenth of the pain that Padre Pio suffers from his wounds, we'd be dead."

Now that the war was finally ended, Dr. Sanguinetti worked diligently and conscientiously, assisting in the planning of the hospital, together with the architect, Angelo Lupi. The chaotic conditions of the country following the post-war years, however, caused numerous problems in obtaining and transporting materials.

The war had hindered the immediate realization of the project, and the directors studied the great problems that had to be solved. There were also the ecclesiastical authorities to deal with and the civil officials of the town. It was not until October 5, 1946, at the end of World War II, that the Society for the Relief of Suffering Project was legally constituted. On that memorable day Padre Pio raised his hands to bless the undertaking of the directors.

Then the work for construction began in earnest. The first step was the blasting of rock. This work took many months, and the force of the blasting was heard for miles around the area. It seemed as though the mountain rumbled and was awakening from a long slumber of inactivity.

When the blasting was finished, workshops were erected so that everything which could possibly be made for the building was done on the premises. A lime kiln was set up for making an immense quantity of artificial stone for internal and external facings. Hundreds of thousands of tiles and iron and metal fixtures were manufactured, and shops for woodwork were constructed. Hundreds of workmen on the jobsite manufactured the tiles for the floors and slabs for the great white facade. These undertakings provided work for many of the men of San Giovanni Rotondo and vicinity, thereby alleviating their economic conditions. Some men donated their services to this project.

But there were endless technical problems to which the three men and the engineer had to find quick solutions. The nearest railroad was about twenty-five miles away in Foggia, and the hospital was about half a mile above sea level. Supplies by rail were often delayed because of the damage suffered by the bombings of the war, and other means of transportation had to be quickly improvised.

A hydroelectric plant for auxiliary power was built. Then difficulties arose in locating water for the institution. Padre Pio was consulted and he suggested that they make special connections with the aqueduct of Apulia. This was done, assuring a steady supply of water, and the work could continue. On May 16, 1947 the first stone was set in place.

Padre Pio's family was on hand, except for one. Orazio never saw that day. He had lived to be eighty-four years of age, and he had died in Padre Pio's arms on October 7, 1946 in Mary Pyle's villa. Padre Pio was saddened by his father's death. Afterwards some of his brothers found him crying.

"Have courage," one of them said.

His brown eyes lifted, and his voice faltered. "It is a father I have lost," he whispered. Orazio Forgione was buried near his wife in the cemetery at San Giovanni Rotondo.

After Orazio died Mary lived alone in her villa with members of her household, four women who worked for room and board. But she wasn't lonely. People from all parts of the world used to write letters to her, and she was submerged in mail daily. Primarily she would be asked to present various needs and problems to Padre Pio. She would then sit at her small desk and for hours answer these letters, relaying Padre Pio's advice, promises of prayers and blessings. It was a tiring and never ending work, and in later years she accepted the assistance of secretaries who volunteered their services.

A year passed this way, and autumn came again to the monastery. A new face appeared, and suddenly everything changed for the better.

Miss Barbara Ward came from London to see Padre Pio for personal reasons. She was greatly pleased with the help she received and wanted to do something for him. Dr. Kisvarday told her about his increasing desire to get the hospital project underway and how badly funds were needed. He also told her how the funds had shrunk considerably with the severe devaluation of the lira. So she decided to intercede for the hospital when she went to America on a lecture tour.

Miss Ward succeeded in obtaining the substantial amount of $325,000 from the United Nations Relief and Rehabilitation Administration (UNRRA), whose director was New York's ex-mayor, Fiorello LaGuardia; his family had come from Foggia. This donation gave the hospital the financial boost it needed. And not to be outdone in generosity, the Italians matched the amount, and the construction of the hospital continued more rapidly. Padre Pio was beaming when the funds were declared.

"I told you it would come," he said to the friars at dinner one evening.

They all smiled. "We never doubted it for a moment," someone said.

It was all going extremely well, although there were a few problems. When donations in large amounts came, the government stepped into the scene, and Dr. Kisvarday's simple system of bookkeeping had to be revised. But his original notebook was kept as a momento.

Because the funds made it possible for the work to progress, the hospital workers designated Barbara Ward as the godmother of the hospital.

In 1948 Mary Pyle made a trip to America to visit an aunt who was dying of cancer. She stayed four months, and while she was in the country her friends persuaded her to speak to different groups about Padre Pio.

When she got back she told him that while she was away she had not missed daily Communion once during the four months.

"Yes," he said, "but you haven't missed it once in four years!"

"I never told you that," she said slyly.

He feigned surprise. "No?" Their eyes met, and they seemed to reflect the joy their long association had brought them.

"I'll go outside and wait for your brother," she said. "He's coming over to visit." Padre Pio smiled and nodded, watching her walk away.

Since his wife died, Michael came daily to the monastery. He reminded Padre Pio of Orazio more and more, with his beardless face and greying hair. Michael was in his late sixties now. He made his home with his daughter, Pia, her husband, and their eight children.

Michael, for the twenty years that he had lived in San Giovanni Rotondo, had faithfully attended Padre Pio's mass at 5:00 A.M., and he was also among the visitors who greeted his brother in the evenings. He would invariably sit by Padre Pio and often in private conversations relate the recent happenings of family and friends.

If he should ever oversleep or come late for mass, Padre Pio would shake a finger and say, "Michael, you'd better get yourself a good alarm clock. You were late for mass this morning!"

After confession one morning a doctor sitting near Michael saw Padre Pio's face contract in pain. A penitent had just revealed many sins to him.

"Are you all right?" asked the doctor, rushing over.

Padre Pio nodded, but a shudder involuntarily rocked his body. "Souls, souls!" he cried, "What a price your salvation costs!"

One day when he wasn't well enough to leave his room, one of his crosses, perhaps the heaviest after not being able to celebrate Mass, was the thought of the crowd which waited for him for confession.

"I am here," he said, "and the people are there waiting for me."

"I wouldn't worry about it," a brother told him, meaning to console him. Padre Pio simply stared at him incredulously.

He wondered sometimes how his life could have gotten so complex and so involved with humanity on such a wide scale. There were days when the thousands of faces he had seen would march through his mind, living and dead, all the timeless faces of souls he had encountered.

Miss Italia Betti was one of them. She was known throughout Italy and in many countries of Europe as an ardent Communist. She lived in Bologna, where she taught mathematics. All the members of her family belonged to the Communist party except a younger sister, Emerita, who had remained loyal to the Catholic faith.

Italia, a stocky muscular woman who always wore a harsh expression, was an avid member of her party and was always the first on the scene on her motorcycle whenever there was a clash between the Communists and the Catholic party. She was ready at all times to fight, and if the occasion presented itself, even to kill.

Then she was stricken with cancer. The doctors gave no hope at all for her recovery. During her illness a friar who said he was Padre Pio appeared to her in a dream and told her to go to San Giovanni Rotondo.

She had never heard of him, but in desperation she, her mother, and her sister went to the mountain village on a glistening December day in 1949. The three of them rented two rooms in a home near the monastery.

Padre Pio warmly greeted her and he began to instruct and console her. He brought peace and light into her heart, and that was something she had never known. She received Communion from his hands and made a public renunciation of her former ways of hatred and violence. During her ten months of excruciating pain, she gave a wonderful example of humility and patience, being completely re-signed to God's will. A year later she died.

Padre Pio remembered another conversion, that of Dino Serge, a popular Italian playright, who used the pen name of Pitigrilli.

Pitigrilli was an atheist living in Buenos Aires. He had a friend, Luigi Antonelli, who was a writer living in Foggia. Antonelli had cancer on the side of his neck and was told by doctors that he had six months to live if he would have an operation and three months without one.

As preparations were being made for the operation, someone suggested that he go to see Padre Pio, who was only twenty-four miles away. Antonelli was desperate and as a last resort consented. Accompanied by Pitigrilli they attended Padre Pio's mass. A complete stranger in San Giovanni Rotondo, Pitigrilli followed the mass in a corner of the church.

Suddenly after mass, Padre Pio turned to the congregation, and said: "Pray, dear people, pray fervently for someone who is here among you today who is in great need of prayer. One day he will approach the eucharistic table and will bring many with him who have been in error like himself."

That day Antonelli confessed, and Padre Pio spoke to him at length. Afterwards he was cured of his cancer. As for Pitigrilli, he became converted through Padre Pio and became a reformed man. He went back to Buenos Aires and began writing articles about his conversion by Padre Pio.

It seemed that every few weeks someone would try to find a way to test Padre Pio's powers. Once a Dominican priest from Pompei went to the church of Our Lady of Grace dressed in civilian garb. He had never seen Padre Pio before, and after mass, when the men were lined up in the sacristy for confession, the disguised priest stood in a corner so as not to be noticed.

All the while Padre Pio was hearing confessions of the men, he'd keep glancing at him. Finally he sent someone to call him over. The disguised priest was puzzled and walked over hesitantly.

"Go and put on your robe," Padre Pio commanded.

The priest smiled and took Padre Pio's hands, kissed them, and said, "This is all I wanted to know. Now I believe."

Later, a woman was complaining to Padre Pio that she was unable to do anything for him.

"Only a general knows when and how to use a soldier," he said. "Wait till your turn comes."

She was the last visitor that day, and he was glad to be going back to his room. He was even happier that he didn't meet anyone in the corridor on the way. He was incredibly tired, but he didn't know if it was the strain of entering a new era or just the fatigue that comes after a long hard day.

# I Confess

*Like the Curé of Ars,* Padre Pio spent most of his priestly life in the confessional. In his early years he devoted as much as eighteen hours a day to hearing hundreds of confessions. Now that he was getting older his failing strength kept the number to about eighty a day.

"That's 30,000 a year!" said a young brother.

"29,100," corrected his companion.

"Do you think we'll be able to do that many when our time comes?" His friend rolled his eyes in a who—would—want—to—fashion.

Two priests were passing near enough to see a woman struggling to reach Padre Pio. She was trying to kiss his hand and touch his habit.

"See that?" asked the one, a large bulk of a man.

The other nodded. "There's the proof. We've got to put up an iron barrier around his confessional to keep them back."

Padre Pio's confessional for women was unusual in that there were no curtains to conceal him. A penitent entered on either side through a swinging door that partially concealed him but left an opening about two feet from the floor. Inside the enclosure the penitent knelt and spoke through a screen. A small door which could be opened by the priest covered the screen.

Padre Pio was completely attentive as he listened. He concentrated on each person's confession, tilting his head first to one side and then to the other. When the confession was completed he closed the door and leaned over to the other side to begin the confession of another penitent. As each woman approached to confess, he let her kiss his stigmatized hand.

The men's confessional, set up in the sacristy of the church, was less elaborate. Padre Pio sat on a chair behind an arch, immediately behind the door of the corridor. To his right he had a hassock on which a penitent knelt. A cloth on a frame served as a divider between confessor and penitent. This confessional stood in a corner, surrounded by a curtain, so it was hidden from curious eyes.

A certain amount of patience was required for those who wanted to confess to Padre Pio. The Capuchins inaugurated a number system whereby men and women had to register for confession and take their turn, waiting for their number to be called. Before this number system was put into effect, men and women waited all through the night at the church door in all kinds of inclement weather. The monastery was becoming known as the "House of Patience." Men waited for confession from three to fifteen days, and women waited from five to twenty-eight days, depending on the season of the year.

Two priests were looking out the window with Padre Pio one day, observing a woman who had been patiently waiting for three weeks.

"I don't know how they can do it," said one. Padre Pio glanced at him without commenting.

"No offense," said the priest quickly, catching his eye. "But you have to admit that some of them wait for weeks and it's not natural." Padre Pio just stared at him.

"Oh, I don't know," the other volunteered. "I think it's *natural* enough. The question is whether a year from now we'll be able to handle the growing numbers."

Padre Pio's eyes turned away from his brothers to settle on the line of people beneath the window. "We will not turn them away," he said quietly. A moment later he walked on.

One of the priests lingering behind watched him shuffle away and shook his head sympathetically. "Personally, I think *he's* worried too."

His companion nodded. "I would be too if I were responsible for all of this." He waved his hand toward the long line of people.

"I don't think we should blame him completely."

The friend raised his eyebrows. "They're not coming to see you or me."

"No, but I don't feel that Padre Pio is entirely responsible. We might give God a little of the credit! And although the entire business has created problems, it *has* been for the best, you know."

"I hope so."

They backed off when a man in the crowd below began pointing at the window where they were standing.

The two priests rounded a corner of the corridor and nearly collided head-long into a young Capuchin. The wide-eyed youth skidded to a halt and panted heavily. Unable to catch his breath he waved his arm frantically.

"What on earth is it?" asked one of the priests.

"Padre Pio!" the boy gasped, between snatches of breath. "He's killing a man!"

The two priests looked at each other for a minute. "We have no time for games, young man," said one of them sternly.

'It's true!" the youth shrieked. He looked terrified.

"Where is Padre Pio?" asked the priest.

"His confessional."

"Men's?"

The boy nodded, and the two priests rushed off toward the sacristy. In the distance, through the partly-open curtain, they could see the brown-robed figure of Padre Pio towering over a slight, emaciated man who was on his knees, his hands gripping the skirt of Padre Pio's habit. They heard Padre Pio rebuking him harshly with his hands on the man's shoulders. Between admonishments he shook the man's shoulders vigorously.

"My word!" breathed one of the priests. He put his hand on his companion's arm. "I had heard he did things like that, but—"

"If you or I did that," said the other, "we would be arrested! But, look." Padre Pio had released the man who was now kissing his hands.

The young boy who had followed the priests edged up behind

them sheepishly. One of the priests turned around and scowled at him. "I hope you've learned your lesson," he growled.

The young boy looked bewildered. "But he had him by the throat!"

"By the *shoulders*, young man. There is quite a difference."

"But—"

"I know you meant well, but how could you suspect our Padre of harming anyone?"

The boy shook his head. "I'm sorry. I just thought something was wrong when he grabbed the man. I'm truly sorry."

"I should hope so."

"May I ask what I saw?" the boy asked timidly.

The priest glared at him again. "You saw Padre Pio chastising someone, of course. A perfectly normal procedure . . . for Padre Pio, that is. And a successful one, I might add." The boy stared at the priests and excused himself.

"But don't you ever try anything like that," the priest called after him.

It was generally well known among the older priests that Padre Pio was not adverse to using rough, harsh, and shocking language, especially in cases of scandal, calumny, impurity, and sins against motherhood. These he did not forgive without a reproach. As a spiritual director, he admonished serious sinners with a warning. Other sinners he refused at first to absolve until they were sufficiently prepared for their absolution. It annoyed him when people approached the confessional without attaching any importance to the Sacrament of Penance, and it annoyed him even more when people came to him merely to test his apparent omniscience.

He often treated a great sinner who was ignorant of the divine law with more pity than those who were convinced of their own perfection. When a young man of the village said to him that in spite of imperfections he considered himself to be good, Padre Pio replied dryly, "Yes, good like boiled beef."

It was obvious that his sometimes brusque manner was a deliberate effort to break down all resistance. It was a style peculiar to him which only he could use. Inevitably the people waited, returned, and humbled themselves, really repentant, to receive absolution. The majority of them were flooded with joy and gratitude. However Padre Pio acted, he had reason. He knew precisely how to discover the intentions of the most tight-lipped penitent. Though this was his style, he suffered and prayed for those who came to him, so that they would receive the grace to bend their head before the divine mercy, and he did the same even for those who were unwilling to be converted.

"I don't give a piece of candy to those who need a cathartic," he once told a colleague, and on another occasion, said: "If a doctor takes pity on a patient, he will make a wound gangrenous."

Even though many confessions brought him great consolation, many of the sins were a secret and perduring agony. Tears flowed down his cheeks when he met repentant hearts. He seemed nearly always to be enlightened when in the confessional as if God allowed him to partake of His own omniscience. If a penitent hid or diminished a sin out of shame, Padre Pio sternly reproved him. To a penitent who attempted such a confession he would say: "There are sacrilegious words on your tongue." He was also very severe with habitual sinners, incorrigible drunkards, and people who constantly sinned against purity. Padre Pio once remarked to a woman of questionable virtue: "If you have the courage to imitate Mary Magdalen in her sins, have the courage to imitate her penances."

A journalist from Rome said that before Padre Pio gave him absolution, he told him in no gentle terms to be on guard against a certain weakness. The knife cut into his soul. On another occasion Padre Pio laid bare another deeply-rooted imperfection, and he progressively corrected himself. Then on his third visit Padre Pio asked him how many days had passed since his last confession.

"Padre Pio," he smiled and replied proudly, "every day I go to church to attend mass and receive Holy Communion."

Padre Pio frowned, and said sharply, "You are here to confess your sins and not to sing your own praises. Have you lost your temper with your sisters?"

The journalist lowered his eyes, his smile disappearing. "Yes," he mumbled.

"That is what you must confess then," said Padre Pio, "and don't do it again." The journalist wondered how Padre Pio knew he had sisters.

Soon thereafter a young woman confessed to Padre Pio that she committed sins against purity. Yet, she knew that when she returned home she would fall into the same temptation and sin again. Padre Pio refused her absolution. Later she returned and repeated the same confession. Again the same thing happened—no absolution. This occurred four times. Finally, before her fifth confession, she thought to herself, *I'd rather die than commit this sin again,* and she had this on her mind all throughout the confession. Padre Pio studied her closely and suddenly absolved her.

After that another woman said she read immoral books. Padre Pio scratched his greying beard, and looked puzzled. "Have you confessed this before?" he asked.

She nodded. "Yes."

"What did your confessor say to you?" he asked.

"I wasn't to do it any more."

Without a word Padre Pio closed the little confessional door, turned away, and began to hear the confession of the next penitent.

The woman began crying and went to confession to another priest, later receiving Communion from Padre Pio. "I'd like to burn all the bad papers and books in the world," she cried before leaving.

Padre Pio was pleased. He *wanted* his penitents to go away from his confessional changed. It was not only big sins but also imperfections that he wished them to put away. He directed the penitents to obey God's laws and trust God for all the necessary help. After confessing to him, some people left consoled, in tears, but with peace of soul and a firm resolution to improve their spiritual life.

One day a young man came to Padre Pio in the sacristy, which was crowded with men going to confession. "Please, Padre," he said, "I would like to confess to you."

Padre Pio looked at him with penetrating eyes, "Hog!" he shouted, while all eyes turned in his direction. Deeply humiliated, the man hastily left the sacristy.

An astonished friar stared at Padre Pio. "Why did you use that *terrible* word?"

Padre Pio shrugged. "If I had not thrust that word into his face, he would have been condemned forever. He lives in concubinage and this is a horrible abomination before the Lord. That humiliation was for his benefit. He will come back again in a few days. If I gave him absolution, he would have entered without repentance and a firm purpose of amendment, and he would have had to leave without absolution."

After a few days the young man returned to the sacristy as Padre Pio had predicted. He had not eaten or slept for several days and suddenly it had become extremely difficult for him to continue his illicit relationship. When he saw Padre Pio he fell to his knees and started weeping.

Padre Pio reached down and put his arms around the young man. "See, my son," he said gently, "our Savior now takes great delight in you." The young man smiled through misty eyes and left, firmly resolved to reform his life.

At the far end of the church a priest was listening to a handsome young couple. The young man said that once he was dating a girl, who was now his wife, and when he learned that she was expecting a baby he left her. They did not see each other for two or three years. Her parents turned her out, and she spent many a sleepless night.

"I was desperate," explained the pretty young woman, "on the edge of a precipice, when I heard one day about a convent of nuns who would help me. Sure enough, I had my baby and afterwards they helped me find work with a family that would let me keep my child. It was from those nuns that I first heard about Padre Pio."

The young man nodded. "Young people often make a lot of

silly mistakes," he said. "I had forgotten her and the child. Well, sometimes I thought about them, but then I became engaged to another girl. This girl's family was very attached to Padre Pio. Before the wedding they wanted us to go with them to meet him. So one day she and her parents and I went to San Giovanni Rotondo. I set off light-heartedly, slightly irritated at their infatuation with the friar. The following morning after Padre Pio's mass, I began to feel restless. I felt inexplicably worried. In the afternoon I went with the girl's father to meet Padre Pio in the garden. He was sitting on a low wall, and there were five or six men around him. Another friar was sitting next to him. As soon as I reached the group Padre Pio looked at me. His eyes seemed much bigger than they really are and the expression on his face was serious, severely so. I had the impression that he wanted to cry but couldn't. I tried to be natural. The girl's father introduced me and explained that I was about to marry his daughter and would like to have his blessing.

" 'My blessing?' Padre Pio sighed. 'My blessing? But what about God's? What about God's blessing?"

"The girl and her mother were curious about the way Padre Pio received us. Her father didn't understand the deep meaning of those words. Their meaning was reserved only for me. I went through a terrible night. The next morning I tried to speak to Padre Pio. I met him in the sacristy after Mass.

" 'My son,' he said, smiling, "do you understand what you have to do?' "

"I grasped his hand and kissed it. I rushed back to the hotel then and wrote a long letter to the girl and her parents explaining my difficulties. Then I left for Rome and began looking for the girl I had abandoned. It wasn't easy to find her."

The young woman dabbed at her eyes with a handkerchief. "It must have been about seven one evening," she continued. "I was alone in the house. My baby was in his chair. I heard the door bell and thought the owners had come back. I opened the door and saw him. I almost passed out."

"The baby smiled and rang the bell for me," said the young

man. "He didn't know I was his father, but from that moment our life began."

The priest couldn't think of anything to say, so he cleared his throat and smiled at them.

## II.

Padre Pio had an unpleasant duty to perform. He was talking with a recently-widowed woman. Her husband had once left her and their two children to live with another woman for over three years. Unexpectedly cancer had claimed his life. Before his death, after urgent appeals, he had consented to receive the last Sacraments of the church.

The woman, short and plain, nervously adjusted the kerchief on her head and finally asked the inevitable: "Where is his soul, Padre? I haven't slept, worrying."

Padre Pio watched her with troubled eyes. He could almost feel her grief filling his own heart. "Your husband's soul is condemned forever," he whispered.

The woman shook her head and her eyes clouded with tears. "Condemned?"

Padre Pio nodded sadly. "When receiving the last Sacraments he concealed many sins. He had neither repentance nor a good resolution. He was also a sinner against God's mercy, because he said he always wanted to have a share of the good things in life and then have time to be converted to God."

Before she left, he comforted her as best he could, but it all hung heavily on his mind throughout the day. The others at the monastery could see his distress and preoccupation. It seemed as if a huge cloud had settled just overhead and was casting a dark and depressing shadow that obliterated every ray of light.

"You are troubled today?" asked one of the friars, a gentle quiet man, as he caught up with Padre Pio on the way to lunch.

Padre Pio kept his eyes glued to the floor. His feet were aching. "It is a troubled world," he replied solemnly.

"That it is," the friar agreed. "Hundreds of persons are waiting to see us today for that very reason."

Padre Pio nodded. "They come with heavy sorrows. Many ask me to take away their crosses, but very few ask me for the strength to carry them."

The friar caught Padre Pio's arm as he paused suddenly and reached out for the wall to support himself.

Padre Pio managed a faint smile. "I am getting old."

Now that he was in his sixties, Padre Pio found his list of aches and pains growing. They all seemed minor, though, compared with the never ending pain from his wounds.

The seasons disappeared, one into another, until they all appeared to merge indistinctly together. A new spring had settled in and was already nudging summer.

"This is my year," Mary Pyle told Padre Pio one sunny morning. He had been strolling in the monastery's cypress gardens.

Padre Pio's brown eyes twinkled. She had a way of dissipating all dark clouds. "Are you planning to keep it all to yourself?" he asked.

"You know I'm not," she scolded. "But it's no secret I'm happy about the new monastery and church in Pietrelcina. Wasn't the dedication this month absolutely perfect?"

He nodded. "I'm very happy for my friends and family in Pietrelcina—the ones who are still there." His eyes misted for a moment as he thought how pleased Giuseppa and Orazio would have been. "And I'm happy for you," he added.

"I was told that long ago when you were a young cleric you predicted that there would be a new monastery in Pietrelcina."

Padre Pio laughed. "You must not ask an old man to remember back so far." They paused outside the monastery. It had rained the night before and the grass, still wet, looked dark and silky.

Her clear blue eyes smiled at him and his still handsome face softened with delight. Age had solidified their long association and had brought the ease and comfort that old friends experience in each other's company.

Progress was evident in San Giovanni Rotondo as well as in Pietrelcina. By 1952 Padre Pio and his three collaborators were deeply involved with his hospital project.

"How's it going?" asked a priest at lunch one day, just when it wasn't going particularly well.

"Some problems now and then," Padre Pio acknowledged, "but it's coming along." Several of the friars stopped eating to listen.

"What's this we hear about the thirty million dollar donation?" someone asked.

"It's three million," corrected the friar at Padre Pio's left. "Isn't it?"

Padre Pio nodded without commenting. He would just as soon they didn't meddle in unsettled matters. Inevitably things got exaggerated and distorted.

A bald, round-faced man with a short, red beard stared at Padre Pio. "As I understand it," he said, "the three million from Dr. Mario de Giacomo's estate may end up in some state hospital instead of in the Home for the Relief of Suffering. Dr. de Giacomo's lawyers say his will stipulated that in case Padre Pio abandoned his plan to build the hospital or refused to accept the inheritance, the property would go to the state hospitals in Naples. The lawyers are claiming now that at the time of his death there was no Home for the Relief of Suffering in existence." He kept looking at Padre Pio, trying to catch his eye. "Isn't that right, Padre?"

Padre Pio finally lifted his brown eyes and looked over in the priest's direction. "I'm sure there will be no problem," he said.

"I don't know about *that*," said the priest, "but I think they may soon be celebrating in Naples with your three million dollars!"

Everyone nodded. They watched Padre Pio concentrate on a slice of bread, as if he were alone in the room.

A trial was finally set to settle the matter. The two lawyers contesting the will came to ask Padre Pio for his prayers and blessing.

"If you speak the truth, there will be no difficulty," he assured them, "and I will pray for you."

The court ruled that at the time the will was made, the hospital was under construction.

Hearing the news, two priests poked their heads through the doorway of Padre Pio's cell. "Congratulations!" they called.

Padre Pio was sitting in his chair, meditating. He smiled and motioned for them to come in.

One of them, the bald, round-faced priest with a red beard, smiled broadly. "You must be pleased."

Padre Pio agreed that the court's ruling was good news for the hospital.

"For a while," said the other priest, "I thought the Home for the Relief of the Suffering had lost."

"Faith, my friend," said the round-faced priest, "have a little more faith." Padre Pio hid a smile.

"Of course," continued the priest, "for every good thing, something bad must fall." He put a hand on Padre Pio's shoulder. "I just learned that the church has now banned a total of eight of the books written about you."

Padre Pio shrugged. "There are enough books in the world—"

"Yes, but—"

"And most of them more interesting than any written about me."

"Well, I don't think *that's* true."

Padre Pio asked if they would excuse him as he had to prepare for mass. He didn't want to get into a discussion of why the books were banned because that would lead to a discussion of his miracles and cures, and that was one of the topics he preferred to avoid completely.

### III.

The land had gone green on May 4, 1954 when a ten-year-old boy arrived with his father who wanted to have the boy blessed by

Padre Pio. The youth was suffering from the last step before total blindness. Padre Pio's heart ached when he saw the boy's sad, unsmiling little face. He heard his confession and suddenly reached out to touch the clouded, dark eyes.

The next morning at Padre Pio's mass the father noticed that his son was looking curiously around the church. He was surprised. The boy had never done anything like that before.

"I can see something on the wall!" the boy whispered excitedly.

The father rushed him out of church after mass and asked him to tell him all the things he saw. He could see everything.

"How can we thank you?" the father asked Padre Pio. "It is a miracle! What can we say? My boy can see! He is cured! I don't know how to—"

Padre Pio lifted his hands. "Please," he said, trying to calm the man, "please don't make a fuss."

It wasn't long after that, in another town, that a child about six years old fell from a fourth story window and was almost crushed.

"Help me!" screamed the child's distraught mother, rushing to the lifeless form.

"I will help you," said a soft, gentle voice. She looked up at a man with a grey beard and a long brown robe.

"I'm Padre Pio," he said. "Don't be alarmed. The child will be well again." Suddenly he was gone, and she couldn't explain any of it.

"Pray to the priest," said a nurse the next morning. She held out a photo of Padre Pio. "They say he has miraculous powers." The woman prayed, and the child recovered.

Word of the incident reached the monastery, and someone had stopped a doctor just outside the monastery door where the usual crowd of visitors had collected.

"Is it true?" asked a tall man with a thin, long nose. He had short sandy hair that stood nearly straight up on the top of his head.

"So I'm told," said the doctor, a friendly, jovial man.

"I don't understand how he does it," the tall man said, shaking his head. "How does he do things like that—make people walk or see? And how can he be in two places at once?"

The doctor smiled. "Those are rather difficult questions."

The man agreed. "But doesn't anyone know how he does those things?"

The doctor winked at him. "You can be certain that God knows."

A ripple of laughter went through the crowd, but the sandy-haired man frowned. He liked straight answers to straight questions. "Is it true he can predict if an unborn baby is going to be a boy or girl? I read that he tells people to call a baby "Francis" or "Maria" and that he's always right."

The doctor nodded, growing serious. "I can tell you this much. Once I was having my third son baptized when Padre Pio asked me, 'Where's Paul?' I didn't know what he was talking about and told him I didn't have any child named Paul. I didn't have any *then*, but early this year we had our sixth baby—a boy, and what do you think we called him?"

"Paul!" cried several women standing beside the doctor.

He nodded and laughed. "Yes, Paul."

"I heard," continued the sandy-haired man, "that his eyes grow luminous and he looks different somehow at times—as if part of him has gone elsewhere to be with someone who needs him." The doctor agreed.

"I know a young woman who teaches school," said a man's voice in the crowd, "who once heard robbers breaking into her home. She prayed to Padre Pio and just when they were ransacking the house, his voice thundered out of nowhere and they fled!"

"That reminds me of what I heard," someone else said. "There was a young man in Rome who was ashamed of his usual custom of tipping his hat when he passed a Catholic church. He was afraid his companions would make fun of him. But once he heard Padre Pio's voice in his ear, saying: 'Coward.' Later this young man really met Padre Pio—in person—and without mentioning this, Padre Pio suddenly said to him, 'Next time it will be a sound box on the ear!' "

"There are many famous persons as well," said the doctor, "who have been moved in some mysterious way by Padre Pio. One is the Mexican-American composer, Alfonso D'Artega, who claimed that

Padre Pio knew all about his past, present, and future, and that
changed his life forever."

A great "aaaah" escaped the lips of the bystanders.

"Benjamin Gigli," said the doctor, "was a Metropolitan Opera
star, and he said that even though he had met the greatest world
rulers, no one impressed him so much as Padre Pio. And Graham
Greene, the English writer, says he inspires men to pray."

The sandy-haired man was listening somewhat impatiently. "I
still would like to know," he said, "how he does all those strange
things."

"Wouldn't we all," said the doctor. He waved at the crowd
and went inside the monastery, meeting Padre Pio on his way out
for a breath of fresh air. "They're eager today," he said in passing.

Padre Pio's eyes were twinkling. "They're always eager," he said.

Shouts went up as the people caught sight of the brown habit
in the crowd. The years had left Padre Pio still handsome, though
his hair had thinned and his beard was grey now. Everyone recognized the sensitive, gentle face and the penetrating brown eyes.

"Touch me, Padre, touch me!" screamed a woman.

He looked at her and continued walking, mumbling to himself,
"I've never touched a woman in my life, and I'm not going to start
now!"

An elderly woman with a long black dress clutched the sleeve
of his habit and he stopped to look down into her intense brown eyes.

"Please, Padre," she begged, "tell me how to pray. I am always
distracted."

"You must not be distracted voluntarily," he warned. "But if
you are distracted, continue to pray, and you will have great merit,
for Our Savior knows that you are not an angel praying to Him,
but a poor woman. Go on praying without ceasing. And when you
find it difficult to concentrate, don't waste more time stopping to
consider the why and the wherefore. It's like a traveler who loses
his way. As soon as he realizes he is on the wrong road, he immediately sets himself on the right road again. So you must continue

to meditate without stopping to reflect on your lack of concentration."

"Please tell us more," the crowd urged.

Padre Pio thought about suggesting that they attend his mass, but changed his mind when he scanned the open and hopeful faces.

"The graces and the pleasures of prayer are not water of the earth," he said, "but of heaven. All our efforts are not sufficient to bring down God's graces. But it is necessary that we prepare ourselves with diligence, with the soul humble and calm. We must keep our hearts open towards heaven and await its dew. Do not forget to take this into consideration when you pray. In this way you will draw closer to God and place yourself in His presence."

He explained that one should place himself in God's presence at prayer for two main reasons. "The first," he said, "is to render to God the honor we owe Him. This can be done without Him speaking to us or us to Him. Our obligation of honoring God is fulfilled in recognizing that He is our God and we His humble servants, prostrate in spirit, awaiting His commands. Many courtiers, for instance, come and go, hundreds of times, in the King's presence, not to talk to Him or listen to Him, but merely to be seen by Him. In this way they show themselves to be true servants of the King. Putting ourselves in God's presence in this way attests to our will to be God's servants. The second reason is that we may speak to Him and hear His voice through His inspiration and illumination. Normally one does this with great satisfaction, for it is a sign of grace to speak to a great Lord. When God answers us, He spreads over us a thousand precious soothing and fragrant oils which bring great joy to the soul.

"Prayer must be insistent inasmuch as insistence denotes faith. The prayers of the saints in heaven and of just souls on earth are perfume that will never fade. When there is little time, though, meditation is more fruitful and preferable to vocal prayer. Whoever does not meditate acts like one who never looks into a mirror and does not bother to put himself in order, since he can be dirty without knowing it. The person who meditates and turns his thoughts to

God, the mirror of the soul, seeks to know his defects and tries to correct them. He controls his impulses and puts his conscience in order."

The crowd had grown silent. He blessed them and went back into the monastery.

"All that wisdom," murmured a woman. "Such a beautiful person. Surely he is a saint."

The tall, sandy-haired man was by now on the brink of total frustration. He stared at the quiet, peaceful, and contented faces around him.

"I would still like to know," he insisted, "how he does all those funny things."

## IV.

Alberto Festa, an attorney, was a cousin of Dr. Giorgio Festa, the doctor who had examined the stigmata of Padre Pio. The attorney had heard his cousin speak many times about Padre Pio and from the beginning thought it was all an exaggeration. In addition, the attorney was one of the leaders of Masonry at Superba, near Genoa, and so he had little if any sympathy for priests, monks, or any men of religion. But one day he went to San Giovanni Rotondo to see if he could witness a miracle.

Padre Pio was on his way to the sacristy when he saw him. "Why are you here among us?" he asked. "Aren't you a Mason?"

"Yes," replied the lawyer. His dark eyes studied Padre Pio with microscopic intensity.

"What duty have you in Masonry?"

"To combat the Church on political matters," answered Festa.

Padre Pio smiled at him, took his hand, and spoke kindly about the prodigal son, the infinite mercy of the Lord, and the great good he could obtain by approaching the Church.

Attorney Festa went outside to mull it all over. Suddenly he made up his mind. He rushed back and asked Padre Pio if he could confess.

Padre Pio said, "Of course," and he watched the transformation taking place as Festa's face began to relax and a new sparkle lit his eyes.

Before leaving Festa asked Padre Pio what he should do about publicly casting away his badge of Masonry.

"Do nothing now," said Padre Pio. "When the opportunity presents itself, the Lord will inspire you."

Attorney Festa returned to Genoa and immediately wrote to his cousin, Dr. Festa, and thanked him for showing him the road to Padre Pio. He was full of zeal and even made a pilgrimage to Lourdes in Franciscan simplicity, travelling in the train with the sick and infirm and acting as one of the stretcher-bearers. But when he got back, an Italian Socialist newspaper published an article about Mason Festa at Lourdes. He was bitterly attacked, bestowed with abuse, and threatened with sanctions. As soon as the lawyer learned that his former friends were holding a secret meeting he decided to attend. The morning of the meeting he unexpectedly received a letter from Padre Pio which said: "Do not hesitate to speak about Christ and his doctrine; now is the time to combat openly. The doctor of every good will give you strength."

Festa went to the lodge meeting and spoke openly and zealously before the surprised group about God and the religion of Christ. He gave an eloquent speech. The members quietly listened to him in utter amazement.

It was more than a beginning. Alberto Festa was prepared to spend the rest of his life living as a fervent Franciscan tertiary.

Padre Pio was pleased, and it showed. But he made the mistake of telling one of the brothers how well it had turned out.

"Too bad they all don't turn out that way," the brother remarked. "But for every one like that there are a dozen others who—"

Padre Pio raised his hands to cut him off. He made a suitable excuse to leave and hurried away. *There is something incredibly frustrating about human nature,* he thought.

A fisherman was the first to confess to him that day. "Padre," said the man, "I don't believe in God."

Padre Pio raised his eyebrows and shook his head. "But God believes in you!" The man agreed that there was something worth considering in that.

The next man said: "Padre, I have sinned too grievously; I have abandoned hope."

"My son, God relentlessly pursues the most obstinate souls," he assured him. "You have cost Him too much for him to abandon you. He did not abandon you when you fled from Him; much less will He abandon you now that you wish to love Him."

A man who had followed him into the sacristy appeared next. Padre Pio frowned and suddenly recoiled. "Go away," he cried, "and marry the woman you are living with, and then come back." The startled man stopped in his tracks and then ran for the door.

Later that day a woman appeared. Padre Pio remembered that a year ago she had come with her husband who was having an illicit relationship with another woman and even was plotting to kill her, making it look as though she had committed suicide. But she had sensed that something was wrong and had persuaded him to accompany her to visit Padre Pio.

When they arrived at Our Lady of Grace the young man felt attracted by a magnetic force toward the sacristy at the opposite end of the main altar. There he saw Padre Pio with a group of men. The young man hadn't uttered a word, and was standing in a corner. Suddenly he felt himself taken forcefully by the arm and pushed at a distance.

Padre Pio started shouting at him: "Get out! Get out! Don't you know that you cannot stain your hands with the blood of your wife!"

The man was totally stunned. He rushed out, pushing his way through the crowd of shocked on-lookers. For two days his soul was in a terrible tempest. Finally on the third day he went back to Padre Pio and asked if he could confess.

Padre Pio confessed him, and at the end affirmed: "You have

been without children, hoping for a son. Go home now and your wife will conceive a son."

Now, a year later, the woman was back with her young son. She confessed to Padre Pio that her husband was acting strangely again and she feared for her life.

Padre Pio reassured her that everything would be alright. "Be calm," he said gently, "your husband no longer plans to kill you."

One of the friars saw the woman and later asked Padre Pio, "Wasn't that the wife of the man you chased out of here once?" Padre Pio feigned shock.

"I think it was," said the friar. "I see she has a child now."

Padre Pio patted his arm. "There is certainly nothing wrong with your eyes."

"Uh, no—what I meant was—not that you should tell me anything privately revealed to you, but didn't you publicly and openly accuse the man of wanting to kill her?"

Padre Pio's eyes widened. "Did I?"

The puzzled friar nodded. "Yes, Padre, you did. I was there the day you called out something about staining his hands with her blood."

"There is clearly nothing wrong with your memory either."

"If there's anything I shouldn't know, that you don't want to tell me, just say the word, Padre."

Padre Pio smiled. "Consider it said."

"Oh." The friar smiled back at him weakly, wishing he had kept his mouth shut.

Padre Pio went about his business chuckling. But by evening he was unusually weary, and his mood had grown sober. As the days passed, the friars started asking him if he felt alright. The effort of trying to convince them that he was fine was almost as exhausting as his daily routine.

The next day he got a letter from a friend of Rosetta Polo Riva from Bolzaneto who had suffered from a serious constriction of the heart from the time she was twelve years old, and the doctors had never been able to alleviate any of her pain.

One day a friend had visited her and asked, "Have you tried writing to Padre Pio?"

"What can he do for me?" the sick girl had wondered hopelessly. Her friend said she had already written to Pietrelcina requesting a special blessing for her.

Two weeks later, one morning when Rosetta's bedroom window was open, something that looked like a white cloud entered the room. And all at once she saw a Capuchin with a brown habit standing near her bed. She was absolutely terrified and tried to call for help but couldn't make a sound.

"Do not be afraid," a comforting voice was saying.

"Who are you?" she asked, relaxing a little.

"I am Padre Pio, Rosetta. Instead of writing you a letter I have come in person to visit you. Aren't you pleased?"

His voice calmed her and she nodded. "Yes, Padre, I am so pleased. Will you bless me?"

"I will tell you, Rosetta," he said, "that you will receive grace from the Madonna."

Her eyes opened wide. "When, Padre?"

"August 28," he told her, "at eight o'clock in the evening."

Then the white cloud and Padre Pio evaporated. When she awakened on the morning of August 28, she felt better. On an early autumn day, two weeks later, she was completely cured.

Fall had arrived early, and the days had turned warm and dry and the nights had turned cool. Padre Pio was watching the clouds building overhead one day. He could sense the subtle daily changes. Soon the early winter winds would snatch away the last leaves, leaving only the tall pines to color the hillsides. And the snow would follow.

That night he stayed awake, sitting in his chair, meditating. It was late when there was a soft rap on his door and a young, solemn faced brother stepped just inside.

Padre Pio lifted his eyes. "Yes?"

"Excuse me, Padre, but I bring bad news. Dr. Sanguinetti has had a stroke. He is dying."

Padre Pio's face grew dark. He couldn't remember if he thanked the boy or not. Wearily he pulled himself up, grimacing as his weight fell on his swollen feet. It was a long walk to Dr. Sanguinetti's room, and the pain prevented him from rushing. When he got there, a number of priests and young brothers were standing outside the door in the corridor, talking in hushed voices. When they saw Padre Pio, they all fell silent.

Padre Pio glanced from face to face. "Is he gone?"

They nodded quietly and watched him shuffle hesitatingly away toward the church. "May I help you, Padre?" someone called. Without turning back or stopping he shook his head.

"I think Dr. Sanguinetti was more to him than just the director of his hospital project," said one of the priests. "I think they were very fond of each other. And the padre feels everything so deeply. All the sorrow and agony and loneliness of the world is his own." Everyone agreed but no one knew what to do so they didn't do anything.

# Gargano's Citadel

## I.

*Padre Pio's hospital* cost five million dollars. But he disliked debts and had no peace until all of them were paid.

"It is simply immoral to accept these high interest rates," he said, and on the day of inauguration the books were balanced.

The Home for the Relief of Suffering was dedicated on May 5, 1956. Over 15,000 persons were present when Padre Pio together with Giacomo Cardinal Lercaro, cut the traditional ribbon for the inaugural ceremonies. It all attracted world-wide attention, and a large group of the foremost heart specialists in the world were present and later attended a symposium on coronary diseases in the hospital's lecture hall.

Padre Pio celebrated mass that morning at 7:00 o'clock on a portable altar on the portico of the Home to mark the beginning of the ceremonies. During the mass a slight breeze caused the three hundred flags atop the hospital to flutter. The American flag was in the center, immediately next to the Italian flag. Afterwards, military planes from Manfredonia flew overhead as if it were a national holiday.

Many of the highest officials of the Italian government, local authorities from Foggia and San Giovanni Rotondo, and dignitaries from the Vatican and elsewhere were present. Six hundred representatives of Prayer Groups from various cities in Italy were there, and three hundred more came from Spain, India, Argentina, France, United States, Brazil, and other countries.

Throughout the ceremonies Padre Pio sat between Cardinal Lercaro and the father general of the Capuchin Order.

"Is Angelo here?" he asked a fellow Capuchin. He was looking for Signore Angelo Lupi, the gifted engineer who was responsible for the actual construction of the hospital.

"Yes," replied the Capuchin. "He's on the other side."

The mayor of the town thanked Padre Pio as the moving spirit of the whole undertaking; the superior general of the Capuchins read a message from Pope Pius XII, who sent his Apostolic Blessing and referred to the new hospital as a work inspired by a profound sense of charity.

When Cardinal Lercaro spoke, he summed up the spirit of the Home for the Relief of Suffering with the words: "It is superfluous for us to address you in a place where things talk most eloquently. . . . I am reminded of the words of our Sacred Liturgy: 'Where charity and love dwell, God is there!' It is equally true that where God is, there charity and love are found together. . . . Have you not noticed it here in San Giovanni Rotondo? Yes, the whole world has noticed it! God is here! Manifestly, therefore, charity and love dwell here."

Finally Padre Pio stepped to the microphone: "Gentlemen and Brethren in Christ. The Home for the Relief of Suffering is completed. I thank all the benefactors from every part of the world who have in any way cooperated toward it. I now present to you this institution which Providence, with your help, has created. Admire it and join with me in blessing the Lord God.

"A seed has been sown, which He will nurture with the rays of His love. A new militia, founded on self-denial and love is about to rise in the glory of God and the comfort of the sick. Do not deprive us of your help. . . . Lend us your support in this apostolate of bringing relief to suffering humanity, and the divine charity, which knows no limit and is the very light of God and of life eternal, will amass for each one of you a treasure of grace to which Jesus on the Cross has made us heirs. This institution which you behold today is in its first year of life. But to grow and mature, it needs to be nourished. Hence I appeal to your generosity to prevent it from perishing, so that it may become a center having the most up-to-date clinic and at the same time be permeated with the spirit of militant Franciscanism. May it become a place of prayer and of science,

where the human race may find its center in Christ Crucified, as one flock under one Shepherd.

"The first stage of our journey has been reached. Let us not check our progress, not halt on the way. Let us respond to the call of God for the good cause. Let each one of us fulfill our duty. My duty, that of a useless servant, is offering up incessant prayers to our Lord Jesus Christ. Yours, by an earnest desire to embrace the whole of suffering humanity, is to entrust this hospital to the mercy of our heavenly Father, so that enlightened by the action of grace and by your liberal generosity you may persevere in good works with a right intention. Forward then, in humility of spirit, lifting up your hearts to God. May the Lord bless those who have labored, who still labor, and will continue to labor in the future, and may He reward you and all your families a thousandfold in this life and grant you eternal joy in the life to come.

"May the most holy Virgin, Mother of Grace, and our Seraphic Father St. Francis from heaven, and the Vicar of Christ on earth, the Supreme Pontiff, intercede for us that our prayers may be granted!"

Among the thousands of spectators at Padre Pio's mass and inaugural ceremonies was a man whom many could not help noticing, because he was in tears through it all. It was Dr. Kisvarday, the last living member of Padre Pio's team of three collaborators who aided him in the hospital project. At the end of the ceremonies Kisvarday went to Padre Pio, kissed both of his hands, congratulated him in having the hospital built, and then broke down crying.

Padre Pio was moved, and spoke softly to him until he gained his composure. "Carletto, let us thank God together," he said.

Among the many distinguished doctors in attendance for the inauguration ceremonies and who later attended a convention were: Dr. Gustav Nylin, President of the European Society of Cardiologists; Dr. P. Valdoni, Rome; Dr. Paul Dudley White, Boston; Dr. O. H. Wangesteen, Minneapolis; Dr. W. Evans, London; Dr. J. Lequime, Brussels; Dr. C. Lian, Paris; and Dr. H. Olivercrona, Stockholm. Other doctors came from Milan, Florence, Switzerland, Argentina, and other countries.

At the conclusion of their convention on coronary diseases, a group of the distinguished visitors went to the monastery and asked Padre Pio to speak to them.

Padre Pio smiled graciously, and said: "What can I say? You, too, have come into this world in the same way as I, with a mission to fulfill. I speak to you of duty, in a moment when everyone only talks of rights. I, as a religious and a priest, have a mission to accomplish. As a religious and a Capuchin, I am bound to accomplish the perfect and strict observance of my rule and my vows. As a priest, mine is a mission of atonement, of propitiating God for the sins of mankind.

"All this may come to pass if I am in God's grace, but if I go astray from God, how can I make atonement for others? How can I become a mediator with the Most High?

"You have the mission of curing the sick, but if at the patient's bedside, you do not bring the warmth of loving care, I do not think that medicines will be of much use. I have seen this proved by my own experience. During my illness in 1916 and 1917, while my doctors cured me, they brought words of consolation. Love cannot do without words. And you, yourselves, how could you, other than by words, bring spiritual comfort to a patient. Later on I went to a specialist, who bluntly told me that I had tuberculosis and that I only had another year to live. I returned home, grieved to death, but resigned to God's will. And as you see I am still here! The specialist's prophecy did not come true.

"Bring God to the sick; it will be more valuable than any other cure. And may the Lord bless you all, your families, and particularly your work and your patients. This is the most ardent wish of a priest's heart."

They had let him speak without once interrupting and appeared spellbound by his words.

Then Dr. Paul Dudley White, President Dwight Eisenhower's cardiologist, stepped forward, and said: "I return to America profoundly impressed with Padre Pio's work. This hospital, more than any other in the world, seems to me best suited to study the relations that exist between the mind and sickness. Here, more than anywhere else, the study of psychosomatic illness can progress."

Padre Pio's brown eyes never left his face. Actually, White was echoing an opinion he had expressed himself when the hospital was first planned. He had said then: "I have noticed that very often the soul and body become ill and recover together. I want to build a large house to receive sick pilgrims who come up here to ask God for a miracle. Faith and hope will help to heal their spirit; charity will provide them with a roof; science if it can will do the rest."

Dr. Evans from England said: "This is the finest weekend I have ever spent in my life, and these are the most important moments of my important weekend." And withdrawing a little, he bowed slightly, and added: "I thank you, Padre Pio." Padre Pio smiled warmly at him. His heart was beating wildly with joy by now.

The president of the European Society of Cardiology, Dr. G. Nylin of Stockholm, speaking in the name of the Society, said: "We bow respectfully before Padre Pio, author of such a magnificent work of charity. With his unshaken faith, his love for mankind, Padre Pio gives us a splendid example of abnegation in the service of our fellow man. This hospital is a tangible proof of the Good Samaritan. With all our hearts we wish that God may bless the noble and charitable intentions of Padre Pio."

Dr. Wangensteen of Minneapolis said: "Everything is beautiful, good and wonderful; however, I have one great regret—that there is only one Padre Pio in this world. What a pity that there are no others!"

After the dedication and convention, one hundred cardiologists went to Rome for an audience with Pope Pius XII. Afterwards the Holy Father spoke to the group informally. He listened with patience and affectionate interest as the doctors spoke about the symposium at the clinic.

Then Dr. Wangensteen reiterated his remark about Padre Pio, and said: "It saddens me to think that in this world there is only one Padre Pio. It is a great pity there are not more."

The pope listened with a benevolent smile, and commented:

"May God send us many good and holy priests." Before the conclusion of the audience Pope Pius XII praised the work of Padre
Pio's hospital and imparted to the group his papal blessing.

The influx of patients into the hospital was gradual. The rich
and the poor were given the same kind of treatment with all of the
hospital facilities at their service. Various communal means of in-
surance and relief aided those who could pay a little. For those who
were unable to pay at all, the management kept a separate fund
to cover the cost of treatment and hospitalization.

The high cost of administration was borne by donations and fees
from the patients, and additional funds from drives and collections
were constantly being received. As another means of raising funds,
the management began the circulation of a periodical called "La Casa
Della Sofferenza," publishing in five languages: French, English,
Italian, German, and Spanish, and selling subscriptions at $2.50 a year.

It had been a long hard road and Padre Pio was more than
a little tired. But he was happy. One thing, at least, had worked out
almost perfectly.

He was especially pleased that Prayer Groups could use the
hospital for international meetings. Soon groups began arriving almost
daily, coming from Manila, Ireland, France, northern Italy, Yugoslavia, and Switzerland; they were accompanied by bishops, priests,
or prominent laymen.

A prayer group from Yugoslavia arrived at the Capuchin monastery then, comprised of sixty-five pilgrims, including fifteen priests.
The priests had a special audience with Padre Pio and each received
his blessing.

"We have the names of those who request your prayers," said
one of the priests.

Padre Pio nodded and sighed. "I do a lot of praying," he said.

Letters began to arrive from all over the world, praising the
Prayer Groups. Priests told them how they aided them in their
spiritual work, and Pope John XXIII sent his special blessing to
a prayer group for one of its celebrations.

Padre Pio watched the progress, sometimes not quite believing everything that had happened over the years. Life on Gargano Mountain was moving very fast these days.

## II.

Wondering where the days had gone, he soon found himself delivering an address on the first anniversary of the dedication of the hospital.

"Blessed be God! Today is the first birthday of the hospital, which last year you saw come into existence. The Home for the Relief of Suffering has already welcomed many thousands of people who were sick in body or soul. All, both rich and poor, have benefited from your charity and received in most generous measure all that you have provided for them.

"With the rays of His love God has warmed the seed which was sown. To be legally established from the time of its coming into being, the hospital has had to ask for charitable contributions from many generous individuals. To all of these I should now like to express my most heartfelt gratitude.

"Today, by favor of the Holy Father, the hospital has attained complete autonomy. The Supreme Pontiff, with prompt paternal care, has decreed that it should have a legal position corresponding to the purposes for which it was founded. The Holy Father has conceded that it should have a new settlement of its immovable property and that its effects should be put at the disposition of the Franciscan Tertiary fraternity of Santa Maria delle Grazie in San Giovanni Rotondo, so that they might take over its administration.

"In the Home for the Relief of Suffering, prayers are fervently and incessantly offered up for the august person of the Vicar of Christ. Today, by this sovereign act, the hospital is duty-bound by an especial sense of gratitude to our Holy Father, who has emphasized its original aims and objects.

"As of today we begin the second stage of the journey we have undertaken. The next step that we must take is this: the institution commends itself to your generosity that it may become in very fact a hospital city, technically adequate to the most searching medical and surgical demands.

"The hospital will have to increase the number of wards and treble the number of beds. Two buildings will have to be added: one for women and one for men, where those weary in soul and body may find God and receive comfort at His hands.

"An international center of studies will enable doctors to further their professional learning and their formation as Christians.

"We must develop the organization of this institution in such a way that it may become a powerhouse of prayer and knowledge, where mankind may find itself again in Jesus Crucified, one fold and one shepherd.

"The spiritual children who come together, in all parts of the world, to pray in the spirit of our Seraphic Father St. Francis, under the guidance and according to the intentions of the Holy Father, are to find here a center for their prayer groups. Here, retreats will be conducted for priests and the spiritual development of nuns and lay people, helping them in their ascent to God, so that, in faith in detachment, and in self-surrender, they may live the love of God, the consummation of Christian perfection.

"Love is the realization and communication of the superabundant life which Christ declared He had come to give us. Let us listen to that Voice: 'As the Father has loved Me, so also have I loved you, continue then in My love.'

"To His activity as divine Teacher, Our Lord added that of a healing physician. Having died once, He reigns, the Author of life for evermore.

"If this institution were only for the relief of physical suffering it would merely be a model hospital, built by means of your great generosity and charity. But it is strongly urged that it must be active principally in drawing souls to the love of God, through the moving spirit of charity.

"Here the patient is to live the love of God by resigning himself to accept his sufferings and serenely meditate on Christ as his ultimate end. The love of God must be deepened in his soul through his experience of the love of Jesus Crucified, a love which emanates from those who attend to his bodily and spiritual infirmities. Here the priests, doctors and patients are to be sources of love. The more abundant this is in a person, the more it will be communicated to others.

"Both priests and doctors, in their work of charity to the sick, to which they have been called, will themselves feel the burning desire to perpetuate the love of God so that both they and their patients may dwell together in Him who is light and love.

"May the whole human race feel itself called to cooperate in this apostolate to suffering humanity, and may all follow the urge of the Holy Spirit. They will receive from our Lord the glory given to Him by His Father, and they will be one in Him: 'While you are in Me, may I be in them, and so they may be perfectly made one. So let the world know that it is you who have sent Me and that you have bestowed your love upon them, as you have bestowed it upon Me!'

"May Mary of Grace, most holy, our Queen, to whom each day we often turn to manifest our love, and whose material help we implore, reign sovereign for ever more in the city destined to rise above her shrine, and may she ever be your protectress. May our Lady intensify the love of her children for the Vicar of Jesus Christ on earth, and may she one day show us Jesus in the splendor of His Glory."

The passing of time didn't cause Padre Pio's enthusiasm for the hospital to weaken. One day he predicted a future hospital city, and he saw the hospital triple in size. He saw buildings erected for an international study center. Land and money were donated towards a rest and retreat house for priests, a house for a prayer group center, and a home for the aged. Soon there was a training school for nurses. There seemed to be no end to it.

Pope Pius XII had appointed Padre Pio lifetime director of the Third Order fraternity at Santa Maria delle Grazie, thus conferring on him the most singular privilege of personally guiding the Home for the Relief of Suffering. The pope also granted him permission to cooperate with the Third Order of St. Francis in the administration of the hospital, and a special decree freed him from his vow of poverty so he could collect money for the hospital.

Contributions were running high one day, and Padre Pio was smiling to himself as he went down the corridor on the way to his cell. He nodded at one of his brothers on the way.

"How's it going?" the friar asked.

Padre Pio laughed and threw up his hands. "What can I say? It is all so wonderful."

The friar smiled approvingly. "I'm glad you're not letting any of the gossip bother you."

Padre Pio hesitated a moment. "What gossip?" he asked, his smile disappearing.

"Oh," said the friar, "I'm sorry I even brought it up. I thought you surely would have heard."

"*What* gossip?" Padre Pio asked again.

The friar shook his head. "Just forget I said it, Padre. Don't give it another thought." Padre Pio's expression darkened. He sighed and turned to walk on.

"Everyone knows," the friar called after him, "that you wouldn't keep any of the donations yourself."


III.


Padre Pio was ill when Don Michele, pastor of a new church in San Giovanni Rotondo, came to him.

"You promised to attend the dedication of our new church," Don Michele reminded him.

"Someone will come to your church who is much more important than I," Padre Pio assured him, begging off.

Don Michele was puzzled. As far as he was concerned, no one was more important. However, a few weeks later, the famous portrait of the Madonna of Grace was brought in procession from the village to the monastery. As the procession passed his church it began to rain, so he invited the leaders to take the portrait into his church. The crowd poured into the church following the picture.

"That's it!" Don Michele suddenly exclaimed. "The Madonna! That's who he meant!"

Padre Pio's failing health kept him in his cell more and more, and his life seemed strangely quiet compared with the mounting activity outside. New buildings were going up everywhere: several children's homes, various shops, and schools. For better or worse Gargano Mountain had undergone a miraculous transformation.

In spite of improvements and additions to the monastery, Padre Pio continued to live in his room attached to the church. The only modern convenience he allowed was an elevator, and that he permitted only because his age and suffering were making it harder each day for him to move around the monastery.

He had been given a room overlooking the garden, close to the terrace. This was to help him enjoy the cool air, as he suffered intensely from the heat. The small room contained only a black wooden crucifix on the wall, a modest desk, two straw chairs, and an iron cot. There was no heat, even in winter. When he combed his hair, he had to use the window for a mirror, and he washed in cold water which harshly attacked his wounds. He refused all types of artificial warmth, electric or gas heaters, or even charcoal brazier for the cold winter nights.

"It wouldn't be Franciscan," he said, refusing each thing offered to him.

In his room, he prayed his breviary and read letters handed to him by fellow Capuchin priests who acted as his secretaries. Every day an average of six hundred letters, and from sixty to eighty telegrams, arrived from all over the world. Once he had answered his own correspondence; later he could personally answer only urgent letters; and now he had to leave the thousands of letters and telegrams to his secretaries. They replied in English, French, Spanish,

Portuguese, German, and Italian. Fifteen of them worked constantly on his correspondence, and four of them were needed for the Italian mail alone.

He didn't answer certain requests. "The Lord," he explained, "makes me remember only the people and things He wishes. At different times the Lord presents people to me whom I have never seen nor spoken to, other than when I prayed for favors for them which were always heard. Sometimes, however, when the Lord does not wish to hear me, He makes me forget to pray for those people, although they had every good and firm intention. My forgetfulness sometimes extends to necessities such as food, etc. I thank God that He has not allowed me to forget things belonging to my priesthood and my Capuchin vocation."

People who wrote to him received a slip of paper in the mail, saying: "Padre Pio sends you his blessing and will pray for your intentions. He urges you to have complete trust in the goodness of God, and to pray always according to His divine will."

Although he didn't officiate at funerals, sometimes while he was kneeling in prayer, a funeral service would be conducted. He would attend mass then and watch the ceremony. When the services were over and the casket was being removed, he would rise and bless the casket.

Once his friends asked whether the deceased should be sent back to his native town.

Padre Pio shook his head. "No," he said emphatically. "Burial must be made in the cemetery of the town where he died. That is where God called the soul."

Later, a few minutes before noon, he showed himself at the balustrade of the old church and recited the Angelus. The crowd beneath responded noisily that day.

Padre Pio's face was masked with annoyance. He wasn't feeling well at all, and this didn't make him feel any better. "You're in church," he reminded them, "not a marketplace."

Padre Pio was seventy-two years old now and his health simply wasn't very predictable any more. He fell unexpectedly and gravely ill one cool spring day. It was the same day a statue of the Madonna arrived in Italy.

The Italian bishops had decided to consecrate all of Italy to the Madonna, and to prepare for the consecration which was to take place on September 13, it was agreed to take the Madonna of Fatima in procession in all the cities of Italy.

Renowned doctors—Valdoni, Mazzoni, and Gasbarrini—were rushed to Padre Pio's bedside. "It's a tumor," they told him.

Padre Pio's brown eyes shifted uneasily from one man to another. "Malignant?" he asked. They nodded

"How long have I?" he asked, suddenly feeling drained of energy.

They gave him only a few months to live, and Padre Pio fell silent. He barely heard the words of comfort as his mind travelled rapidly over days past and days to come. He quietly resigned himself to his condition. Using a microphone, he started to address the faithful who had gathered in the square from his bedside. They knew about his illness, but not the gravity of it.

Spring slid unnoticed into summer that year, and on the first of August the Madonna of Fatima was brought by helicopter to San Giovanni Rotondo, landing on the heliport of the Home for the Relief of Suffering. Accompanying the statue were the two helicopter pilots and Padre Mario Mason.

The statue remained exposed for the veneration of the faithful for a few days, and there was an uninterrupted passage of pilgrims who had come from all parts of Italy and elsewhere to gather in prayer in front of the image and to see Padre Pio. But Padre Pio was in bed, weak and immovable, and still gravely ill, with the terminal diagnosis hanging over him more formidably each day.

On the morning of the departure of the statue Padre Pio begged to assist at the mass that Padre Mason was to celebrate, and the doctors consented. He was brought into the presbytery and they put him near the altar. Then the statue was brought into the church.

Due to his illness the monks wanted to take the Madonna to him, so as not to tire him, but he refused and went to meet her, while the police and monks protected him from the crowd.

He knelt at the feet of the Madonna, kissed her, and then presented to her a gold rosary, and as a sign of his devotion, a dove. There was a mass of people all around the scene, but few could see him. He was exhausted by now; his face hallowed; his forehead was dripping with perspiration; and his breathing was labored. When it was obvious that he could barely speak, they brought him back to his room.

Padre Mason and the two pilots went to see him in his cell. Their visit was short as the doctors had warned them not to allow Padre Pio to speak.

"He will never return to confess or celebrate Mass," a doctor advised them.

They sadly placed the Madonna in the helicopter and headed for Foggia, but when they were quite a distance away, Padre Mason suddenly told the pilots to head towards the sanctuary and stop for a few moments over Padre Pio's cell.

At the same moment while flying over his cell, Padre Pio cried out: "Holy Mother, when you came to Italy, you put me to bed, and now that you are leaving, are you still going to leave me this way?"

Unexpectedly, he began to tremble all over his body. His brown eyes widened, and he pulled himself up in his bed.

"What is it?" asked a worried attendant, reaching for his arm.

"I feel fine," Padre Pio whispered. He smiled weakly at the nervous attendant. "I feel fine," he said out loud.

The doctors hurried to examine him. They left his room shaking their heads in amazement.

"What has happened?" asked a friar waiting outside. "Has something happened to Padre Pio?"

"Yes," said one of the doctors. "Don't ask me what, but he is completely cured."

## IV.

It was inevitable that Pope John XXIII would one day hear about Padre Pio. It was just as inevitable that not all the news would be good news.

He first learned about Padre Pio's work just after World War II when, as Cardinal Roncalli, he was the apostolic representative in France. It was there that he heard the rich and powerful Emanuele Brunatto from Torino, Italy praise Padre Pio with boundless enthusiasm. Brunatto, who was one of Padre Pio's chief propagandists, was clearly electrified by his mentor, and the zeal with which he spoke was infectious. Cardinal Roncalli listened and smiled as he caught himself nodding in agreement. In fact, he was so impressed with what he heard that he never forgot, and one of the first telegrams of his pontificate was a blessing to Padre Pio.

In time he had his thoughts directed to Padre Pio again. Bishop Girolamo Bortignon, the Capuchin bishop of Padua, complained to powerful friends in Rome that the activities of San Giovanni Rotondo would bear investigation. So Pope John XXIII sent Monsignor Carlo Maccari to investigate and make recommendations.

Monsignor Maccari was not surprised to discover that the so-called spiritual daughters of Padre Pio were causing a great deal of disturbance. People squabbled for the first place in church. They came armed with scissors to cut pieces of cloth from Padre Pio's brown robe, and sometimes they tugged at his arm until he cried out in annoyance. There were reports of ferocious battles among them for the cushion on which he knelt during Benediction. And there were complaints of women pushing and shoving in the front of the church door for entrance and a rush for front seats when the doors opened.

At the hospital the Monsignor discovered a poor bookkeeping system, with the record of donations kept in a notebook.

In the village he discovered that many hotels and boarding houses were lining the broad Avenue of the Capuchins, and some men were selling extra confession tickets for impatient pilgrims or arranging to slip them into the sacristy. He learned, too, that a merchant had a trunkful of fingerless gloves exactly like Padre Pio's and had dipped them in the blood of an animal and was trying to pass them off as belonging to Padre Pio.

Monsignor Maccari stayed three months and at the end reported: "The people are fanatics; the administrators are guilty of negligence, disorder, and incompetence."

To top it off, he had a confidant of Padre Pio, Padre Justino de Lecce, transferred to Cerignola, and to control the crowds he insisted that a chain be placed in front of Padre Pio's confessional to keep the people back while someone was confessing. The entire inquest focused world-wide attention on Padre Pio. The Capuchins at San Giovanni Rotondo were shocked.

"It's only routine," Padre Pio told the friars at lunch. "Don't concern yourselves."

A priest across the room sighed. "Routine," he mumbled. "I sincerely hope *not*. These apostolic visits inevitably foretell doom." Padre Pio glanced in his direction but remained silent.

"There haven't been *that many*," someone argued. "This is only the second time the Pope has sent an investigator and the world hasn't ended yet."

"Let's hope not—"

Padre Pio raised his hands to cut them off. He could do without a debate. But the gloom settling over the room was worse than the debate so he was glad when someone laughed awkwardly and broke the silence to say the soup was too weak.

*It's true*, Padre Pio thought, smiling to himself, *The world hasn't ended, and the soup definitely is too weak.*

The world went right along as usual, in fact, although the number of visitors to the monastery was getting larger every day. That fall hundreds of bishops and cardinals joined the usual throng. They had been to the Twenty-first Ecumenical Council in Rome and came from South America, the Philippines, India, Japan, Canada, Poland, Yugoslavia, United States, Madagascar, Vietnam, the Holy

Lands, and other countries. Some stopped at San Giovanni Rotondo before going home. One was an Orthodox Patriarch who hadn't seen Padre Pio since his seminary days in Rome. The bishops usually attended Padre Pio's mass and then celebrated mass either at a side altar or in the chapels at the hospital. On one occasion as many as ten bishops celebrated mass simultaneously. One of the cardinals asked Padre Pio for prayers.

"My first thought in my prayers every day is the pope," Padre Pio told him. "The second person will be Your Eminence."

As if the new hospital and the apostolic visit hadn't focused enough attention on Padre Pio, the controversies over his cures continued endlessly, without pause.

Before any cure is called miraculous, a long and detailed study is made by the Church. In the nearly 125 year history of the famous shrine of Lourdes, France, only 150 cures were called miraculous, in spite of the 5,000 accounts in which persons were relieved of incurable physical pain in a moment. So it was with Padre Pio— in the hundreds of cases reported, only a handful were acknowledged. And not everyone who went to him was cured of his infirmities; however, often when a miracle was performed, the faith of the whole family was restored.

If anyone tried to thank him, Padre Pio usually replied: "I performed no miracle. All I did was pray for you, and God cured you. Thank Him, not me."

Giorgio Bernucci, an editor of the Vatican newspaper, "Osservatore Romano," lived with his elderly mother who was nearly blind. One morning he went to his office feeling very upset, and when his colleague, Mario Cinelli, asked why, he said that his mother had suffered a stroke and the doctors had told him she was dying.

Cinelli offered to go to San Giovanni Rotondo and request a special blessing for her, and before long he was standing before Padre Pio, telling him about his friend's mother.

"What can I do for her?" Padre Pio asked sympathetically.

"Pray," answered Cinelli.

"Very well," said Padre Pio, "I will pray." Cinelli returned to find his friend's mother was already getting better, and in a few weeks she was cured.

The incident caused little stir at the monastery. Everyone there was involved with the dedication of a new church of Our Lady of Grace at the monastery. In comparison with the small and humble seventeenth century church, this monumental temple had a capacity of four thousand.

The unusual marble used freely in its construction came from Sardinia, the Alps, Sweden, Mexico, Peru, Pakistan, and many parts of Italy. A group of Biblical paintings, powerful and clear, represented scenes of the Passion painted by various schools, all fresh, intense, and truly beautiful. The frescoes, the stained glass windows, the colannades, and the altar rail all contributed to the artistry of the church. The sanctuary was built with marble and precious onyx stone, and the background of the presbytery is a vast mosaic of the Madonna of the Grace, a work of the Vatican School, donated by two Swiss sisters, Lillian and Martha Gemsch.

One day on an inspection tour of the new church, Padre Pio was taken to the basement and shown the crypt.

"Padre Pio," one of the men said, "I hope you live to be a hundred years according to what a legend says, but when you die, this is where you will be buried."

Padre Pio listened, looked at the crypt, turned to the speaker, and said, "Why don't you put yourself in it?"

A man standing nearby smiled. "We wish you many more years of life," he said.

Padre Pio frowned. "You wish me ill, then," he said. "Do you want to prolong my exile? My chief desire is to retire to my room and prepare for a good death."

There was a moment of silence. No one was ever quite sure what he was going to say or how to respond once he said it. His reputation for being blunt was firmly established by now.

Women received especially rough treatment from Padre Pio

because of current fashions. He had always been a merciless enemy of feminine vanity.

"Vanity," he said, "is the son of pride, and is even more malignant than its mother. Have you ever seen a field of ripe corn? Some ears are tall; others are bent to the ground. Try taking the tallest, the proudest ones, and you will see they are empty; but if you take the smallest, the humblest ones, they are laden with seeds. From this you can see that vanity is empty."

Padre Pio wouldn't tolerate low-necked dresses or short, tight skirts, and he forbade his spiritual daughters to wear transparent stockings. Each year his severity increased. He stubbornly dismissed them from his confessional, even before they set foot inside, if he judged them to be improperly dressed. On some mornings he drove away one after another, until he ended up hearing very few confessions.

His brothers observed these drastic purges with a certain uneasiness and decided to fasten a sign on the church door: "By Padre Pio's explicit wish, women must enter his confessional wearing skirts at least eight inches below the knees. It is forbidden to borrow longer dresses in church and to wear them for the confessional."

The last warning was not without effect. There was a furtive exchange of skirts, blouses, and raincoats, that took place at the last moment in the half-lit church to remedy any failings.

The women made their adjustments, but perhaps not exactly enough. Padre Pio continued to send some away before giving them a chance to confess. He would glower at them, and grumble, "Go and get dressed." And sometimes he added, "Clowns!" He spared no one, persons he saw for the first time, or his long-time spiritual daughters. Often the skirts were decidedly many inches below the knees, but not sufficiently long for his moral severity.

As the years began to weigh on Padre Pio, his daily hours in the confessional were limited to four, equally divided between men and women. In addition to being dressed properly, they had to know the Italian language, even though he could somehow understand people speaking another language. But he knew Italian, Latin, and very little French, consistently refusing to hear confessions except in Italian or Latin.

Sometimes when Padre Pio refused to absolve his penitents and closed the small confessional door in their faces, the people would reproach him, asking why he acted this way.

"Don't you know," he asked, "what pain it costs me to shut the door on anyone? The Lord has forced me to do so. I do not call anyone, nor do I refuse anyone either. There is someone else who calls and refuses them. I am His useless tool."

Even the men had rules to follow. They were not permitted to enter the church with three-quarter length sleeves. Boys as well as men had to wear long trousers at church, if they didn't want to be shown out of church, that is. But women in short skirts were his prime targets.

Padre Pio's citadel was perhaps the only place in the world where the fashions of the 1930s still ruled in the 1960s.

# The Investigation

## I.

*On a muggy summer morning* in 1960 Padre Pio was in his cell talking with one of the priests, an outspoken young man who was a newcomer to the monastery. A wealthy woman from northern Italy had donated a large precious stone for the benefit of Padre Pio's hospital and someone in the hospital had substituted a fake—all which had nearly brought the roof down on Padre Pio again.

"I'm afraid we have a problem, Padre," said the young friar, shaking his head. "A very *serious* problem."

Padre Pio breathed deeply and leaned back. He was weary after a sleepless night and a hectic morning, and every muscle in his body ached.

"The newspapers are claiming fraud," continued the young friar, "and let's face it—people read. Why, incidentally, did the woman donate the stone in the first place?"

"It was in thanks. She said I helped her."

The young priest shook his head some more. "That's not going to help you." Padre Pio's dark eyes settled questioningly on the young man.

"What I mean is that it ties it all in with you personally."

Padre Pio smiled and shrugged. "Never let it be said that life in a monastery is dull!"

The young man didn't smile back. "I'm not certain it can get much livelier here, or that we can survive if it does."

"You will make it, my boy, and you will discover that there will always be trials and disturbances—even in a monastery."

The young friar tugged at his black beard and watched Padre Pio closely. "This monastery has had its share of disturbances."

Padre Pio stiffened. He didn't blame any of them for feeling uncomfortable each time something like this focused too much attention on them, but he just wasn't in the mood to talk it to death. To end the conversation he suggested they go to lunch, although the thought of eating almost made him physically ill. But if he didn't go everyone would assume he really was ill and they would start fussing over him.

"How is it going today?" one of the friars asked, helping him slide behind the table in the dining hall.

"Fine," said Padre Pio, hoping his young companion would keep his thoughts to himself.

"Not exactly fine," the young priest volunteered. "Padre Pio is just being very courageous."

That did it; all eyes zeroed in on Padre Pio and the concerned young friar at his right. "Aren't you feeling well?" someone asked.

Padre Pio nodded. "Much better today, thank you."

"It's the scandal," the young man persisted, "about the stone."

The friars became quiet. "Is there anything new on that?" asked one.

"No," said the young priest. "All we know is that someone from the hospital has the original and the hospital has the fake. Of course, the newspapers and magazines are making the most of it."

"Oh, oh," called a voice urgently. Padre Pio looked up along with the others.

"What is it?" asked the young priest next to Padre Pio.

"The Holy Office won't sit still for this. You can be certain there will be more investigations and more restrictions." The friar looked sympathetically at Padre Pio. "As if they haven't done enough to you."

Padre Pio held up his hands and shook his head. "No, please, do not criticize the Holy Office."

"I meant no offense, Padre. It's just that we all feel badly about the way you have suffered unjustly in the past."

"Please do not be concerned. At least you might wait until the

Holy Office actually does something. All we have now is a missing stone and a new wave of publicity."

"*Bad* publicity," said the friar.

Padre Pio rose to leave. "It will pass," he said, excusing himself. "It will all pass." The brothers watched him slowly and painfully shuffle from the room.

"It may all turn out right in the end," someone concluded after he was gone.

"And then again, it may not," someone else added.

Padre Pio saw a smiling priest waving at him near the end of the corridor by his cell. "Padre," the priest called. "I have good news." Padre Pio smiled back and tried to quicken his steps.

"They caught the man who took the stone. It's all over. Isn't that wonderful?"

Padre Pio looked sadly at the smiling priest. "It is only beginning for the thief."

"I know, Padre, but for the hospital and for you, things will probably quiet down now."

"That *will* be a nice change. I have been concerned that the incident might weaken the faith of some."

"I wouldn't worry about that." Padre Pio patted him on the arm and went into his room.

The priest went on too and caught up with the others leaving the dining hall. "Did you hear?" he called to them. "They have the man who took the stone."

"I knew they would get him," said the young man who opened the subject at lunch. "*That* was never the question."

"No, but I'm glad it's all over."

"It's not over. There's still the question of fraud and scandal at the hospital—and, frankly, I don't understand how Padre Pio could have entrusted the stone to the wrong person. If he can read souls, as well as he can, why didn't he see through the man who took the stone and anticipate the entire business?" The others fell silent.

"I believe," someone replied, "that he only sees and hears and knows what the Lord wishes." Everyone nodded, looking very much relieved.

Padre Pio temporarily relaxed and turned his mind to other events, some of them unhappy ones. On August 14 Dr. Kisvarday died. He was the last of the three original collaborators on the hospital project. He was buried a few days later in the cemetery beside Dr. Sanguinetti, another of the collaborators. As a memorial to him, his modern air-conditioned office in the hospital was kept just as he left it before his illness, with his large oil portrait hanging on the wall. His servant Paola sent roses from his garden for his desk, since raising flowers was the doctor's hobby. He left his home and personal effects to Paola, with the instructions that after her death they become part of the Home for the Relief of Suffering.

For a while Padre Pio's thoughts settled on his old friends, but the others were soon intrigued with a recent report that came to the monastery.

Vincenzo Martini said that as a youth of San Giovanni Rotondo he had studied to be a hotel manager. Since work was at a premium in his area he accepted a position in Lucerne, Switzerland. There he married and two years later his wife was in the hospital to give birth to a child.

On the day of the event he was called from the hotel by a doctor of the hospital staff who said he was to come immediately, and he did. He was told that a decision had to be made by the doctor in charge either to save the life of the child or that of the mother. Vincenzo decided in favor of the life of his wife. The doctor told him he would have to sign papers for this purpose and he consented.

While in the act of signing the papers a doctor came to him, smilingly, and said, "Congratulations, you are the father of an eight-pound boy!"

Vincenzo said he was dumbstruck and later went into his wife's room. She was still suffering from the after-effects of the medication but later told him a doctor in a brown habit had delivered her baby. Vincenzo asked everywhere in the hospital about a doctor but none could be found. Finally he said he remembered Padre Pio and took a picture of him to his wife, who had never heard of him. "Is this the doctor?" he asked.

"Yes, yes," she replied excitedly, "He's the one—he's the doctor who delivered my baby!"

The couple were so grateful that they returned to San Giovanni Rotondo to live and work near Padre Pio.

Someone asked Padre Pio about it but he was conveniently rushing off to attend to matters concerning his spiritual children.

The international president of the Blue Army, a marianist organization, Monsignor Harold V. Colgan, had requested that Padre Pio adopt all the members—hundreds of thousands—as his spiritual children.

"As long as they behave," he told him.

A poor, widowed woman from Bologna, with five children, arrived at San Giovanni Rotondo soon after that. She had been to see Padre Pio five years before and had then confessed to him and asked him to accept her as one of his spiritual children. In the five years after that, every day she had prayed: "Padre Pio, please watch over my children, protect, and bless them."

Now, during her second visit, she was confessing to Padre Pio, and asked: "Padre Pio, please watch over my children, protect, and bless them."

Padre Pio stared at her. "How many times are you going to ask me this same thing?"

She hesitated and looked bewildered. "Padre," she said, "this is the first time I ever asked you."

He shook his head. "You have been saying this to me every day for five years."

Before she could question him, he closed the window of the confessional and soon he left for the sacristy to hear the men's confessions. He watched their anxious faces and heard their sins and concerns. One by one, he advised and consoled them, sensing each time a part of his strength leave his own body and soul, until at the end of the day he felt weak and exhausted.

The last man that day was Signore DiMaggio, a lawyer from Palmero, living in Rome. As DiMaggio was leaving, he said: "Padre, I am now returning to Rome and the old occasions of sin. What shall I do to keep my promises I made to you? Please help me."

"My son, pray," said Padre Pio. "Don't ever stop praying, and be assured that when I have raised a soul, I never let it fall. A most important thing for everyone is this: Be grateful to God, especially for the gift of faith. The most beautiful belief is that which your heart utters in darkness, in sacrifice, in suffering, in a supreme effort to do good. It is faith like that which dispells the darkness of your soul like a blaze; it is that which leads you to God although a storm is raging." The color had left his cheeks, and they had a chalky hue that merged with his grey beard.

"Hard day?" asked a brother, passing him later on the way out of the sacristy.

Padre Pio smiled weakly. "Are there easy ones?"

## II.

August 10 was Padre Pio's golden jubilee celebration, a gala occasion for the inhabitants of San Giovanni Rotondo as well as for his spiritual children scattered all over the world. Months of preparation went into it. Hotels and rooming houses were engaged many months ahead. Rich and costly gifts arrived at the monastery. A room in the Franciscan auditorium adjoining the new church displayed the vestments and other religious objects used in the celebration of the Mass, and the Third Order Franciscan Tertiaries of the village presented him with an ornamental gold chalice which he used to celebrate Mass.

He celebrated mass at 8:30 A.M. instead of the usual 5:00 A.M. He was dressed in a white alb made from Irish linen and a beautiful gold-colored chasuble and was assisted by Padre Raffaele and Padre Romol, O.F.M. Cap. Three bishops, Viola of Hungary, Palatucci of Salerno, and Carta of Foggia, were seated in the sanctuary;

Padre Amedeo, Provincial of the Capuchins, and other ranking members of the Franciscan Order were also present.

The church of Our Lady of Grace was filled to capacity. There were government officials from Naples and Rome, and representatives from the armed forces: army, navy, and air corps. Some of them had served with Padre Pio during World War I. In addition, many dignitaries were present, as well as doctors from his hospital, children from the orphanages, and visitors from near and far.

At the conclusion of the hour-long mass, the father provincial gave a short talk. He stated that there has been no way to count the number of persons who have approached Padre Pio during this half century, either directly or indirectly. He read a few of the many hundreds of telegrams of congratulations that had been sent to Padre Pio from all over the world. Among them was a warm greeting from Cardinale Giovanni Battista, archbishop of Milan, who was to become Pope Paul VI.

A sixty-page magazine, *Il Fratello*, containing full-color pictures and the story of his life, was given to Padre Pio as a gift from his colleagues. A special dinner was served at the monastery for him and his guests, and in his honor the hospital staff and patients and those at orphanages also had a special menu that day.

In the afternoon Padre Pio returned to the church for services. Assisted by fellow members of his order he said the *"Te Deum"* (Holy God We Praise Thy Name) in thanksgiving for the 50th anniversary of his life as a priest. After the services a fifty-piece orchestra from Foggia gave a concert near the garden of the monastery, and for about two hours they played many arias and well-known Neapolitan tunes. At the close of the day, lights illuminated the monastery and the clinic for miles around.

From the time of his assignment to San Giovanni Rotondo, Padre Pio was available to visitors except for the two years when his stigmata was under investigation. He followed the daily routine of his community, Divine Office, prayer and study, but more and more of his time was taken up with the spiritual and temporal needs of the people who flocked to him.

The focus of every pilgrim's visit was Padre Pio's daily mass which began at 5:00 A.M. Crowds arrived each morning in all kinds of weather and filled the church to capacity. Even those who came merely out of curiosity were usually impressed not by his stigmata, which he kept covered with fingerless gloves, but with the extraordinary devotion with which he offered the Holy Sacrifice of the Mass. He removed the brown woolen gloves only to celebrate this service.

During the mass the congregation watched Padre Pio become completely transformed as he stood at the altar. He seemed to be in pain, but utterly detached from everything around him. His eyes blurred with tears and his movements became slow and labored. Then his body quivered and someone in the congregation said he was reliving the Passion of Christ. A priest watched him and whispered to a friend: "I believe that Padre Pio cannot see or hear anyone. His spirit is not present."

Padre Pio was immersed in the drama of the Lord's death. The wounds on his hands were red and bleeding. At certain parts of the Sacrifice he became oblivious to everyone around him. At the moment of the Consecration he was transfigured, and everyone present with him felt part of a great supernatural wonder.

A cosmopolitan crowd had arrived at the square, using all sorts of conveyances: buses from nearby towns, cars, taxis, and motor scooters. Some also walked up the hill. Some people had been waiting since one o'clock in the morning, sometimes praying and singing, until the doors of the church were opened. At four o'clock a large crowd of several hundred had already gathered. It was warm but a cool breeze blew from the Adriatic Sea, quite unlike the winter months when the breeze turned into a fierce penetrating wind which forced the crowd to huddle close to the buildings.

On a typical day the huge bronze doors of the church opened at 4:30 A.M., and almost immediately the church overflowed with enthusiastic pilgrims, some scurrying for side nave seats, for a better view of the mass.

The church was huge; its very high ceilings were of colorful marble, and along both sides were pillars of red marble, with the side altars behind them. At the end was a spacious sanctuary, dominated by a towering mosaic of Mary of Grace, identical to a sixteenth century icon.

By the time Padre Pio arrived at the sacristy to vest for the Sacrifice, he had already spent three hours in prayer. Two priests helped him put on his vestments, and one of them saw that he had tears in his eyes.

"Why are you crying, Padre?"

Padre Pio lowered his eyes and shook his head sadly. "I am not worthy to celebrate Holy Mass," he said. "I am the most unworthy priest."

"I beg to disagree with you, Padre," said one of the priests, trying to comfort him, but Padre Pio was already walking away.

At the scheduled time, the door of the sacristy to the left of the altar opened. Two men acted as servers, chosen from a long list of names. Cardinals, bishops, and distinguished prelates felt it was a privilege to serve the mass of the first stigmatized priest. They were followed by a Capuchin friar, and then the celebrant, Padre Pio.

The alb, or white linen tunic, had long sleeves, at his request, which came down to the knuckles and partly hid the wounds on his hands. But occasionally during the mass, the sleeves fell back, and the people could see the large red-brown areas covering almost the whole of the palm and back of each hand. A gasp rang through the front row as two women caught a glimpse of the open wounds.

Padre Pio stood almost motionless at the foot of the altar, and made the sign of the cross. The mass began. His face was transfigured as though he had become one with the Creator. He was alone in the midst of all the people present, and he passed into ecstasy. Then he recited the prescribed prayers at the foot of the altar.

Mass was the center of Padre Pio's day and life. Its length was from one hour to an hour and a quarter, double the usual time, owing to his long pauses. He might remain motionless for more than five minutes. The spectators were so absorbed in his movements that they were unaware of any sign of fatigue. Padre Pio's move-

ments at mass were leisurely, but not unduly slow. He did everything with care, but without fuss. He pronounced his words in a
perfectly natural voice. He gave the impression of deepest recollection
with no hint of posing or affectation.

When the introductory prayers were completed, a confrere
helped him up the three altar steps. Because of the wounds in his
feet, he couldn't go up or down steps without support. He made a
low bow, pausing before the tabernacle in contemplation of the mighty
work he was about to perform. The pause was long. Sometimes during
this period he stood motionless at the middle of the altar for as much
as five minutes. He seemed to have to pull himself together before
he could go on with the mass. From the Introit until the Communion
he labored under a strain, which subsided only after he received
Holy Communion.

He opened the book, made the sign of the cross, and began the
first mass prayer. He knew the mass from memory and was even
able to continue when electrical failure put the lights out, which
sometimes happened at the reading of the Epistle or the Gospel.
The Introit ended and the "Lord Have Mercy" began. Nine times
he invoked the mercy of the Lord.

When the server carried the mass book to the gospel side, Padre
Pio went to the middle of the altar, bowed and prayed, and again
made a long pause. Coming back to life, he read the gospel with
great devotion. His voice was warm and alive. Whatever he prayed
was reflected in his countenance, which for the most part was great
pain.

At the next part of the mass, Padre Pio said: "Let us pray,"
and he read the Offertory prayer. Then he uncovered the chalice,
but before he offered the unconsecrated wafer on the paten, he
ran his fingers around the Host to make sure there were no loose
particles. He then lifted the host on the paten with both hands.
and offered it to God, gazing at the crucifix for a long time. Again
he fell into ecstasy and often spoke in a low voice as though talking
to someone. He seemed to put on the paten all the requests which
people wrote or told him about.

He slowly walked to the right side of the altar for the wine and a little water. Then he went to the center of the altar and lifted the chalice to eye level, again delaying as with the offering of the host. When he returned to the side of the altar, he washed his hands, a gesture symbolic of purity.

The next part of the mass was the "Pray Brethren," a prayer eagerly awaited by those watching him, because now he turned to the people with arms up, showing the palms of his hands as he uttered these words. This was the only part of the mass in which the people saw his reddened perforated hands quite distinctly. There were large areas of dried blood covering the wounds. The scabs of blood made the wounds appear larger than the people expected. The dried blood extended over the backs and palms of his hands and part way up his fingers. The red of the blood contrasted sharply with the whiteness of his hands. His face was drawn and tense.

During the mass Padre Pio wept four times. He took a white handkerchief from the altar where he had placed it and wiped away the tears. In the interval from the Consecration to the Communion, his pain-etched face radiated his all-absorbing union with God. Just before the Consecration, he gazed at the crucifix and once more the tears began to fall. He took the Host, blessed it, bent forward, and said: "This is my body." At these words the substance of the bread was changed into the Body of Christ. At that instant his body began to twitch with pain. At the same time the people could see blood begin to trickle from the wounds in his hands, and his movements showed he was trying to ease the pain in his side.

He elevated the Host in both hands after the Consecration, high enough to be seen by everyone in the church, with great difficulty. His eyes steadily watched the elevated Host as though beholding another crucifixion, and his eyes suddenly glowed with love. He took the chalice in both hands and began the prayer that would change the wine into the Blood of Christ. "This is the Chalice of my Blood." Then he set down the chalice and genuflected. In a low voice he repeated the divine promise: "As often as you do these things, you shall do them in memory of Me." He elevated the chalice with great intensity and looked at a particular spot for a long time. The silence was profound.

When the Host and chalice were lifted, the sleeves of Padre Pio's tunic moved up a little and the nail prints in the hands could be seen more distinctly. The backs of the hands showed the same dried blood as the palms. Part way up the fingers, fresh blood was trickling down his fingers.

After the Consecration, Padre Pio's expression of pain was not as vivid, but it did continue. He recited the Lord's Prayer with great devotion, in preparation for his Communion. When he broke the Host, his fingers trembled. He hesitated as though the veil had been rent for him and the reality of what he was doing became too intense. Before taking the two broken halves of the Host, he was lost in colloquy with God. He moved his head as if nodding assent and he spoke abruptly.

Then, leaning forward, he struck his breast, and said: "Lord, I am not worthy." He repeated these words three times, each time striking his breast with strong strokes. His voice faltered, and there were tears in his eyes again. Then he partook of the Holy Communion. He remained almost motionless for about ten minutes, very peaceful —far from this world.

When he drank the contents of the chalice he hesitated for a few seconds. His lips quivered before he drank it and set it on the altar. Taking the ciborium of smaller consecrated Hosts he gave Communion to the people. They could see the fresh blood trickling down between his fingers and there was an odor of either perfume or carbolic acid around him. Padre Pio had often distributed Holy Communion each morning for nearly two hours, and sometimes longer, but to conserve his strength he now gave it only when special permission was granted by parish priests.

When the people's Communion was over, he returned to the altar. Before he gathered up the fragments of the Host, tears streamed down his cheeks once more. He couldn't hide them, and he didn't try.

The blood on his hand was clearly evident when he turned to

face the congregation before the last blessing. He gazed at the cross before the blessing, and pilgrims from all over the world knelt for his priestly blessing.

Before he left the altar, one of the Capuchin padres gave him a pair of brown woolen fingerless gloves, and then he was again assisted down the altar steps. Once down the steps, he managed to leave the altar unassisted and walked slowly with a slight wobble to the sacristy.

The sun still had not risen over the horizon of the Manfredonia Sea when his mass was over. After mass he went into the sacristy and took off the sacred vestments, paused for a moment in meditation, and then passed to a kneeling bench for thanksgiving. His head was bowed in his hands: his face was taut; and he remained this way for some time, perfectly quiet. His breathing was regular, but every so often he was shaken by a tremor, as brief and light as a sigh.

After a few minutes many men entered (women were not permitted in the sacristy) to await his blessing and wish him a good day. They moved silently so as not to disturb him. Some remained standing; others knelt with their hands clasped. They waited in silence, their eyes fixed on the stooped figure with his gloved hand held above his head.

Suddenly he lifted his head, took a handkerchief, and pressed it to his eyes. He was still withdrawn, and didn't notice that he was the center of attention. A confrere gave him a glass of water, and helped him up. His face was pale and beaded with perspiration, and his gaze was frozen, his suffering still evident. A bishop tried to whisper something, and he stopped and nodded, but then moved away without speaking. He was somewhere else, someplace not of this world.

## III.

Monsignor Maccari continued his investigation. Padre Rosario da Aliminusa, the superior at the monastery, talked with Padre Pio about it. He was a small, thin man wearing brown shell-rimmed glasses.

"Although it is merely a formality," he said, "we are instructed to place you under guard."

Padre Pio's chin drooped and his brown eyes widened. "Under guard?"

The superior nodded. "I'm afraid so, but as I say, it is only a formality."

"Under guard, only a formality? Then I'm not *really* under guard?"

The superior hesitated. "Uh—yes, you *are* to be placed under guard, but—"

Padre Pio shook his head uncomprehendingly. "But what have I done? And what is it you think I will do? Flee?"

"Oh, it is not what *I* think at all. In my opinion this is all, shall we say, incorrect. But if you look at it from their side, the Holy Office does have an obligation to satisfy itself or the Church that nothing improper has occurred. And the only way to do that is through a routine investigation of the hospital—and you. Naturally, certain procedures must be followed."

Padre Pio sighed. "At least I may celebrate Mass and...." He paused. The superior was staring at him, looking almost as miserable as he felt. "I may *not* celebrate Mass?"

The superior shook his head. "No. I'm most sorry, Padre. Nor may you perform weddings or baptisms."

"What may I do?"

"Oh, anything. Anything else, that is. Merely restrict yourself to the monastery and do not celebrate Mass or perform weddings or baptisms."

"*Merely* restrict myself?"

"I am *most* sorry, Padre, believe me."

Padre Pio smiled faintly. "Yes, of course, you are, and I am sorry too. I shall obey without further question."

He left for the sacristy to hear the men's confessions, but the investigation weighed heavily on his mind. He glanced about, hearing Monsignor Maccari's voice.

"Oh, there you are, Padre," Maccari called, coming over. "Do you have a minute?" He smiled uneasily.

Padre Pio kept on walking and let Maccari fall in beside him. "The men wait for me," he said.

Monsignor Maccari nodded. "With your busy schedule it's difficult to find time to visit with you. I was meaning to ask you the other day, and forgot. You have a great deal of property in your name. The hospital, I mean. What is it you intend doing with all of this—wealth?"

Padre Pio caught the accusing tone and for a second was tempted to let him wonder, but he replied, "I have intended to leave it to the church."

"Oh, how *very* generous of you. My compliments, Padre!"

Padre Pio breathed deeply and looked away. "Excuse me," he said quietly. "The men wait."

A man was waiting who had not confessed since he was seven years old. Padre Pio put the investigation out of his mind and listened intently. Little by little, as the man freed his conscience of the weight of his sins, Padre Pio's face became pale. Perspiration collected on his forehead and his mouth twisted unnaturally. The penitent watched him sympathetically and decided not to prolong things. "Listen, Padre," he said, "I feel I came with honesty and openness. It is useless to answer any of your questions. I will tell you now that I have committed all the sins except four, and I will tell you what they are."

Padre Pio looked at him in amazement, and answered, "It is really true, as you say."

"But I am attached to my sins," the man explained. "For me they are a necessary way of life. Help me find a remedy." Padre Pio gave him a prayer to be said to Saint Michael the Archangel every day for four months.

As soon as he was finished, another penitent came to take his place but Padre Pio, perspiring and suffering, rose, raised his hands, and exclaimed, "Enough! Enough for now!"

He couldn't endure any more, and he went to the garden for some fresh air. The air was brisk, and the sun had vanished behind a sheet of grey stratus clouds edging across the sky. Fall was dying, and fierce winds of winter would soon be whipping around the monastery.

"It's cold today, Padre," said one of two government officials who were chatting in the garden. They had their collars turned up against the wind. Padre Pio smiled and looked at the sky.

"Tell me, Padre," said the official, "what would you tell the people who are afraid Rome will go entirely Communist? We've been debating what there is to say that will assure them the Christian Democrats will be in power."

Padre Pio raised his dark eyebrows and shrugged. "Tell them the Pope will save Rome." The man stared at him, speechless for a moment.

"And," Padre Pio added, "I will say the prayers of our Lady."

"Thank you," said the other official. "I'm sure that will be helpful, and I hope you're right. But when people see communism around the corner, or think they do, they sometimes look at Russia and become afraid."

Padre Pio nodded. "Yes, though Russia is like a tree with sick leaves, but with healthy roots."

"One of our bigger problems is not the threat of communism but the injustice in the Christian Democratic party and the way some party members neglect their duty. There are some things we should have done but we didn't. What do you think we should do now?"

"Take the consequences," said Padre Pio. He excused himself and strolled on to look for a spot to be alone.

The days grew shorter, and soon the first snows came to Gargano Mountain. It was a sad and lonely winter for Padre Pio, until the investigation ended, and restrictions were relaxed somewhat.

Earlier Monsignor Maccari had accused Padre Pio's followers

of fanaticism, the hospital administrators of negligence, and he objected to the hospital's bookkeeping system, the disorder among the Spiritual Daughters, and a number of other things.

As it turned out, Monsignor Maccari had his way. The hospital was given a new bookkeeping system and an administrator was appointed by the Vatican. A man who was selling gloves dipped in animal blood, claiming they were Padre Pio's, drifted away, and the spiritual daughters were shorn of their powers. Finally, a chain was placed around the altar, and no one was permitted to approach it until Padre Pio left the sanctuary.

When Monsignor Maccari returned to Rome and submitted his report to a group of high ranking ecclesiastics, including Pope John XXIII, the Pope said, "They have chained the saint and let the wild beasts out." The conclusion reached by this distinguished group was that Padre Pio was not responsible for the insipid activities around the monastery, but the people who surrounded him were the guilty ones.

"I'll bet you feel a lot better now, don't you?" asked a brother, smiling broadly at Padre Pio.

Padre Pio smiled back. "I am happy whenever I am free to do the Lord's work."

# The People

## I.

*Padre Pio never read newspapers,* watched television, or listened to the radio. "I must detach myself completely from the world and its pomp," he said. He never opened books, only his breviary, the gospel, the missal, and the Bible. But he always knew everything.

His Franciscan concern for souls was dominant. He spent long hours in the confessional, directed tertiaries and prayer groups, and promoted his hospital. At 2:30 A.M. every day he got up to pray over the thousands of letters that came to him from every part of the world. His mass began at 5:00 A.M. and ended at 6:00 A.M., and shortly thereafter he distributed Holy Communion and heard confessions, having had no breakfast. After hearing confessions he returned to his room, passing along a narrow corridor where sick people and women lined to catch sight of him, receive his blessing, or kiss his hand.

Everyone at the monastery wondered about one thing—how he could survive with so little food each day. When his health allowed he joined his brothers in the dining room, but it was a symbolic gesture more than anything, because he consumed only a few grams of food a day, and that only once a day.

"I don't understand," said one of the brothers, "how a body so poorly nourished can carry such a work load."

"I don't know either," the friend agreed. "But his physical appearance shows no trace of undernourishment. I think he looks rather husky, in fact."

"Yes, but his dinner consists of no more than a small dish of green vegetables, or fish or cheese, and a half glass of wine or one glass of beer. He never has meat or liquids except for something prepared in the monastery kitchen."

"True, and if the greens are missing he takes an egg and about a spoonful of macaroni or rice, a crust of toasted bread, and a little fruit, such as fresh figs."

"Incredible."

"And on hot days when he works at his table he takes a large glass of water."

One of the priests started to chukle. "Did you know that at certain times he opens a bottle of beer and before midnight the bottle is empty because he keeps offering it to his visitors?"

The other nodded. "But his favorite drink, you know, is water with a little sugar and lemon juice. I think it soothes his stomach."

"I heard him tell a confrere once that the greatest gift the superior could give him would be to dispense him from eating."

"Shhhhh," said one of the priests. "I hear him coughing. He must be on his way to hear confessions."

Padre Pio appeared from around the corner. He nodded at the two priests and went on. His wounds were especially painful and he felt unsteady. He was glad to reach the confessional, just to sit down and take the weight off his swollen feet.

An Irish-American woman from New York City was waiting and told him that she had two daughters, both divorced and both alcoholics. "What shall I do?" she asked. "They both make their home with me."

Padre Pio nodded understandingly. "Because you are charitable," he said, "the Mother of God is interceding for you. I advise you to send your two daughters out of your home on their own. Let them assume their responsibilities as wives and mothers."

Later Padre Pio's eyes brightened as he spotted a Countess, Eleonora from northern Italy. Once she had told him she wanted to do some worthwhile work in her life, and he advised her to found the Order of Franciscan Sisters of the Adoration. She converted her home into a convent and eventually this new order began to care for orphans. Later it was moved near San Giovanni Rotondo in the district of Santa Croce where it began to flourish.

He was always happy whenever he saw the fruits of church workers. He thought about Padre Dominic Labellarte, a secular priest who organized a group of lay persons to alleviate the burden of priests through clerical work, instructions and maintenance, in order to give them more free time to administer the sacraments. Their religious vows of poverty, chastity, and obedience are binding for only a year, and each year the vows are renewed so that if any desire to leave this state to marry they are free to do so. The young people wear no special habit, but dress modestly. The number of Padre Dominic's group had increased, and they were now becoming a missionary group.

"When I am discouraged," Padre Dominic once said, "I think of something Padre Pio told me many years ago: 'Do you know of any work better than placing souls on the altar of God? Don't you know that good is obtained as a fruit of tears and suffering?'"

Padre Pio had rather strong convictions about suffering. "If people would only understand the value of suffering," he said, "they would not seek pleasure, but only to suffer."

Once he heard that his sister Pia suffered considerably as a nun trying to live a saintly life. "Doesn't she know that's why she became a nun—to suffer?" he asked.

The Capuchins were always concerned with Padre Pio's health and tried gradually to alleviate his heavy burdens. He was seventy-five years old now and he no longer conducted the afternoon Benediction services, though he still knelt in prayer in the chancel of the church while the services were being conducted.

When the afternoon services were over he retraced the route to the friary, along the corridor lined with men, some standing, others kneeling, who waited for him as he passed. For the men of Gargano, their monk was an image of holiness. Padre Pio usually answered them with love, but he didn't like to be pressed for favors.

"Padre Pio," a man called when he was passing. The man leaned close and whispered something in his ear. Padre Pio frowned and shook his head.

"But it is such a small thing to ask," the man persisted, running after him.

"You give me a headache," Padre Pio grumbled, walking on.

In the outer corridor the women were waiting. He smiled at them and offered blessings, as well as a severe reproach on occasion.

A middle-aged woman was standing nearby, her face masked with distress. "I cannot pray anymore," she told him. "I am losing my faith." She said all of this happened because her husband had committed suicide by throwing himself in a well.

Padre Pio nodded sympathetically. "But now you must think of saving your own soul," he said.

A woman from Stockholm stopped Padre Pio to tell him that, thanks to him, her son was living a healthy, normal life. He had been suffering from a cancerous brain tumor and Padre Pio had advised her to have the operation performed.

"If Padre Pio said to operate, I want the operation done," she had told the doctor, "and I'll take the consequences." The doctor had marvelled at her faith and performed the operation. It was successful.

After many hours dedicated to his ministry of prayer, Padre Pio allowed himself a short recreation in the monastery garden. These moments were not actually a rest but rather intervals between one task and another, relaxation and calm, when people didn't crowd in on him. At these times a privileged few had a chance to speak to him with greater freedom.

Waiting for him was an industrialist from Milan who was extremely upset. He belonged to Padre Pio's spiritual family and during one of his visits to the monastery he had commented to Padre Pio: "I am undecided as to whether to leave Tuesday or Wednesday."

"Why don't you stay here and leave on Wednesday?" Padre Pio had suggested.

But when Tuesday morning came it was such a beautiful day

he had decided to leave for home. While he was driving in Perugia a young girl darted in the path of his car, and he couldn't avoid hitting her. The girl was brought to the hospital and was pronounced dead on arrival.

Padre Pio comforted the man and went on to listen to a young local policeman, another spiritual child. He was sad because he had been transferred to Sardegna.

"For the children of God there is no distance," Padre Pio told him, "and if you need me, call for me. I shall arrive in good time."

Padre Dominic approached, shaking his head and laughing. He handled the American mail for Padre Pio. "Padre," he said, "listen to this. A woman wants to know if she sends her Guardian Angel to you, does he come?"

Padre Pio listened without smiling: "Tell her that her angel is not like she is. Her angel is very obedient, and when she sends him, he comes!"

That evening, far from San Giovanni Rotondo, an elderly woman who lived alone in an apartment in Ireland went out to buy bread. When she got back she became sick and dizzy. She sat on a chair and said: "Padre Pio, I know you are far away, but please send someone to help me."

A short time later two girls living in the upstairs apartment came down, and asked: "Did you call us?"

## II.

On a warm summer day during recreation several priests were huddled together, talking about their sermons.

"I say it is absolutely necessary to thunder from the pulpit," insisted one of them, "to threaten God's punishment, to shake Christians in this age of moral and religious decline."

Padre Pio was sitting on a bench beside them. Suddenly he shot to his feet, and burst out: "Stop it! It's time to end this shouting and threatening from the pulpit. God isn't only justice. He is above all

mercy. God is love!" The priests fell silent and stared at him.

"Of course, Padre," someone agreed. "We didn't mean to suggest that God is anything else."

Padre Pio watched their serious, startled expressions. He began to smile. "The day is too beautiful for such solemn thoughts." They glanced at each other and smiled weakly.

"Let me tell you a story," said Padre Pio, "that I heard this morning: In the Naples railway station an old priest and a peasant boarded a train. When the train stopped at the next station, the compartment became full of smoke. The peasant began to cough. Between one cough and another, he called out, 'Now, where are we going?' The priest said, 'To hell!' And the peasant promptly replied, 'Ah, well, at least I have a round trip ticket.' "

The friars broke up in laughter, and Padre Pio left them slapping their knees and shaking their hands.

He went on out of the garden. Today was election day, and a police escort was waiting to see him to the polls. Padre Pio thanked the two policemen who helped him into a waiting car. The car moved slowly down the long stretch between the people lining each side of the road. Some of them surged towards the car, others ran on ahead, while still others thronged noisily behind. There was no way to hurry, and the car crept along. Occasionally Padre Pio lifted his hand at the window.

After he registered his vote, everyone drew close to him again. Instead of making way for him to pass, the crowd pressed around him, happy to see him and eager to hear what he had to say. He was patient and smiling, and he blessed them. Women tried to kiss his robe; youngsters wanted to touch him; men took off their hats and stared in awe at him.

A few moments later he was out in the street, once more surrounded by a wall of people. When the car moved through San Giovanni Rotondo many people threw flower petals on it.

Padre Pio asked the driver to stop at the home of his niece,

Pia, on the Avenue of the Capuchins. He wanted to visit his ailing brother. Michael had been an invalid for some years now.

"It's so good to see you," Michael told him.

Padre Pio sat by the bedside and tried to cheer him but Michael was clearly old and tired and ill. Padre Pio could see his days were ending, and he left him reluctantly.

From Pia's home the car went around the Home for the Relief of Suffering. This gave Padre Pio an opportunity to look at the progress of the new additions. The patients and workers of the hospital were alerted that it was election day, and they waited for Padre Pio's arrival. After a short inspection he went back to the monastery.

The election district usually voted Christian Democrat, but some of the Communist members succeeded in winning office. Padre Pio didn't consider politics his business, but when someone asked him how they should cope with the Communists, he said, "If Christians were more Christian, there would be no need for Communism."

A Communist approached Padre Pio and started to say something.

Padre Pio cut him off, asking, "May I see your membership card?" The man pulled it from his wallet and handed it to him.

"Thank you," said Padre Pio, and he tore it up. "You do not need this in Heaven," he said.

"But—my card! I need it for a job," argued the astonished man.

Padre Pio shook his head. "You do not need it; neither can you live on promises. Accept work from Saint Francis. Go now and come back ready to go to work at the clinic."

The man stared at him, his jaw dropping. He started to say something again, but Padre Pio was disappearing in the crowd.

Just as Padre Pio entered the monastery an assistant handed him a telegram from the sister of an injured man. Desiderio Magnani of Padua, a laborer, had been badly burned in an accident. His face had been completely and horribly disfigured and he had a very high fever. His condition had grown worse and he was near death.

That night Magnani had a marvelous dream where Padre Pio appeared at his bedside. He was smiling at him, and gave him his blessing. Four hours later he opened his eyes, feeling hungry. His condition improved day by day and although none of the doctors could explain it, by the time summer was gone, he was completely cured.

Summer had ended abruptly it seemed. The leaves were suddenly yellow, and soon the branches would be bare. The parents of eleven-year-old Maria Panisi had just learned that she was suffering from tuberculosis. When she began to have frequent hemorrhaging, her parents took her from one specialist to another. Finally, Dr. Moscato, from he University of Naples, told them that by the time the leaves would fall their daughter would have passed to a better life.

Padre Pio was from Pietrelcina too, they thought, and decided to go to see him.

He met with them and Maria. He quietly listened and then gently patted Maria on her shoulder. "What do you mean by saying you are sick? Your lungs are made of steel!" All at once Maria's eyes brightened. She sat forward and smiled at Padre Pio. Something was happening. The days passed and the hemorrhaging stopped. Maria recovered.

During the feast of the Holy Name of Mary that same September, a large procession took a portrait of the Madonna into the new hospital church and placed it on a side altar. At 4:30 P.M. Padre Pio had Benediction of the Most Blessed Sacrament. As he was leaving the altar, he shook his finger at a crippled middle-aged woman who was leaning on two crutches near the altar.

"Why didn't you kneel at the Benediction of the Most Blessed Sacrament?" he asked. Without waiting for a reply, he continued to walk into the sacristy. A group gathered around the woman, and someone asked her if she knew what he had said.

She said that she did, because although she was Belgian, she spoke French and Italian too. Tears started streaming down her cheeks. "How can I kneel when I walk with two canes and the muscles above my knees are stiff?" she asked, sobbing. "I haven't moved them in four years since my automobile accident."

One of the women who had drawn close said, "If Padre Pio says 'kneel' you should kneel."

She looked puzzled but painfully and slowly attempted to kneel. All at once she relaxed and found she could move her limbs. Suddenly she was kneeling and easily was able to rise without assistance. Then she discovered she could take some steps and minutes later she disposed of her canes while the crowd clapped and cheered.

The woman tried to find Padre Pio but he had gone to meet the doctors from the hospital. Each day after vespers they came from the hospital, still dressed in their white frocks.

Padre Pio smiled when he saw them. "Tell me about your day's work," he said. He eyed one doctor who had two gravely ill patients. "How are your patients progressing?" he asked

The doctor shook his head. "I'm afraid we must operate, and surgery will be dangerous. I came to ask for your prayers."

Padre Pio's eyes began to dilate and they filled with tears. He gave a sigh and a cough, suffocating a sob. Everyone grew quiet, and they decided to leave him alone.

"It is beyond human understanding," one of them said when they were out of earshot, "to see him so tormented by the emotions of his heart and flesh for someone whose name he has never even heard."

The days had been unusually difficult for Padre Pio recently. He suffered more than usual. He was worried about his brother's failing health; the sadness of the people he saw seemed to affect him more every day; and he could sense his own health ebbing.

Padre Mondrone met him the next day in the monastery garden. They were strolling casually when Padre Pio began to move hesitantly.

"Take my arm," Padre Mondrone offered, and Padre Pio quickly accepted. "You look a little tired."

Padre Pio glanced at him for a second and shrugged. "Only a little." But he leaned heavily on Padre Mondrone's arm.

"I think it is more than a little."

Padre Pio paused, breathing with difficulty. "My dear brother," he whispered, "I can hardly go on."

### III.

On June 3, 1963 Pope John XXIII died. The new Pope was Padre Pio's old friend Giovanni Baptiste Montini, Archbishop of Milan. Among the first things he did as Pope Paul VI was to reject all accusations against Padre Pio.

Life changed swiftly for Padre Pio and many of the men who had made things so difficult for him were consigned to obscure positions. Among them was Monsignor Maccari, who was sent to a small parish in Piemonte.

"The longer the trial to which God puts His elect," said Padre Pio, looking back on his trials, "the greater His goodness in comforting them during oppression and exalting them after the struggle."

When the news was out that Pope Paul had acted in favor of Padre Pio, many people gathered in a field adjacent to the monastery garden, near a small white farmhouse among cows and donkeys. They recited the Rosary and sang hymns. In every hand was a handkerchief.

As the sun set, the windows of the monastery were thrown open and Padre Pio appeared. The crowd waved handkerchiefs, and shouted: "Eccolo il Padre! There is the Padre. We love you, Padre. Don't forget us! Remember we belong to you! Goodnight! Sleep well!"

Padre Pio smiled happily, raised his gloved hand in benediction, and returned their greeting by waving a large white handkerchief of his own.

He rested a little better that night and the next morning some color had returned to his cheeks. His brown eyes were clearer and his walk a little steadier. A woman came to him, and he remembered her from a visit two years earlier.

"I am completely well," she told him, and he smiled approvingly.

Two years before she had asked him: "Why am I ill? I have been ill for thirty years. It is true, I can do my housekeeping, but only with difficulty. Will I always be this way?"

Padre Pio had nodded, saying, "This is a great favor. The Lord has chosen you to suffer. You have two brothers who lead a very bad life and your other relatives are not much better. You will expiate their sins for two more years and you will be cured. Then you will have saved all those souls, for every cross is a favor, although we do not understand it."

A man who followed her wanted to hear a prediction concerning his aging parents. They wanted to go to America and make their home with his brother. Because of their age he was worried about the journey.

Padre Pio hid a smile. "Are they going on foot?" he asked.

"Of course not!" said the man.

"Then why are you asking me? If they want to go, let them." He turned away, seeing a priest he knew from Ireland.

"How are you, Padre Pio?" the priest asked, smiling broadly. "I wanted to tell you something. Do you remember I had a hearing problem and once came to see you?" Padre Pio nodded, smiling, and watching him closely.

"When you put your pierced hand to my ears I felt moved to ask God only that I might have a good hearing aid and not a complete cure of my hearing. I did not ask Him to take away this affliction and humiliation, but just to let me do the work He had given me to do. So I received a hearing aid in Ireland. Later on, in England, the National Institute for the Deaf gave me an extra one free, telling me to come back for another one when it should wear out. This spare is doing duty right now. The decision not to ask for a cure but just to carry on has naturally been the butt of a joke among some, but I believe it was right. Apart from helping me to keep my native pride in its place, the use of the hearing aid has another providential purpose, which only recently struck me forcefully. On my rounds to visit the old and infirm Christians of Africa, I met some people who couldn't hear. But when I put my receiver into their ears, they could. That way they could receive words of encouragement as well as instructions on how to prepare for a good confession and for meeting the Lord."

Padre Pio looked pleased and congratulated the priest before he left. His spirits were high by now, but one of the brothers interrupted.

"Padre, I wondered if you heard about the priest that was here yesterday—the one who told us about his sister leaving him. She was widowed, a mother of eight children, and was his housekeeper for ten years since her husband's death. The chronic illness of a married daughter with three small children was forcing her to leave him, and he was so upset. Do you remember? You told him to prepare for a long journey."

Padre Pio nodded and looked away. "Yes."

"Well, I just heard on the radio he had a heart attack in the train station and died."

Padre Pio nodded again, still looking off in the distance. "Yes."

Another friar standing nearby walked over. "You look far away, Padre."

Padre Pio glanced back at him. "I am here."

"I just told him about how a parish priest that was here yesterday died," said the brother.

The friar rested his hand sympathetically on Padre Pio's shoulder. "There is also good news, Padre. We received a letter from Mr. and Mrs. Rocco Falatico in California. Two years ago their son Rocco underwent brain, surgery at the Los Angeles Medical Center, and the doctors said they had removed only a part of the tumor because it was touching the brain, and if totally removed it would leave their son like a vegetable. The doctors also said that the part of the tumor that remained would become large and be fatal to the boy in a matter of months. As I understand it they came to see you."

Padre Pio smiled. "Yes, such a frail little boy."

Padre Pio remembered how he had placed his wounded hand on the boy's head, and said: "I pray for this boy not only with my hands but with my whole body."

At the time they had only two children and decided it unwise to have others. However, before leaving San Giovanni Rotondo they asked Padre Pio if they should have more children.

He immediately replied, "You must have more children. The cure of Rocco depends upon it."

The friar pulled a letter from his habit and opened it. "The good news, Padre," he said, "is that they have a third child now and little Rocco is doing wonderfully. His mind is sharp. His coordination is much improved. He can walk up and down the stairs and he can run. He couldn't walk at all after his operation. He has now started to go to school. His parents are thoroughly convinced that your prayers brought about the cure of their son."

"The Lord heals," Padre Pio answered. "I only serve the Lord."

Some men from San Giovanni Rotondo were trying to get Padre Pio's attention, and he glanced at them, beckoning one of them over.

"Padre," the man asked, "we have been wondering about the assassination of the American president, John F. Kennedy. Can you tell us how he appeared before God?"

"He appeared before God as a good Christian," said Padre Pio, "and the other appeared before God as his assassin."

The villagers disappeared, leaving the priests alone. A visiting priest had joined the group. Padre Pio smiled and chided: "How fat you are getting!"

The priest started laughing, rubbing the layers of flesh in his neck bulging above his habit. "No, Padre, it's only my face.'"

A solemn-faced brother stepped over to Padre Pio. "Excuse me, Padre, but may I speak with you a moment?" Padre Pio followed him to a quiet corner.

"It's your nephew, Padre. I know he's an epileptic, and some of us were wondering whether you might not offer prayers for a cure."

Padre Pio frowned and looked annoyed. "I have already spoken with him on that subject. God would grant me the favor of a cure if I should ask Him for it, but I would not be able to answer for it before the Lord. He would love the world too much and go astray, and his soul would be lost."

The friar listened intently but couldn't think of a good argument. He nodded and smiled. "Whatever you say, Padre."

# If I Die

*One Good Friday* Padre Pio was on his bed crying. "If I die," he asked his two assistants, "will you celebrate Mass for me?"

"Courage, Padre," said one of them, trying to smile reassuringly, "Good Friday is almost passed."

Padre Pio nodded, rubbing his gloved hand over his reddened eyes. "Yes, but remember, in every week there is a Friday."

There was little they could say. The world suddenly looked very dark to Padre Pio. He was seventy-nine years old and his health had become unsteady and unpredictable.

But the snows had melted. It was spring on Gargano Mountain once again, and the promise of warmer weather was encouraging. By the time the tenth anniversary of the Home of the Relief of Suffering arrived he was feeling more optimistic. It was also time for the second International Prayer Group Meeting. On May 5, 1966, after a mass celebrated by Padre Pio, Cardinal Lercaro offered mass. Ten years ago he had blessed the original departments of the hospital. The Cardinal's mass was televised throughout Italy and the rest of Europe.

Various speakers in reviewing the history of the Home told how almost a billion and a half liras had been spent and this was all paid when the hospital was inaugurated.

In criticism some people said: "Who would even think of planning a hospital on that rocky spur of a mountain, and who would be expected to be treated up there?" And after the hospital was built they said: "How can a building so colossal survive in a dried up country with only 20,000 inhabitants?"

But after ten years of activity the Home for the Relief of Suffering had not failed the mandate received from Padre Pio. Originally built as a three-hundred-bed hospital, the capacity had increased even on an international plane.

Like a giant octopus it was gradually extending into San Giovanni Rotondo. Work continued regularly to enlarge it from the 45,000 square feet to over 135,000 square feet. Plans were in effect to triple all the sections of the hospital, and double the medical and orthopedic departments.

Prayer Group leaders, under the general direction of Don Giancarlo Setti, held a second international meeting on the occasion of the tenth anniversary of the dedication of the hospital. The years had given growth to prayer groups, both in size and location, having nearly doubled in Italy and being scattered in many more countries.

Padre Pio said to them in a speech: "My dear children from Italy and the world, to all of you, near and far, the Lord's peace and blessing. As I speak to you on this solemn and memorable day, my soul is filled with emotion at the thought that in these ten years divine providence has manifested itself so generously towards the Home for the Relief of Suffering. On looking back to the humble origins and thinking how everything began from nothing we see the miracle of faith and charity to which this work bears testimony to the whole world.

"Let us render infinite thanks to the Lord and to the Holy Virgin, and blessed be all those who have in any way whatsoever cooperated in the birth and the development of the work.

"My beloved children, I thank you with all my heart for the gift of your generosity, for the sacrifices made, for the interest and solicitude shown, because you have been instruments in God's hands for the achievement of this Home in which the souls and the bodies of so many of our sick brothers are cared for and healed, through the priestly, medical, spiritual and social work of the whole of the hospital organization.

"My thoughts and gratitude also turn to those who from the first moments collaborated in bringing about this work and who continue to give their spiritual aid to the Home from heaven, where they have gone to receive the rewards of their generous charity.

"But my thoughts are especially turned to the Prayer Groups, now spread across the whole world, and gathered here today on the tenth anniversary of the Home for their second International Convention. Side by side with the Home, they are the advance positions of this citadel of charity, generators of faith and love, in which Christ Himself is present every time they gather together for prayer and the eucharistic Agape, under the guidance of their priests and spiritual directors. It is prayer, this united strength of all good souls, which moves the world, restores consciences, sustains the Home, comforts the suffering, heals the sick, sanctifies work, elevates health, gives moral force and Christian resignation to human sufferings, and spreads God's smile and blessing over every human weakness.

"Pray a lot, my children, pray hard always, because it is to prayer that I entrust this work. This is what God desires and which will continue to support and prosper the Home. Thanks also to the help of divine providence and the spiritual and charitable contributions of all those souls who pray. The omnipotent and merciful Lord, who accepts as for Himself all good done to brothers who suffer, will repay you a thousand times and again, in full measure, full to overflowing.

"In pledge of my gratitude I offer for all of you my daily prayer and suffering, my thoughts for you in the holy Sacrifice of Mass in which I present you at the throne of the divine majesty, imploring grace and blessings for all, especially for the sick of the Home and for all the sick in the world, spiritually united in one single family by the bonds of suffering and charity, exhorting them to endure their suffering in a Christian way in union with the sufferings of Jesus and the Holy Virgin. Praised be Jesus and Mary."

The theme of all the prayer group leaders was the same: imitation of Padre Pio in prayer, in sacrifice, in suffering. The activities of each group differed little one from the other. Some passed an hour of adoration, some said the rosary, some attended mass, some listened to a good sermon, some added to the life of the group by means of a cultural contribution, but the thing of essence was to gather and pray.

Don Giancarlo Setti asked Padre Pio what the essential points of the Prayer Groups ought to be.

"The program for all," he said, "is a program of prayer, a program of charity, a program of obedience to the hierarchy and a program of perseverance in good. Charity must dominate these gatherings. No good work has value if it is begun but not completed."

Padre Pio was so absorbed in the activities that there were moments when he almost forgot his pain and fatigue. But never for long. And each time they returned, it was with the fierceness of a raging storm that left him near collapse.

## II.

Michael Forgione died on May 9, 1967 at the age of eighty-five and Padre Pio had him buried in the cemetery near his parents. For days Padre Pio was shattered with grief.

In the months ahead he occupied himself as best he could, although his health had slid a little farther back again, and there were times when he had no alternative but to be confined in his cell. Once, in the night, he fell and badly bruised himself, so that the superior even had to order him to cease rising at night to pray. A year passed this way, and things didn't improve.

Mary Pyle celebrated her eightieth birthday on April 17, 1968 and was stricken with an intestinal obstruction. She was taken to the Home for the Relief of Suffering. After a few days of apparent improvement, at 11:00 P.M. on the night of April 26, 1968, against all expectations, she surrendered her soul to God.

All the friars from the monasteries of Morcone, Larino, Manfredonia and Pietrelcina, besides those from the two monasteries of Foggia, went to her funeral. Six Capuchins carried her casket on their shoulders from her home to the monastery church. Padre Carmelo, the superior at San Giovanni Rotondo, delivered a moving eulogy.

Her body was laid to rest near the bodies of Padre Pio's parents and brother. Inscribed in gold letters on her tombstone were the words:

"O Mary
Full of charity and of seraphic virtues
Rest forever in the grateful memory of
Pietrelcina, to which you donated the monastery
Of San Giovanni Rotondo,
Which for more than four decades admired you,
Gentle spiritual daughter of Padre Pio and
Of the Capuchin Fathers who desire to have you
In their chapel."

Two days before her death she left funds for a gymnasium and a new heating system for the seminary at Pietrelcina. In her last testament she also requested to be clothed for burial in the Franciscan robe, cord, and sandals. All her possessions she willed to the Capuchins, including the house in San Giovanni Rotondo and two cottages in Pietrelcina which had once belonged to the Forgione family. It was decided to keep the house in San Giovanni Rotondo as a memorial to her, just as she left it at the time of her last illness.

"She was a person of exceptional spiritual stature, worthy of canonization," said one of the friars later to Padre Pio.

Padre Pio nodded. "She was always a good religious and the Lord knows how to give the just reward to those who have merited it."

The sky was overcast that day and the wind had a chill to it. Padre Pio felt every part of him aching with sadness. Nothing was the same any more, and he knew his own life was almost over. The sun came out suddenly, yellow and warm, and Padre Pio tried to hurry.

He felt a new sense of urgency, that prodded him on. Time was so short and he had so much to do. And as always the people were waiting.

Padre Pio was greatly devoted to the Blessed Mother, and he recited many rosaries every day. Inside the monastery, one of his brothers caught up with him, and asked: "How many rosaries do you say each day, Padre?"

"About forty," he replied.

"Forty by fifty Hail Marys is two thousand!"

"What? Is the rosary made only of five decades?" A complete rosary consisted of fifteen decades of Hail Marys and fifteen Our Fathers.

He once said to one of his spiritual children, "Always hold the weapon of Mary tight in your hand. It will bring you victory over your enemies."

"What is this weapon?" she asked.

"It's on my Capuchin habit."

"But I don't see any weapon. I see only your rosary beads."

"And isn't that a weapon?" asked Padre Pio.

Padre Onorato was also waiting for him in the corridor. "Tomorrow I'm going to Lourdes," he said, "and I wish your blessing and that you assist me in the trip." He smiled, and added, "Why don't you come, too?"

"Well," said Padre Pio, shaking his head, "I am old and then I never go anywhere. In Lourdes, though, I have been there many times. Nevertheless, to Lourdes one does not only go by train or automobile, one goes in even another manner."

Padre Onorato laughed, but decided not to press him on his reputed bilocation. "So," he joked, "Bravo, you leave the monastery, take a nice trip, and return excommunicated because you leave without the permission of the superior!"

Padre Pio feigned shock and threw up his hands. "Mad, you are mad! Have you ever seen me leave the monastery? All of you watch me night and day and you know well I do not move." He shook his head. "It seems you understand nothing."

Padre Onorato chuckled and went on, catching a glimpse of something yellow in Padre Pio's hand as he turned. He was clutching a single yellow rose. "Ah, ha" he called back. "You have a special admirer, I see."

Padre Pio's brown eyes twinkled. "It's about time, don't you think?" He walked on slowly and paused in front of a door leading to Padre Gerardo's office.

The door was closed. Usually Padre Gerardo could hear Padre Pio's steps from afar, halting and dragging, and from time to time he could hear him stop and have hard spells of coughing. And Padre Pio usually stopped at his office, knocked, and entered. He always had something: a letter, an address, and offering for the clinic, an offering for the celebration of Masses.

"If I die unxepectedly," Padre Pio told him once, "remember in this pocket," and he indicated the one on his right, "there are offerings for the clinic. In the other pocket," and he motioned to the left of his habit, "there are offerings for the celebration of Masses."

It was Padre Gerardo's birthday, and he was expecting Padre Pio to stop. He was occupied with work when he thought he heard a faint cough near his door. He got up and opened it, seeing Padre Pio who was smiling but a little embarrassed.

"Best wishes," Padre Pio said, taking the rose from the door lock where he had inserted it, and handing it to the tall, handsome priest.

Padre Gerardo, his eyes misting, thanked him and kissed his hand, while Padre Pio blushed and hurried on towards the chancel of the church. Fatique was overtaking him rapidly and before long he knew he had to go back to his cell.

Something had been on his mind ever since the Capuchins had an audience with Pope Paul VI, and he decided to write to the Pope one day.

"Holiness, I wish to take advantage of your meeting with the fathers during the chapter to join spiritually with my fellow friars in laying at your feet my affectionate homage, all my devotion to your august person, in an act of faith, love and obedience to you, because of the dignity of the Person whom you represent on earth. The Capuchin order has always been foremost in love, faith, obedience and devotion to the Apostolic See. I pray God that this may always be so and that it may continue in its tradition of seriousness and austerity, evangelical poverty, faithful observance of the Rule and of the Constitutions, while renewing itself in vitality and internal spirit according to the decision of the Vatican II Council in order to be more and more ready to run to the aid of the Mother Church at a sign from Your Holiness.

"I know that your heart is suffering greatly these days because of your concern for the destiny of the Church, peace in the world, and the many needs of the people of the world, but above all the lack of obedience of some, even Catholics, to the important teaching that you, with the aid of the Holy Spirit, and in the name of God, give us. I offer you my daily prayers and sufferings as a small but sincere thought from the least of your children, that the Lord may comfort you with His grace and help you to continue along the straight and difficult path in the defense of the eternal truth that does not change with the changing of the times. Also in the name of my spiritual children and of the Prayer Groups I wish to thank you for the clear and decisive words you pronounce, especially in the last encyclical *Humanae Vitae,* and I once more affirm my faith and unconditional obedience to your enlightened commands.

"May God grant the triumph of the truth, peace to His Church, tranquility to the people of the world, health and prosperity to Your Holiness, so that these temporary clouds may be dissipated and the Kingdom of God may triumph in all hearts through your apostolic work as Supreme Pastor of all Christianity.

"Prostrate at your feet, I implore your blessing together with my fellow brothers, my dear spiritual children, the Prayer Groups, my sick ones and for all the good works that in the name of Jesus and with your protection we strive to do."

> San Giovanni Rotondo
> September 12, 1968
> Padre Pio, Capuchin

## III.

Friday, September 20, 1968 was the fiftieth anniversary of Padre Pio's stigmata. There were fifty vases of red roses on the altar.

"It seems to me to be a garden," said an attendant.

The day was glorious. Visitors greeted Padre Pio all day. In the afternoon he was in the church for the Benediction services and towards evening there was a big torchlight procession, followed by fireworks. His superiors had requested that he make an appearance at each event, and he did.

The next morning he was too fatigued to celebrate his usual 5:00 o'clock mass. However, as soon as he gained a little strength he showed himself for the noon Angelus. In the afternoon he surprised everyone by hearing a few of the men's confessions. He was also present for the late afternoon Benediction services and was seen at the window of his room in the evening, blessing, and waving to the crowds that had gathered.

There was the Prayer Group Convention on Sunday, September 22. Hundreds of thousands of people came from all parts of the world. The church was packed with Padre Pio celebrating mass. Afterwards he remained seated for a few minutes, withdrawn into himself, as was his habit during the past few years. He rose, then, assisted by his brothers. Suddenly he collapsed. He would have fallen if they hadn't held him up bodily.

"The wheel chair!" someone cried. "Bring the wheel chair! Quickly!"

This was the first time the wheel chair had appeared in the presbytery. In fact, Padre Pio always walked from the sacristy to the church. As they wheeled him along, he gazed almost desperately at the lines of faithful and stretched out his arms to them as if trying to embrace them.

"My children, my children," he kept murmuring. His voice was faint and his face had turned ashen so that it was almost impossible to tell his flesh from his beard.

At eight o'clock in the morning on September 22, a mass for the Prayer Groups was concelebrated by fourteen priests, presided over by Bishop Antonio Cunial, apostolic administrator of the Diocese of Manfredonia. On his left was Padre Carmelo of San Giovanni in Galdo, O.F.M. Capuchin, appointed by the Holy See as director of the Prayer Groups. His appointment marked the triumph of the spiritual work of Padre Pio. The Prayer Groups were thus recognized by the Vatican as being useful and good for the soul. The other concelebrants were spiritual directors of these groups.

Immediately after the mass, Padre Clemente blessed Padre Pio's burial crypt, an act which Padre Pio once said would foretell his death was near. After this ceremony, crowds of prayer groups flowed into the church square to hear the speeches. At about 10:00 o'clock Padre Pio appeared at the window of the old chapel of the church to bless the crowd.

A fellow friar advised him to give up the idea, but Padre Pio insisted: "I want to greet my children for the last time."

His face was marked with suffering. He set out to hear the men's confessions, but had to go back to his room and to bed. Here he remained alone except for his assistants who would look in his room frequently, to check on him. Around noon his brothers had gone to their noon-day meal.

At midday, in the mystic silence of his room, Padre Pio recited with unusual strength and in a high voice the "Our Father," scanning every word. It was an act of humble thanksgiving for all of his life.

In the afternoon a solemn "Way of the Cross" was conducted after which Padre Pio blessed the first stone for a new monument: Way of the Cross. After the ceremonies it was announced that sculptor Francesco Messina, who had undertaken to make the bronze figures, portrayed Padre Pio in the fifth station in place of Simon of Cyrene who had helped Jesus carry the cross.

At four in the afternoon Padre Pio was in his usual place in the chancel. He was obviously ill, but he didn't want to disappoint his spiritual children.

When the moment came to leave, he got up with great difficulty, leaned his arm on the iron balustrade, and remained bowed, looking at the crowd. One of the friars gently lifted his arm. Padre Pio traced a sign of blessing, then another, and another. It seemed as if he never wanted to stop. He was tired, worn out completely, but the will to show his love for his spiritual children urged him on.

Later that evening, members of the Prayer Groups with candles sang and prayed, waiting in the field for Padre Pio to show himself at the window of his room. The wait was long. At last his familiar figure shadowed the window and his hand lifted in blessing. Then the waving of hundreds and hundreds of lit candles beneath his window marked the end of a gesture that had been repeated year after year.

He stayed longer than usual, waving and smiling. But friars who were standing next to him saw tears in his tired old eyes.

Shortly after nine o'clock that night Padre Pio called his assistant, Padre Pellegrino, to his room on the intercom. Padre Pio was in bed, and his eyelids were reddened from tears. "What time is it?" he asked.

This happened time and again, until midnight. Each time he asked, "What time is it?" and each time his eyes were red from weeping.

At midnight he begged Pellegrino: "Stay with me, my son." All the while he kept asking the time. Then he asked: "My lad, have you said mass?"

"Padre, it is still too early for mass."

"Well, this morning you will say it for me."

Later Padre Pio asked to confess, and at the end, he said: "My son, if the Lord calls me today, ask my brethren to forgive me for all the trouble I have given and ask my brethren and my spiritual children to pray for my soul."

Padre Pellegrino's large brown eyes gazed helplessly at Padre Pio. He put his hand gently on Padre Pio's shoulder, trying to comfort him. "Padre, I'm sure the Lord will let you live for a long time, but if you are right, may I ask for a last blessing for the brethren, for the spiritual children, and for your patients?"

"Yes," Padre Pio said, "I bless them all, and ask the superior to give them this last blessing for me."

Padre Pio began smiling all at once, and he asked to repeat the act of religious profession. By this time it was 1:00 A.M. "Listen, son," he said, "I can't breathe properly here in bed. Let me get up. I will be able to breathe better on the chair." A combination of asthma and chronic bronchitis had made it difficult for him to catch his breath lately.

Padre Pellegrino started to help him but Padre Pio shook his head and held up a hand. He stood up straight and began to walk as quickly and surely as a youth. Padre Pellegrino stepped aside and stared at him.

"Let's go onto the balcony for a while," Padre Pio suggested, and he turned on the light, sat down in an arm chair, and looked curiously around, searching for something. After five minutes he wanted to return to his room.

Padre Pellegrino tried to help him up, and Padre Pio suddenly felt the strength go out of him. "I can't manage," he whispered.

"Wait," Padre Pellegrino called. He rushed to bring a wheel chair and wheeled him back to his room, helping him into a chair as quickly as possible.

Padre Pio pointed to the wheel chair, and said: "Take it outside." Beads of perspiration began dotting his brow, and his face had paled again. His lips were becoming livid and he continuously repeated: "Jesus, Mary." Padre Pellegrino watched him, growing alarmed.

"Don't call anyone," Padre Pio said, seeing he was about to leave. "The one whom you must call has already called me."

"I must go," Padre Pellegrino cried. He called Fra William Martin and telephoned Padre Pio's personal doctor.

When Dr. Sala saw Padre Pio he hastily gave him an injection, while Padre Pio kept repeating, "Jesus, Mary," his voice steadily growing weaker.

Dr. Sala hurriedly called a number of persons: Mario Pennelli, Padre Pio's niece's husband; the director of the hospital, Dr. Joseph Gusso; his assistant, Dr. Giovanni Scarle; the father superior of the monastery, and the other friars.

The doctors began oxygen inhalation, bronchial dilators, and cardioactivators. All this seemed to cause a slight improvement, and Padre Paolo of San Giovanni Rotondo administered the anointing of the sick, while the other friars knelt around him in prayer.

But at five minutes past 2:00 o'clock a waxy pallor spread over his face and hands. His feet, hands, and face became cold, his pulse weaker, and his breathing stentorous. His eyes were shut.

"Padre, Padre," someone called anxiously, and he raised his eyelids, looked at everyone, and closed them again.

There was no muscular contraction of his face but his heart suddenly stopped at 2:10 A.M. Immediate treatment brought a weak heartbeat, and his breathing, which was superficial with the aid of a mechanical respirator, seemed to improve. But his response to stimuli was practically nil. At 2:30 A.M. his head turned to the right and his lips parted slightly with a weak sigh.

Outside, the morning of September 23 was beginning just like any other. By 3:30 A.M. the men and women were huddled against the church door, waiting for it to swing open an hour later. Some were reciting the rosary, others waiting silently. But the doors didn't open. By the time the sun was high in the sky, the crowd was restless and fearful. All at once a large, deep-toned bell rang ominously, drowning out the excited voices. Then it stopped, and the people grew still.

Over the loudspeaker came the solemn voice of Padre Carmelo, the father guardian of the monastery, telling them that Padre Pio had left them forever.

The September sun warmed them as they listened quietly, and for a long, lonely moment only the endless power of Padre Pio's infinite love filled the deep silence.